Women Leaders of Europe and the Western Hemisphere

Women Leaders of Europe and the Western Hemisphere

A Biographical Reference

Guida M. Jackson

To order additional copies of this book, contact:
Xlibris Corporation
1-888-795-4274
www.Xlibris.com
Orders@Xlibris.com
52112

Preface

The first part of this book has at its core European rulers of the original *Women Who Ruled*, although half again as many completely new biographical entries were added for the second book, entitled *Women Rulers Throughout the Ages*. These included not only women rulers who had come upon the scene in the decade since the publishing of the original work, but many more culled from historical records by dedicated researchers. In addition many entries in the original work were revised, expanded, and updated. The result was a biographical listing of every known ruling queen, empress, woman prime minister, president, regent ruler, defacto ruler, constitutional monarch, and verifiable ruler from the oral tradition of the world's kingdoms, islands, empires, nations, and tribes since the beginning of both recorded and recaptured oral history down to the time of the publication of *Women Rulers Throughout the Ages*.

In the decade since the appearance of the second volume, women's participation world-wide in all levels of government has mushroomed, such that it now seems logical to include not only rulers, but other leaders in government. The entries in this two-volume collection are arranged regionally: African, Asian—which includes India, the Middle East and the Pacific in the first volume, and European and the Western Hemisphere in the second. Within these geographical sections, the entries are arranged alphabetically according to leaders' names, dictionary style. Each entry is supported by sources for further reading at the end.

In the case of rulers, the name of each woman ruler is followed by a title or titles and, in parentheses, the year(s) during which she ruled. In the case of entries that give more than one title, the additional title will help to distinguish that ruler from other women in history with similar names; to designate either a title different from that which the ruler held while ruling or a title that was not the usual one held by a ruler of that particular place; or to clarify for the reader the type of title used in a certain time and place.

Such a compilation could not possibly be a history based on original research of primary sources in their hundreds of languages. It must rather be a gathering together from secondary sources, from the works of others from many cultures. As such, if it cannot be an original work, it carries an added obligation that a history does not, and that is to provide information in some cases even beyond historical fact, so called.

Since gray areas are inherent in a categorization as broad as "women rulers," there will be questions about certain inclusions or exclusions. In broad terms, I have sought to include the name (or when the name has not survived, the identifying clan, dynasty, or even locale) of any woman who held the reins of power, regardless of the extent to which she exercised it, and regardless of her official sanction to do so. To include only those who presided from a recognized seat of government, however, would omit certain tribal leaders. Yet there is a difference between "leaders" and "rulers." Joan of Arc, certainly a leader, did not preside from a recognized seat of government and would not be termed a ruler, although she was certainly an inspirational leader.

Far more open to controversy is my inclusion of certain women behind the throne, such as Diane de Poitiers, to the exclusion of others like Marie Antoinette who doubtless influenced history to a greater degree. My inclination has been to omit these powers behind the throne unless history indicates that they dominated the designated rulers and their decisions.

In addition, with some ambivalence, I have included the names of a very few legendary rulers about whom no firm historical or archeological evidence survives, whose embroidered histories may or may not have been based on the lives of actual (albeit far less colorful) persons. These inclusions are clearly labeled as legendary and are included because of the unique information that they provide, which in some cases may link the historical to the legendary or may contain some elements that coincide with known historical data.

Diacritics, particularly in accounts of rulers of recent times, have been kept to a minimum for the sake of a particular fluid robustness which a clean page allows; however, in the case of certain of the more exotic and distantly removed entries, where names have not been Anglicized by current usage, the use of diacritics seems preferable and even unavoidable. It is hoped that what fluidity is lost due to their inclusion is compensated for by the edaphic flavor they lend.

In this ongoing endeavor, I am indebted to those who brought newly elected rulers to my attention, who lent or located research materials, and who offered editing assistance, inspiration, and encouragement: John Hume, William H. Laufer, James Tucker Jackson, Patty Wentz, William

A. Jackson, Mary Gillis Jackson, Jeffrey A. Jackson, Linda J. Jackson, Annabeth Dugger, Steve Dugger, Glenda Miller Lowery, Davis Lowery, Daniel Ramos, Julia Mercedes Castilla de Gomez-Rivas, Ida H. Luttrell, Gregory A. Jackson, Jeana Kendrick, Ashley D. Ramos, Elizabeth A. Jackson, Patsy Ward Burk, Karen Stuyck, Jackie Pelham, Vanessa Leggett, Louise Gaylord, Sue Volk, Lynne S. Gonzales, Mattie R. Jackson, Troy B. Lowery, Ann Anderson, Christopher Michael Ramos, Irene Bond, Bobbi Sissel, Eleanor Frances Jackson, Stephanie L. Noggler, David Bumgardner, Jim Elledge, Ron Pearson, Jan Matlock, Kenny Noggler, Rance J. Lowery, Trinity Alexis Noggler, Jace Lowery, Olivia Orfield, Gloria Wahlen, Carol Rowe DeBender, Joyce Pounds Hardy McDonald, Donn Taylor, Joy Ziegler, Beverly Herkommer, Judith Sherbenou, Bob Davis, Addison McElroy, George Thomen, Joan Winkler.

Houston, Texas 2009

PART I

Europe

Introduction

Although the Parliament of the European Union, created by the largest democratic election outside India, is considered the most advanced governing body ever convened in the world, there are still inequities for minority women.

As of 2007, there were 785 members from 27 member states who sat in chambers in Brussels and Strasbourg. Elections are held every five years. The next European Union election was in 2009. The number of MEPs is determined by each country's size, so Germany had 99 and Malta had five. There are 492 million potential voters spread among these 27 countries, and it is estimated that at least 25 million citizens are non-white—and this number is rising. In 2004, however, only 45.5% of the potential voters actually cast a ballot. They elected a body of MEPs consisting of 776 whites and only nine non-whites.

Livia Jaroka was one of them. She is a center-right Hungarian MEP, one of eight million Roma in the EU. In 2006 she was nominated for a parliamentary award for her conscientious work within and outside of Parliament. However, a Bulgarian observer, Dimitar Stoyanov, who had not yet taken his seat since Bulgaria had not yet officially joined the EU, objected, e-mailing the other MEPs: "In my country there are tens of thousands of Gypsy girls way more beautiful. In fact, if you're in the right place at the right time you even can buy one (around 12-13 years old) to be your loving wife. The best of them are very expensive—up to E5,000 apiece, wow!"

Although the e-mail was widely condemned, Stoyanov was allowed to take his seat in 2007 as a full-fledged MEP, representing a new far right faction that includes fascists and deniers of the Holocaust.

Neena Gill, the only Asian woman in Parliament, was elected from Great Britain as a Labour MEP more than eight years ago. In a *Guardian* (London) article, she admitted to feeling "uncomfortable" if seated next to a neo-fascist. The far right group, "Identity, Tradition, Sovereignty," is represented by 19 members in Parliament from various European countries. Gill, Indian by heritage, said, "I've got used to it now, but initially I felt quite intimidated. It's threatening. This man thinks I shouldn't be here. If he was in power, you don't know where they would stop . . . . they don't see you as an equal . . . ." (1)

One is left to wonder whether this far right element most objects to Gill's color or her gender.

Still, by far the most women rulers and other leaders of whom we have record presided in Europe, where a tradition to include women has existed since legendary times. One has only to look at the ancient Arctic race still in existence, the Lapps, to imagine the attitudes of other European ancestors. The position of Lapp women has always been better than that of some women in the United States. Lapp women marry at about the age of 20, maintaining their maiden name and retaining their own property. A suitor is expected to give presents, and in order to "earn" the right to marry his bride, he and his new wife may live with her parents for a year. (2)

Even before the time of Canute, the Vikings record a Queen Asa. Snorre Sturlason records a Queen Gyda, ruling in England, whom the famous Viking king, Olav Trygvason, took for a wife. (3) Canute himself, unable to govern everything at once, left his English mistress Aelfgifu in charge of Norway. Queen Margrete united the kingdoms of Denmark, Norway and Sweden under one rule for the only time in history. The right of female succession in many countries during feudal times boosted the number of female rulers. In the latter half of the Twentieth Century Northern Europe could boast of having the first woman to be elected president in her own right (Vigdis Finnebogadottir), ten prime ministers (Thatcher, Bruntlandt, Cresson, Suchocka, da Lourdes-Pintasilgo, Plavsic, Indzhova, Bergmann-Pohl, Bjerregaard, Merkel), several more presidents (Robinson, McAleese, Dreifuss, Barbara), several Co-captains regent of San Marino, and four queens (Elizabeth, Margrethe, Juliana, and Beatrix). A queen has held the throne of Holland for more than a century.

In the rest of Europe, the Seventh Century became a period of boy-kings and female rulers among the Franks under the Merovingians. The notoriety of the bloodthirsty Fredegond rivals Wu Chao (see Asian Introduction in the companion volume). From an account of Fredegond's crimes, it is barely conceivable that she had time to think of anything else but methods of revenge. During the Middle Ages, although few women ruled in their own right, many regents, such as Blanche of Castile, made a tremendous impact upon history. Some queens, such as "King" Jadwiga of Poland, exercised far less personal power.

During the Roman era, co-regents with full powers had the title of Augustus, which was an official designation awarded only to men. Augusta was an honorary one. Several women, among them Empress Faustina I (Annia Faustina), wife of Antonius Pius (r. A.D. 138-161) was named Augusta of Rome (A.D. 138-140/41) (4)

Some extremely powerful women were neither queens, "kings" or regents, but duchesses and rulers of their own smaller domains. During her time, there was not much that the Papacy did that was not first sanctioned by the powerful Matilda of Tuscany. The Renaissance flowered under the tutelage of a number of women. It was women who ruled Europe while their men marched off on the Crusades (except Eleanor of Aquitaine, who insisted on going along), and it was women who ruled when their men didn't come back. They fought wars of conquest as well as of defense; they negotiated treaties, murdered enemies, arranged mergers, instituted reforms, squandered fortunes, inspired their countrymen—and had babies.

Women have always stirred many pots at once. The mention of offspring in the account of a woman's life is essential, particularly any woman born prior this century, because throughout whatever else she was doing, the bearing of children did not stop until she could have them no longer. Today's rulers, while neglecting neither their political responsibilities nor motherhood, find time to demonstrate their creative versatility: Queen Margrethe is a renowned illustrator whose best known work is of *The Lord of the Rings*, but whose other work is respected as well. She also wrote a book with her husband. Gro Harlem Brundtland is a doctor; Queen Beatrix, a sculptor. Queen Liliuokalani wrote a song recognized world-wide, "Aloha Oe."

When we come to the realization that war is no longer an option and preserving our planet's resources is of primary importance, more of the creative skills which have made women so versatile must be the qualities we seek in our leaders. Women will continue to have a share, as always, in guiding our destiny, and perhaps, as has happened in Native American nations, that share may even grow.

Notes:

(1) Patrick Barkham, "Minority Report." *Guardian Weekly*. February 23-March 1. pp. 17-18.
(2) Edward Weyer, Jr. *Primitive Peoples Today*. (Garden City, NY: Dolphin/ Doubleday, n.d.), 143-158.

(3) Snorre Sturlason. *Heimskringla, or The Lives of Norse Kings*. tr. A. H. Smith. (New York: Dover Publications, Inc., 1990) 137-138, 471.

(4) Gwyn Jones. *A History of the Vikings*. (Oxford: Oxford University Press, 1984), 137.

(5) Diane Bowder. *Who Was Who in the Roman World*. (Ithaca, NY: Cornell University Press, 1980), 18, 197-198.

Europe Section A

Adela

Countess of Blois and Chartres, regent (c. 1097-1109)

The daughter of William I the Conqueror of England, Adela (b. c. 1062) inherited his strong will and interest in politics. She married Count Stephen of Blois and Chartres and governed alone when her husband left for the Holy Land on the First Crusade, ca. 1097. In the spring of 1098, Stephen became discouraged and decided to return home. On his way, he met Byzantine Emperor Alexius and convinced him that the attempt to take Antioch was hopeless, so Alexius also turned back. Steven's advice was to cause Alexius difficulties later, for when the remaining crusaders learned he had turned back, they felt no obligation to return Antioch to him. Steven's return without fulfilling his crusading vows was a source of great humiliation to Adela, reared in the tradition of the great William the Conqueror. It was said that behind the doors of their bedchamber she shamed him for his cowardice and urged him to redeem his honor. Stephen could not argue that he was needed to rule Blois, for Adela had always actually ruled. Against his own better judgment, Steven set out on another expedition in 1101. This time he survived the seige of Antioch and continued the pilgrimmage to Jerusalem. The crusaders' ship was blown ashore off Jaffa, where, under the command of Jerusalem King Baldwin, they planned to attack the approaching Egyptian army, believing it to be much smaller than it was. Steven saw the proposed attack as precipitous, but his comrades, remembering his past cowardice, ignored his advice. Too late, they realized their mistake, but they went into battle bravely. Steven redeemed his honor but lost his life (1102). After his death Adela continued to serve as regent until 1109, when her oldest son Theobald reached majority and she had him made count. During the years of her regency she worked to strengthen her fiefdom so that her son would have an increasingly important role to play in European affairs. It was due to her efforts, through her friend the bishop St. Ives of Chartres, that her younger brother, King Henry I of England, was able to reach a compromise with the archbishop of Canterbury over the lay investiture of churchmen. The schoolmaster Hildebert of Lavardin (1056-1133), who became archbishop of Tours, earned the ardent admiration of Adela because of his classical Latin poetry. She addressed many love songs to him, as did the Empress Matilda. Adela's third son, Stephen, became king of England, based on her claim of inheritance following Henry's death. She died in 1137.

Suggested Reading:

(1) Runciman, Steven. *A History of the Crusades*. Cambridge: Cambridge University Press, 1952, 1987. vol. 2, *The Kingdom of Jerusalem and the Frankish East*. pp. 20, 48, 78.

(2) Heer, Friedrich. *The Medieval World*. tr. Janet Sondheimer. New York: The New American Library, Inc., Mentor Books, 1962. p. 124.

Adelaide

Queen of Italy, regent of German Empire (983-995)

She was born in 931, the daughter of King Rudolph II of Burgundy and Bertha of Swabia. She married King Lothair of Italy in 947, at about age 16. Lothair died only three years later and Adelaide ruled alone, briefly. However, the following year, her kingdom was threatened with siege by Berengar of Pavia. She was imprisoned but, because she was a beautiful woman of strong character, she found many willing to help her. After being confined for four months, she managed to escape. She offered herself in marriage as reward for helping her regain her Italian throne. Several nobles sought to intervene, but it was Otto (Otto the Great, Saxon emperor of the German Empire) who stepped to her rescue. Seeing an opportunity to expand his holdings, he came to Adelaide's aid, defeated Berengar's forces and declared himself king of the Franks and Lombards. Adelaide, glad to have Otto's protection, and envisioning for herself a larger kingdom, married Otto and ceded Italy to Berengar in exchange for Istria, Friuli, and Verona, which became part of Bavaria. Otto and Adelaide were crowned emperor and empress of the Western German Empire in 962. Their son, Otto II, succeeded to the throne upon his father's death in 973. Only ten years later, three-year-old Otto III, son of Otto II and Theophano, inherited the throne. Adelaide, his grandmother, served as co-regent, sharing the duties with her daughter-in-law from 983 to 991, when Theophano died. She then governed alone until Otto came of age in 995. After his coronation, she devoted herself to founding churches and monastaries. She died in 999 at the age of 68 and was buried in Seltz, Alsace, where miracles were reported to have occurred. She was made a saint of the Catholic Church; her feast day is December 16.

Suggested Reading:

(1) Previté-Orton, C.W. *The Shorter Cambridge Medieval History.* Cambridge: Cambridge University Press, 1952, 1982. vol. 1, *The Later Roman Empire to the Twelfth Century.* pp. 436-437.

(2) Kinder, Hermann, and Werner Hilgemann *Atlas of World History.* tr. Ernest Menze. Garden City, NY: Anchor/Doubleday, 1982. p. 143.

Adelaide of Salona (or Savona)

Countess, regent of Sicily (1101-1112)

Adelaide was the daughter of the Marquis Manfred and the niece of Boniface of Salona. She married the great Count Roger I of Sicily in 1089, becoming his third wife. When Roger died two years later, she assumed the regency for Simon, who died in 1105, and thereafter for her son Roger II, who went on to become one of the most remarkable rulers of the Middle Ages. Queen Adelaide's immense wealth attracted the attention of the Frankish King Baldwin I of Jerusalem, who had cast aside his dowerless second wife and was looking for a new wealthier queen. Adelaide had just retired from more than a decade of her regency and was looking for a new husband. Baldwin sent word asking for her hand; Adelaide accepted, providing the king would agree to the terms of her contract: that if no baby was born of the union—and the ages of both suggested little possibility—the crown of Jerusalem would pass to her son, Roger II. Her terms accepted, Adelaide sailed the Mediterranean in the elegant splendor reminescent of Cleopatra, with a fleet of gold—and silver-trimmed ships carrying all her personal treasure. Baldwin met her with equal pomp, and ordered his entire kingdom adorned for her arrival.

However, once he had spent her dowry to pay off his debts, his ardor cooled, as did hers, when she found that Jerusalem was a far cry from her luxurious Palermo palace. In 1117 Baldwin fell seriously ill, and his confessors reminded him that he might die in a state of sin, since he had never legally divorced his second wife. When he recovered, he announced the annulment of his marriage to Adelaide. Now alone, scorned, stripped of her wealth, Adelaide sailed back to Sicily in humiliation. Baldwin's insult would cost the kingdom of Jerusalem dearly in the ensuing years, but Adelaide's marriage contract would be the basis for her son's claim upon the lands of Jerusalem. Roger II never forgot Baldwin's dishonor of his mother. In 1117, two lunar eclipses and the appearance of the aurora borealis were taken as foretelling the death of princes. In the following months, in 1118, King Baldwin, his patriarch Arnulf, Pope Paschal, Iranian Sultan Mohammed, Baghdad Caliph Mustazhir and ex-Queen Adelaide all died.

Suggested Reading:

(1) Smith, Dennis Mack. *A History of Sicily*. New York: Dorset Press, 1968. vol.1, p. 24.
(2) Runciman, Steven. *A History of the Crusades*. Cambridge: Cambridge University Press, 1952, 1987. col.2, *The Kingdom of Jerusalem and the Frankish East*. pp. 102-5, 199, 207, 251-2.

Adele

Co-ruler of Vendome (c. 1017-1031)

She was the wife of Bouchard I, count of Vendome, Paril, and Corbeil, ruler of Vendome from 958 to 1012. The couple had three sons, Renaud (bishop of Paril), Bouchard II, and Foulques d'Oison. When Bouchard I died in 1012, the oldest son ruled for four years. Following his death in 1016, a nephew, Eudes, son of Landry, count of Nevers, ruled briefly because Bouchard II was too young and quite possibly Adele was again pregnant. Bouchard II assumed the rule sometime after 1016 with his mother, but apparently he died soon after. The youngest child, Foulques d'Oison, then ruled with his mother until 1031, when Adele, in financial straits, sold the duchy to Foulques' uncle, Geoffri Martel, count of Anjou.

Suggested Reading:

(1) Egan, Edward W., Constance B. Hintz, and L. F. Wise. *Kings, Rulers and Statesmen*. New York: Sterling Publishing Company, 1976. p. 162.

Aethelburgh, Queen of the Saxons

Army leader (722)

Accoprding to *The Anglo-Saxon Chronicles*, Queen Aethelburgh's forces destroyed the City of Taunton in 722.

Aelfgifu (or Eligifu) of Northumbria

Regent of Norway (c. 1029-1035)

She was the daughter of an ealderman of Northumbria who in 1006 was murdered at the order of King Aethelred II. In ca. 1013 she met and became the mistress of Canute (the Great), son of Danish King Sven I Fork Beard, who invaded England that year. Canute became king of Denmark when his father died in 1014, was elected king of England in 1016, and became king of Norway in 1028. Aelfgifu bore two sons, Sven (Sweyn) and Harold (Harefoot). However, in 1017, to bolster English support in case of an attack by Aethelred, Canute married Emma, the mother of exiled King Aethelred's sons. Emma was also sister of Duke Richard II. After Canute became king of Norway, he assigned Haakon as his regent; but Haakon soon died. He then put Norway in the hands of Aefgifu as regent for their son Sven. Aelfgifu and Sven remained in Norway for some six years before they were driven out. They escaped to Denmark, where Canute had put his legitimate son by Emma, Harthacnute (Hardecanute), in charge (1035). Canute died the same year, and Aelfgifu returned to England to champion the cause of her second son, Harold I Harefoot, as king. He ruled as regent from 1035 until his death in 1040, when his half-brother ascended to the throne.

Suggested Reading:

(1) Derry, T. K. *A History of Scandinavia*. Minneapolis: University of Minnesota Press, 1979. p. 39.

(2) Langer, William L., ed. *World History*. Boston: Houghton Mifflin Company, 1940, 1980. pp. 182-183.

Aelfwyn

Queen of Mercia (918-191)

The daughter of Aethelred II, who ruled from 879 to 911, and Queen Aethelflaed, who ruled following his death until 918, Aelfwyn briefly ascended to the throne upon her mother's death but was deposed in 919 when Mercia was annexed to West Saxony.

Suggested Reading:

(1) Morby, John. *Dynasties of the World*. Oxford: Oxford University Press, 1989. p. 66.

Aethelflaed (or Ethelfleda, "Lady of the Mercians")

Queen of Mercia (c. 910-918)

Mercia was an Anglo Saxon kingdom located in Central England. Aethelflaed was the daughter of Alfred The Great. She married Aethelred, ealdorman of the Mercians, and became the effective ruler in his stead long before he died. When Aethelred died in 911, she anomalously succeeded him, having already become firmly established as ruler. She became known as the Lady of the Mercians. She rivaled her brother Edward the Elder, ruler of West Saxony (899-924), in both war and organization, and she assisted him in overcoming the Danish armies which controlled great portions of Eastern England. While Edward spent six years (910-916) fortifying the southeastern midlands, Aethelflaed was doing the same for Mercia. In 913 she erected the great earthen mound near presentday Warwick Castle as a fortress. By 917 the two of them had amassed large forces for a joint assault against the Danes. She captured Derby easily and went on to occupy Leicester in 918. She had already extended her boundaries into Wales on the west and Northumberland on the north. She obtained a promise of submission from the Danes in Northumberland; however, before she could gain complete victory, she died (918) in Tamworth, now in Staffordshire, leaving Edward to win the final victory against the Danes.

With his sister gone, Edward claimed her lands, and thus nearly all of what is present-day England was united under his control.

Suggested Reading:

(1) Whitelock, Dorothy. *The Pelican History of England.* Harmondsworth, Middlesex: Penguin Books, 1952, 1976. vol. 2, *The Beginnings of English Society.* pp. 76-77.
(2) Previté-Orton, C. W. *The Shorter Cambridge Medieval History.* Cambridge: Cambridge University Press, 1952, 1987. vol. 1, pp. 385-389.
(3) Grun, Bernard. *The Timetables of History.* New York: Simon & Schuster, 1979. yr. 913.

Agnes de Dampierre

Baroness, ruler of Bourbon (1262-1287)

Agnes ruled Bourbon during that period in French history in which so-called "feudal anarchy" existed. The French kings actually ruled a small area around Paris and Orleans while the heads of the great duchies and baronies maintained their independence. Agnes was the daughter of Dame Mahaut I and Gui II de Dampierre and the sister of Baroness Mahaut II, who ruled from 1249 to 1262. Mahaut II married Eudes de Bourgogne and Agnes married his brother, Jean de Bourgogne. She succeeded to the Barony when her sister died in 1262.

Suggested Reading:

(1) Egan, Edward W. et. al., eds. *Kings, Rulers and Statesmen.* New York: Sterling Publishing Company, 1976. p. 153.

Agnes de Nevers

Countess, ruler of Nevers (1181-1192)

Nevers was located in the modern day *Departement* of Nievre in central France, south-southeast of Paris. Agnes succeeded Count Guillaume V, who ruled from 1175 to 1181. She married Pierre de Courtenay and they had a daughter, Mahaut, who succeeded her mother in 1192.

Suggested Reading:

(1) Egan, Edward W. et. al., eds. *Kings, Rulers and Statesmen*. New York: Sterling Publishing, 1976. p. 159.

Agnes of Dunbar (Black Agnes)

Countess of March, ruler of Dunbar (c. 1338)

She was the daughter of the great Randolph, earl of Moray, who had been fighting off the British for years. In 1338 the English troops of Edward III attacked Dunbar castle; Edward had never been happy about the Treaty of Northampton (1028) making Scotland an independent realm, and he intended to bring it back under English control. Agnes held out triumphantly for five months, successfully defending the castle until the English retreated. Fortunately for the Scots, Edward, attempting also to gain the French throne, took his army to France.

Suggested Reading:

(1) Mackie, J.D. *A History of Scotland*. Harmondsworth, Middlesex: Penguin Books, 1984. p. 80.

Agnes of Poitou

Duchess of Bavaria (1056-1061), regent for Holy Roman Emperor Henry IV, (1056-1062)

She was born c. 1024, the daughter of William V the Pious, duke of Aquitaine, a descendant of the kings of Italy and Burgundy. She married Henry III on Nov. 1, 1043, becoming the second wife of the Holy Roman emperor, and forming an allegiance cementing the empire's relations with its neighbors to its west. She and Henry III had a son, Henry IV, for whom Agnes assumed the regency when her husband died in 1056. However, although she was descended from kings both of Italy and Burgundy, she had no talent for leadership; she was, in fact, characterized as being pious and colorless. She gave away the duchies of Bavaria, Swabia, and Carinthia to relatives. An opponent of church reform, she allied herself with Italian dissidents and helped lect Cadalus as Antipope Honorarius II to oppose Pope Alexander II, elected by the reformers. In 1062 Archbishop Anno of Cologne, with the help of several princes, succeeded in kidnapping the young king and bringing him to Cologne, out of his mother's grasp. He jumped overboard but was rescued and recaptured. As ransom for her son, Agnes resigned as regent and Anno took her place. She spent the remainder of her life in a convent.

Suggested Reading:

(1) Previté-Orton, C. W. *The Shorter Cambridge Medieval History*. Cambridge: Cambridge University Press, 1952, 1987. vol. 1, p. 460.

Aigner, Ilse

German Minister in Merkel's Cabinet (2008-)

Ilse Aigner was born on December 7, 1964 in Feldkirchen-Westerham, Rosenheim, Bavaria. She is a member of the Christian Social Union of Bavaria, and as such, was tapped by German Chancellor Angela Merkel to join her grand coalition cabinet in 2008. She is Federal Minister of Consumer Protection, Food, and Agriculture. She replaced Horst Seehofer when he was elevated to Minister President of Bavaria.

Alix of Anjou

Ruler of Brittany (1203-1221), regent (1221-1237)

She was the daughter of Constance, daughter of Conan IV the Younger (r. 1156-deposed in 1166) and her second husband, Guy of Thouars. She inherited Brittany when her half-brother, Arthur I, died in 1203. In 1213 she married Peter I, Mauclerc, son of Robert II of Dreux. The couple had a son, John I the Red, who came to the rule when Peter died in 1221, with Alix as his regent. She died in 1250.

Suggested Reading:

(1) Morby, John. *Dynasties of the World*. Oxford: Oxford University Press, 1989. p. 83.

Alix of Vergy

Countess, ruler of Burgundy (1248-?)

She was the daughter of Count Otto II and his wife, Countess Beatrix, daughter of Count Otto I. Ailx's brother, Otto III became Count in 1234, and she inherited Burgundy, located in present day eastern France, upon his death in 1248. She was married to Hugh of Chalon, and their son, tto IV, inherited Burgundy upon her death sometime before 1290. Otto IV, in financial straits after protracted conflicts with the emperor, concluded two treaties (1291 and 1295) with King Philip IV of France wherein he ceded Burgundy to France.

Suggested Reading:

(1)   Heer, Friedrich. New *The Medieval World*. York: Mentor/NAL, 1962. p. 318.

Amalswinthe (or Amalsuntha or Amalsontha)

Queen, regent of the Ostrogoths (Italy, Western Roman Empire) (526-534), then co-ruler (534-535)

She was born in 498, the daughter of King Theodoric the Great of the Ostrogoths and Audofleda, sister of King Clovis. Even by today's standards, she was an extremely well-educated woman. She studied both Greek and Latin and became a lifelong patroness of literature and the arts. In 515 she married Theodoric's distant relative, Eutharic. They had a son, Athalric, and a daughter, Matasuntha. Eutharic died in 522 and Theodoric died four years later, after which Amalswinthe served as regent for her ten-year-old son. She chose to continue the pro-Byzantine policies of her father, even though they were unpopular with the Ostrogoth nobility. Recognizing he danger her policies put her in, she took the precaution of arranging with Byzantine Emperor Justinian that if she were deposed she would transfer herself and entire Ostrogothic treasury to Constantinople. In 533 she successfully quelled a rebellion and put to death three of its instigators, Ostrogoth noblemen. Upon her son's death in 534, she shared the throne with her cousin Theodahad; however, he fell under the influence of the forces which opposed her, and he ordered her banished to an island in the lake of Bolsena (Tuscany, Italy), where in 535, at the behest of the Empress Theodora, relatives of the three noblemen she had put to death strangled her in her bath.

Suggested Reading:

(1) Gibbon, Edward. *The Decline and Fall of the Roman Empire.* New York: The Modern Library/Random House, n.d. vol. 2, pp. 554-556.

(2) Previté-Orton, C. W. *The Shorter Cambridge Medieval History.* Cambridge: Cambridge University Press, 1952, 1987. vol. 1, pp. 139-40, 190.

Anna (or Anne) of Savoy

Regent of Byzantine Empire (1341-1347)

She was the wife of Andronicus III, by whom she had a son, John V Palaeologus (1331). When Andronicus died in 1341, John V was only nine years old. A dispute broke out between Anna and John Cantacuzenus, the Grand Domestic, chief minister under Andronicus III, the late ruler's nearest friend and the real power. John asserted his claim to the regency, but he left Constantinople to battle the Serbs in Thrace. In his absence Anna had him declared a traitor and imprisoned his supporters. For a time Anna was formally recognized as senior sovereign in Constantinople. Her likeness appears on seals and coins of the period. Anna made vigorous attempts toward a reunion of the churches of Rome and Constantinople, even more decisive than those efforts of her late husband, but without lasting results. In 1341 John Cantacuzenus had himself declared Emperor, but he held to the principle of legitimate seccession, placing the names of Empress Anna and Emperor John V before those of himself and his wife Irene. At the beginning of the civil war which followed, Anna pawned the crown jewels in Venice for thirty thousand ducats with which to defend her throne. The loan was never repaid. In 1345 John Cantacuzenus, giving the Empress Anna the office of Despot, asked the Ottoman Turks to come to his aid, even marrying his daughter Theodora to the sultan Orhan. By 1346 John was confident enough of victory to have himself crowned Emperor in Andrianople. Although Anna's power was now limited to Constantinople and the immediate vicinity, the ambitious empress would not give in. She negotiated with the Turks for assistance. Instead of attacking John

Cantacuzenus, they invaded and plundered Bulgaria, then one the way home did the same to outlying Constantinople. Despite last-minute appeals to the hesychasts (a sect of mystics), Anna was forced to surrender in 1347. John was crowned co-emperor with John V, and he ruled alone for ten years until John V was nineteen. To assure that Anna would wield no further influence over her son, John married his daughter Helena to John V.

Suggested Reading:

(1) Ostrogorsky, George, *History of the Byzantine State*. New Brunswick, NJ: Rutgers University Press, 1969. p. 510, 518, 520, 526, 535.

Anna Palaeologina

Despina, regent of Epirus (1335-1340)

She was the wife of John Orsini, Despot of Epirus from 1323 to 1335, and had a son, Nicephorus II. In 1335 Anna poisoned her husband and, with her son, took over the government. She immediately entered into negotiations with the Byzantine emperor, hoping that, once having recognized Byzantine suzerainty, she would be allowed to continue to rule unmolested. However, the emperor did not want anyone so closely tied to Epirian independence to rule Epirus, so Byzantine troops marched into Eprius and replaced Anna with an imperial governor. Anna and her son were compelled to move to Thessalonica. Much later, Nicephorous II attempted to win back his rule and undertook an extensive and fairly successful campaign in both Epirus and Thessaly, but he died in 1358 while fighting the Albanians.

Suggested Reading:

(1) Ostrogorsky, George. *History of the Byzantine State*. New Brunswick, NJ: Rutgers University Press, 1969. pp. 508, 534, 579, 581.

Anna Palaeologina-Cantacuzena

Despina, regent of Epirus (1296-c. 1313)

She was the daughter of Princess Eulogia (Irene), sister of Byzantine Emperor Michael VIII. She married Nicephorus I, Despot of the Greek principality of Epirus from 1271 to 1296. They had two children: Thomas of Epirus and Thamar (Tamara), who married Philip of Tarento. She became Regent for their son Thomas when Nicephorus died in 1296. With her close ties to the Byzantine Empire, the pro-Byzantine party of Epirus gained control. In 1306 anti-Byzantine forces under the leadership of Philip of Tarento joined forces with the Catholic Albanians, seized Dyrrachium and were intent upon overthrowing Anna, but their campaign failed. Anna ruled until Thomas reached his majority, c. 1313.

Suggested Reading:

(1) Ostrogorsky, George. *A History of the Byzantine State*. New Brunswick, NJ: Rutgers University Press, 1969. pp. 510, 518, 520, 526, 535.

Anne

Duchess, ruler of Brittany (Bretagne) (1488-1514)

She was born in 1477, the daughter of Francois II (1458-1488). Anne inherited the duchy of Brittany upon her father's death, whereupon a French army invaded. Various countries sent aid, but the French forces prevailed. Anne was then forced to promise to marry only with the consent of the king. But she married Maximilian of Austria without such consent, touching off a new French invasion, after which the crown annulled her marriage. In 1491 she married Charles VII, king of France. When he died in 1498, King Louis XII obtained a divorce from his wife Jeanne, and married Anne in order to keep this duchy for the crown. They had a daughter, Claude who married King Francis I of France. When Anne died in 1514, Brittany became a part of France.

Suggested Reading:

(1) Egan, Edward W. et. al. *Kings, Rulers and Statesmen*. New York: Sterling Publishing, 1976. p. 154.
(2) Langer, William L., ed. *World History*. Boston: Houghton Mifflin, 1940, 1980. pp. 409-410.
(3) Morby, John. *Dynasties of the World*. Oxford: Oxford University Press, 1989. p. 83.

Anne

Queen of England and Scotland (1702-1714)

Anne (b. 1665), the second daughter of King James II and Anne Hyde, did not impress her father as a particularly promising offspring. For one thing, she did not embrace his Catholicism. For another, her father and indeed her public considered her dull and common, partially due to the fact that she was sickly, plump and plain—in later life, she was to bear a close resemblance to Queen Victoria who would rule a century later. From Mary Queen of Scots the Stuart line had inherited the blood affliction called porphyria, which plagued Anne all her life. During her childhood, at the insistence of her Protestant uncle, King Charles II, Anne lived away from court, estranged from her father, who himself has been described as arrogant, unattractive, humorless and boorish. She developed an abiding friendship with Sarah Jennings Churchill, who wielded enormous influence over her for over 20 years and who convinced her to favor William III of Orange over James when William arrived on England's shores to claim the throne from Anne's Catholic father. William and Mary, Anne's sister, became constitutional monarchs in 1683, and Anne was placed in line for succession to the throne. That same year, at age 18, Anne married a handsome fair-haired, blue-eyed prince, who soon became as fat and phlegmatic and as fond of drink as she. He was Prince George of Denmark, by whom she had subsequently had 17 pregnancies, most ending in miscarriage or infant death. Only one child survived to age eleven. During the six-year reign of her sister, with whom she quarreled bitterly—primarily over Anne's devotion to Sarah Churchill—Anne continued to live in exile from court. However, following Mary's death in 1694, William welcomed her and her unpopular husband, and Sarah as well, at court. Shortly before his death, William embarked on the War of the Spanish Succession, which was his legacy to Anne. When Anne came to the throne at age thirty-seven (1702), she suffered from obesity, gout and premature aging brought about by her blood disorder. Too ill to walk to her coronation, she made a heavy burden for the bearers of her sedan chair. Despite her obesity, or possibly because of it, her subjects perceived her as good natured and dubbed her "Good Queen Anne." Her husband Prince George attempted to assist her in her royal duties, but he was unpopular with the English people. In 1704, partly due to her friendship with Sarah but also due to John Churchill's illustrious victories in the continuing war, Anne named Sarah's husband the first duke of Marlborough. Eventually, however,

Sarah became more queenly than Anne, even throwing a royal tantrum in Kensington Palace. Queen Anne dismissed her and soon after, the Duke as well. The death of her beloved George in 1708 left her with few personal allies. But her political future was bright: When the war ended in 1713, England towered as the world's greatest power with many new far-flung acquisitions. England forged a legislative union with Scotland, forming the nucleus of the United Kingdom. In addition, Anne accepted the principle of a constitutional monarchy, a system which England maintains to this day. She was the last monarch to veto an act of Parliament, or to preside over the majority of the Cabinet meetings. Although she showed no interest in the literature, drama and art which flourished during her reign,—she felt taxed, in fact, by prolonged attempts at intellectual conversation—she established a receptive climate for the arts. Anne was also the last monarch to practice "touch healings" of her subjects for the lymphatic tubercular condition called scrofula. She died in 1714 leaving no heirs, a widowed and friendless old woman at age forty-nine, the last of the Stuart line.

Suggested Reading:

(1) Hodges, Margaret. *Lady Queen Anne.* New York: Farrar Straus & Giroux, 1969.

(2) Kenyon, J.P. *The Stuarts.* Glasgow: William Collins Sons & Co., Ltd., 1970. pp. 186-207.

(3) Hudson, M.E. and Mary Clark. *Crown of a Thousand Years.* New York: Crown Publishing, Inc., 1978. pp. 114-117.

Anne of Austria (Anne d'Autriche)

Queen regent of France (1643-1651), governor of Brittany (1647-1666)

Anne was born in 1601 in Madrid, the daughter of Philip III of Spain. In 1615, at the age of fourteen, she became the wife of Louis XIII of France. The royal couple had two sons, the future Louis XIV and Philippe, future duc d'Orleans, but they lived apart for 23 years as a result of the meddlings of Cardinal Richelieu, who, for political reasons, wished to alienate the king from his wife. In 1636 she was named Governor of Paris. When the king died in 1643, Anne had his will, which deprived her of right of sole regency, annulled and became the queen regent for her son Louis XIV, who was only five years old. Although she was inexperienced, she exercised shrewd judgment by choosing as her minister Cardinal Mazarin, a wise and diplomatic manager who helped her maintain the absolute power of the monarchy that Richelieu had established for Louis XIII. Louis XIV was only five years old when his father died, and thus Anne served as Regent for almost a decade, preserving a close relationship with the Cardinal, her favorite,—some have concluded that they were secretly married—and thus establishing on firm grounds her young son's throne. In 1647 she became governor of Brittany, the second female to govern a major province. She continued to exercise influence over her son's decisions and to govern Brittany until the time of her death in 1666.

Suggested Reading:

(1) Durant, Will and Ariel. *The Story of Civilization, Part VIII, The Age of Louis XIV*. New York: Simon & Schuster, 1960. pp. 3-45.
(2) Harding, Robert. *Anatomy of a Power Elite*. New Haven: Yale University Press, 1978. pp. 127, 221.
(3) Sédillot, René. *An Outline of French History*. tr. Gerald Hopkins. New York: Alfred A. Knopf, 1967. p. 209.

Anne of England (or Anne of Hanover)

Regent of the Dutch Republic (1751-1766)

Anne was the eldest daughter of King George II of Great Britain and Caroline of Ansbach. She was married to William IV of Orange-Nassau who ruled the Dutch Republic from 1748 to 1751. When he died, their son, William V, was only five years old. Queen Anne acted as regent until William was 18 years old.

Suggested Reading:

(1) Langer, William L., ed. *World History*. Boston: Houghton Mifflin, 1940, 1980. pp. 475-476.

Anne of France

Defacto regent of France (1483-1491)

She was born in 1461, the daughter of King Louis XI of France. She was more intelligent and politically astute than her brother Charles (VIII), nine years her junior, and than the man she married, Pierre de Bourbon, seigneur de Beaujeu. The couple had a daughter, Suzanne, who was named heir to her father's Bourbon lands. When King Louis died in 1483, Charles was singularly unfit to ascend to the throne. He was 13 years old, with modest intellectual capacities and delicate health. Anne and her husband assumed the reigns of power in an effort to surmount problems with many wealthy noblemen caused by her late father. To mollify these noblemen, she restored lands which had been confiscated under her father's rule, and she dismissed many of her father's court favorites who had been responsible, in the eyes of the noblemen, for their grievances. In 1483, by negotiations already begun before the death of Louis XI, Charles was betrothed to Margaret of Austria, duchess of Savoy. From this betrothal, he received Artois and the Franche-Comte; however, Anne had a more profitable union in mind: one which would bring the duchy of Brittany under France's dominion. In 1491 she persuaded Charles to repudiate his engagement to Margaret in favor of marriage to Anne of Brittany. After the marriage, Charles' wife and his friend, Etienne de Vesc, persuaded him to free himself from the influence of his sister. In addition to holding the reigns of government for seven years, Anne had been the effective overseer of her husband's Bourbon lands during the whole of their marriage. When he died in 1503, she continued to administer her daughter Suzanne's lands, knowing from her own experiences the penchant of royalty for expanding their domains. Anne died in 1522.

Suggested Reading:

(1) Previté-Orton, C. W. *The Shorter Cambridge Medieval History.* Cambridge: Cambridge University Press, 1952, 1987. vol. 2. p. 484.

Anne Marie Louise d'Orleans

Mademoiselle de Montpensier, ruler of Auvergne (1617)

She was the daughter of Marie de Bourbon Montpensier and Jean Baptist Gaston, duke of Orleans, who ruled from 1608 to 1617. She was the granddaughter of Henri de Bourbon, who ruled from 1602 to 1608. She was the last ruler of Auvergne, which became part of France.

Suggested Reading:

(1) Egan, Edward W. et. al., eds. *Kings, Rulers and Statesmen*. New York: Sterling Publishing, 1976. p. 151.

Arsinde

Countess, ruler of Carcassonne (934-957)

She was the daughter of Acfred II, count of Carcassonne, which was located in what is now southwestern France. Arsinde ruled during a time when Carcassonne went its own way. It was not until the reign of Philip III the Bold (1270-85) that walls were built (1272) and royal power firmly established in southern France. Arsinde married Arnaud de Comminges. The couple had a son, Roger, who succeeded his mother, ruling as Count Roger I in 957.

Suggested Reading:

(1) Egan, Edward W., et. al., eds. *Kings, Rulers and Statesmen*. New York: Sterling Publishing, 1976. p. 156.
(2) Langer, William L., ed. *World History*. Boston: Houghton Mifflin, 1940, 1980. p. 247.

Asa

Queen of Norway (mid-9th century)

Queen Asa is known to have lived in Viking Norway in the middle of the 9th century and to have died at about age 25 or 30. In 1904 the bodies of two women were found in an elaborate burial ship in a grave in Oseberg, South Norway. The highly decorated vessel was the kind probably used by a king or chieftain, so one of the bodies was believed to be that of Queen Asa. With her was buried an older woman of about 60 or 70, possibly a bondswoman who sacrificed herself so as to serve her mistress in the afterworld.

Suggested Reading:

(1) Donovan, Frank R. *The Vikings*. New York: American Heritage Publishing Co., 1964. p. 89.
(2) Wilson, David. *The Vikings and Their Origins*. London: Thames and Hudson Ltd., 1970. pp. 57, 122.

Europe Section B

Balthild

Regent of Neustria (657-664)

Neustria was located in the northeastern portion of present-day France. The daughter of Anglo-Saxon royalty, Balthild, being a Christian, was kidnapped as a child and made a slave. She escaped and eventually married King Clovis II (Chlodwig), ruler of Neustria and Burgundy (639-657). When he became deranged, she ruled in his stead. When he died in 664, Balthild became regent for Clothar III (Lothair), king of Neustria (657-673), king of all Franks (656-600), until he came of age in 664. Balthild, remembering her own tragic childhood, forbade the sale of Christians as slaves. She founded a monastery and made efforts to establish communication between Christian converts in Neustria and those across the English Channel.

Suggested Reading:

(1) Bolding, Elise. *The Underside of History, A View of Women through Time.* Boulder: Westview Press, Inc., 1976. p. 396.

Barbara, Agatha

President of Malta (1982-1987)

She was born March 11, 1924 in Zabbar, Malta. Visually challenged, she nevertheless pursued careers in teaching and in politics as a member of the Malta Labour Party. In 1947, at the age of 23, she was elected Malta's first woman MP, representing the Second District. In 1955 she became the first and only woman to hold cabinet rank when she became Minister of Education, a post she held until 1958.

Although Malta gained independence from Great Britain in September, 1964, at the citizens' request, during a transition period Queen Elizabeth II was named Queen of Malta, and British forces were allowed to remain on the island for ten more years. In 1971 Agatha Barbara became Minister of Education and Culture and held the post until 1974.

On December 13, 1974, Malta became a democratic republic within the British Commonwealth, and the office of president was established. Sir Anthony Mamo, formerly Governor-General, became the first president. Agatha Barbara became Minister of Employment, Labour and Welfare. In December 1976 Dr. Anton Buttigieg was elected president; he served until 1982.

Following a two-month period when Dr. Albert Hyzler served as acting President, Agatha Barbara became Malta's first woman president in 1982. She served until 1987, when the Nationalist Party defeated the Labour Party and gained control of the government, a position it continues to enjoy.

Ms. Barbara continued to maintain a keen interest in politics and also in sports; she had previously been named Honorary President of St. Patrick's Football Club. Now retired, she resides in Zabbar, Malta.

Suggested Reading:

(1) Misokova, Cynthia, National Tourism Organisation—Malta, http://www.tourism,org,mt; cmiso@tourism,org,mt, March 1998.

(2) Ernest Kay, ed. *The World Who's Who of Women*, Third Edition. Cambridge, England: International Biographical Centre, 1976, p. 50.

Beatrice, Countess

Ruler of Provence (1245-1267)

Beatrice was the daughter of Raymond Berengar V (r. 1209-1245). She inherited the rule of Provence upon his death in 1245. In 1246 she married Charles, count of Anjou, who in 1266 became Charles I, king of Naples and Sicily. However, he lost Sicily in 1282. Beatrice had a son, Charles II the Lame. She died in 1267 and her husband continued to rule until his death in 1285. Thereafter Charles II inherited the rule of Provence.

Suggested Reading:

(1) Smith, Denis Mack, *A History of Sicily*, Vol. 1. New York: Dorset Press, 1968. pp. 66f-104.
(2) Morby, John E. *Dynasties of the World*. Oxford; Oxford University Press, 1989. p. 87.

Beatrice

Regent of Tuscany (1052-1076)

Tuscany was located in present day northwestern Italy. Beatrice was married to Count Boniface of Canossa, Marquess of Tuscany. They had three children, two of whom died early. Boniface was considered by Holy Roman Emperor Henry III to be his most dangerous enemy in Italy. When Boniface was assassinated in 1052, the youngest child, Matilda, age six, became heiress to the house of Attoni, founded by her grandfather Atto Adalbert. Beatrice ruled Tuscany alone until 1054, when she married Godfrey the Bearded, duke of Upper Lorraine. Godfrey stood in no better stead with Henry III than Boniface. In 1055 Henry arrested Beatrice and Matilda and sent them to Germany, while Godfrey went into hiding. In time, Godfrey had made peace with Henry, and in 1056 Beatrice and Matilda were released. Beatrice returned to Tuscany to rule over her daughter's lands. In 1069 GodfreyCastile, coerced Ferdinand to accept an arranged marriage between his infant daughter and John I of Castile so as to bring Portugal under the eventual dominance of Castile. When Ferdinand died in 1383, Leonora acted briefly as Beatrice's regent, but she was forced to acknowledge John I as king of Portugal as per the terms of the marriage agreement. In 1387, to strengthen a claim for the Castilian crown, John was married a second time to Phillipa of Lancaster, daughter of duke John of Gaunt. Thus from infancy onward Beatrice remained a helpless pawn in the drive for Castilian power.

Suggested Reading:

(1) Langer, William L., ed. *World History*. Boston: Houghton Mifflin, 1980. p. 306.

Beatrix de Bourgogne

Ruler of Bourbon (1287-1310)

She was the daughter of Agnes de Dampierre and Jean de Bourgogne. She married Robert de France, Comte de Clermont, and succeeded as ruler of Bourbon when her mother died in 1287. She died in 1310.

Suggested Reading:

(1) Egan, Edward W. et. al., eds. *Kings, Rulers and Statesmen*. New York: Sterling Publishing Co., 1976. p. 153.

Beatrix Wilhelmina Armgard

Queen of The Netherlands (1980-)

Beatrix was born in 1938 in Soestdijk, Baarn, the oldest of four daughters of Queen Juliana and Prince Bernhard. Because of the hardships of Nazi occupation of their country during World War II, the royal family was sensitive to public sentiment against unnecessary extravagances by the monarchy, even though the royal family continued to be much loved by the Dutch people. The daughters were reared in a much more democratic fashion than their counterparts in Great Britain. Beatrix attended Baarn grammar school and the State University of Leiden, where she earned a doctor of law degree (1961). In 1966 she made an unpopular marriage to Prince Claus von Amsberg, a German diplomat whose participation in the Hitler Youth Movement and the German Army during World War II did not make him a prime candidate in the eyes of the people. That he had been exonerated by an Allied court did not clear him in the opinion of the Dutch subjects. However, the union produced the first male heir to the House of Orange since the time of William III (d. 1890) when Willem-Alexandre was born in 1967, and much of the public opposition to von Amsberg disappeared. Two other sons were born in 1968 and 1969. At the age of 42, when her youngest son had reached the age of 11, Beatrix succeeded her mother upon Queen Juliana's abdication (1980), taking an oath as "king." Beatrix describes woman's role in Holland as much like her own: "She can do a lot but she can't decide. There's a traditional limit on all women." Described as having a "strong handshake" and as "stylish, magnetic with plumb-line posture," the queen does not engage in social controversy, understanding that her main function is to be a symbol of unity and of continuity with the past. Her concern for the preservation of the historic led her to take great care in equipping the room of her seventeenth century palace which she uses for her sculpture studio. The royal family, which engages in a certain amount of foreign diplomacy on an informal level, has enjoyed wide popularity throughout Europe. The Netherlands has now had a woman ruler for 100 years.

Suggested Reading:

(1) *Who's Who in the World, 1997*. New Providence, RI: Marquis Who's Who/Reed Elsevier Inc., 1996. p. 144.
(2) Langer, William L., ed. *World History*. Boston: Houghton Mifflin, 1980. p. 475.
(3) Bart McDowell. "The Dutch Touch." *National Geographic* 170. October 1986: 500-525.

Beckett, Margaret Royston

British Foreign Secretary (2006-)

She was born Margaret Mary Jackson on January 15, 1943 in Ashton-under-Lyne in Lancashire. Her father was English, a carpenter; her mother was an Irish Catholic. She had one sister who became a nun. She was educated at the Notre Dame High School for Girls in Norwich and the University of Manchester Institute for Science and Technology, where she became a metallurgist. She also studied at the John Dalton Polytechnic Institute, which is now Manchester Metropolitan University.

In 1961 she became a student apprentice in metallurgy at Associated Electrical Industries. She became a life-long member of the Transport and General Workers Union in 1964. Two years later she joined the metallurgy department at the University of Manchester as an experiment officer. She became a researcher in industrial policy for the Labour Party in 1970 and in 1973 was selected as a Labour Party candidate for Lincoln in an attempt to defeat Dick Traverne. She lost in the 1974 February General Election and afterwards went to work for Labour MP Baroness Judith Hart as a researcher.

PM Harold Wilson called for another election in October of 1974, and this time Jackson defeated Taverne for the seat in Lincoln. By then, Hart was Minister for Overseas Development, and Jackson became her Parliamentary Private Secretary. In 1975 Harold Wilson made her Whip, and the next year James Callaghan promoted her to Parliamentary Under Secretary of State at the Department of Education of Science, replacing Joan Lestor, MP for Eton and Slough, who had resigned in protest over spending cuts in her district. In the 1979 General Election Jackson lost her seat to a member of the Conservative Party.

Shortly after her defeat, she married Lionel (Leo) Beckett, a local Labour Party official in Lincoln. She has two step-children. She went to work in 1979 for Granada Television as a researcher. In 1980, as Margaret Beckett, she was elected to Labour's National Executive Committee. In 1983 she became a Member of Parliament for Derby South, a position she continues to hold as of 2006.

By 1988 Beckett had moved more to the center of her party and had become a front bencher as spokesperson for Social Security (since 1984). She became Shadow Chief Secretary to the Treasury in 1989. In 1992 she was elected Deputy Leader of the Labour Party and under John Smith served as Shadow Leader of the House of Commons. The following year she became a Member of the Privy Council. When John Smith died in May of 1994 she briefly headed the Labour Party. When Tony Blair was elected Leader in July of that year, Beckett had hoped to become Deputy Leader, but she came in behind John Prescott. Thereafter, she became Shadow Secretary of State for Health and in 1995 Shadow Secretary of State for Trade and Industry. Following the 1997 General Election, she became Tony Blair's Secretary of State for Trade and Industry, a position she kept until 1998, at which time she was appointed President of the Council and Leader of the House of Commons until she was replaced by Robin Cook in June of 2001. After the 2001 elections, a new department, the Department for Environment, Food, and Rural Affairs (DEFRA) was created and Beckett was selected to lead it. She held this position until May of 2006, when she became the first woman to hold the post of Secretary of State for Foreign and Commonwealth Affairs, replacing Jack Straw, who had condemned Israel for the Qana bombings.

Beckett described the government as "united" around the goal of ending the conflict between Lebanon and Israel. However, in August of 2006, 37 members of her constituence left the Labour Party and joined the Liberal Democrats in protest to her stance on the Lebanese-Israeli conflict. Meanwhile, criticism from within her department about her near-invisibility since taking office. She was reported as rejecting nearly all proposed trips and interviews that have been proposed to raise her public profile and shunning the kind of shuttle diplomacy that were the trademarks of both Robin Cook and Jack Straw. Yet, she was criticized in April 2006 when the details of ministers' use of RAF aircraft for official travel were published. Beckett was discovered to have taken 134 flights on ministerial business between 2002 and March 2005, flying 102,673 miles. The press noted also that Lionel Beckett frequently accompanied her on trips, leading to his being described as the "political equivalent of a WAG" (an acronym used to describe the wives and girlfriends of England football players). Diplomats also complained about the frequent presence of her husband Leo in the Foreign Office. While the *Spectator* was calling on her to resign, describing her as "at heart, an old isolationist, pacifist Leftist," and she was described by correspondents at the Rome Summit as "nervous," Beckett has climbed up the ranks the hard way, becoming the first woman to hold the position of Foreign Secretary and only the second woman to hold one of the four Great Offices of State. She is also only the second woman to serve as Leader of a major party.

Suggested Reading:

(1) *The New York Times.* July 23, 2006.
(2) *www.TheyWorkForYou.com*—Maragret Beckett MP.
(3) "Blair and Beckett Face Internal Revolt" by Ewen MacAskill, Will Woodward and Tania Branigan. Guardian Weekly. August 4-10, 2006.

Bergmann-Pohl, Sabine

President of the Parliament of German Democratic Republic (April 5, 1990-October 2, 1990)

Following World War II, Germany was divided into four zones by the Allies. In 1949 the zones administered by the Western Allies became the Federal Republic, or West Germany, a democratic republic, while the German Democratic Republic, or East Germany, was established under Soviet auspices as an independent communist state.

East Germany was led for more than a quarter of a century by Walter Ulbricht. Thereafter, no single leader dominated the government, although

Erich Honecker functioned as head of state from 1976 to 1989, when he was forced to resign. After the communist government collapsed in 1989 and the reunification of Germany was anticipated, the Socialist Unity Party, a communist organization, held free elections for a new People's Chamber, which took office in March, 1990. The charge to the Chamber was to work out the economic and political merger of East Germany with West Germany.

Sabine Bergmann-Pohl, born April 20, 1946 in Eisenach, studied medicine in East Germany. A Protestant, in 1981 she joined the conservative CDU party and was elected to the Volkskammer (parliament) in March 1990. On April 5 she was elected President and served until October 2 of that year. The following day, East and West Germany were formally reunited. Prior to the reunification, she met with President Rolald Reagan and said, "Mr. President, we have much to thank you for." She served as the last head of state of East Germany and its only women leader. After reunification, she was named Minister Without Portfolio, as a member of the Bundestag (parliament). From 1990 to 1991 she was Federal Minister for Special. From 1991 to 1998 she served as Under Secretary for Health. She retired in September 2002.

Suggested Reading:

(1) *Funk & Wagnalls New Encyclopedia*, vol. 11., 1986. "Germany" pp. 355 364

Bianca

Queen, vicar of Sicily (1410-1412)

She was the wife of Martin I, king of Aragon from 1395 to 1410. On the death of John I, who ruled Sicily from 1387 to 1395, Martin I, ruler of Aragon (1395-1410) and regent of Sicily, left his only son, also named Martin, as king, or viceroy, of Sicily. The latter, then also called Martin I, I died in 1409, willing the kingdom to his father, just like any other item of personal property. The kingdom went to King Martin I of Aragon, who then became known also as Martin II, king of Sicily. He, too, died the following year, and as neither Martin had left an heir, the vacant throne of Sicily fell to Martin II's widow Bianca. Count Cabrera of Modica, Grand Justiciar, defied Queen Bianca, hoping to secure the throne for himself. In addition, in each region, powerful feudal barons reasserted their rights and witheld revenues, so Queen Bianca had to resort to private borrowing to keep the kingdom running. Even the citizens of Messina, which supported her rule, took advantage of the situation by occupying the royal castles at Syracuse and Catania. A committee was appointed to select a candidate for king. Out of a list of six, the committee chose Ferdinand, king of Castile, who in 1412 proclaimed himself king of Sicily before the citizens of Sicily had even been consulted.

Suggested Reading:

(1) Smith, Denis Mack. *A History of Sicily*. New York: Dorset Press, 1968. vol 1, *Medieval Sicily*. pp. 91-92.
(2) Langer, William L., ed. *World History*. Boston: Houghton Mifflin, 1980. p. 306.

Bianca Maria

Duchess, regent of Milan (1466-1468).

She was the illegitimate and only child of Duke Filippo Maria Visconti of Milan and Maria of Savoy. In 1433 she became betrothed to Francesco Sforza, whom she married in 1441. The couple had a son, Galeazzo Maril Aforza, born in 1444. Blanca thought she was the legal heir of Milan when her father died (1447), but instead he had named Alfonso of Aragon, king of Naples, as his successor. Francesco battled Naples, Venice, Montferrat and Savoy for the right to rule Milan in his wife's name. In 1450 he achieved that right and ruled until his death in 1466. Bianca ruled with her son for the first two years of his rule, but following his marriage in 1468 to Bona of Savoy, she retired and became a patron of the arts.

Suggested Reading:

(1) Langer, William L., ed. *World History*. Boston: Houghton Mifflin, 1980. p. 321.

Bjerregaard, Ritt

Premier of Denmark (1995)

She was born in Copenhagen in 1941 and entered politics as a member of the Danish Parliament in 1971, and has held a seat ever since. A member of the Social Democratic party, she was appointed minister of education in 1973. In the election of December 1973, because of dissension among the left-wing parties, the non-Socialist parties gained a majority. The Social Democratic government resigned, and Poul Hartling, of the Venstre (Liberal Democrat) party, headed a minority government. An outspoken critic of French leadership and French policies, Bjerregaard was relieved of her position after criticizing French conservative Jacques Chirac, who was chosen in 1974 by French President Valéry Giscard d'Estaing as his prime minister, saying that she didn't think Chirac would grow in stature with his post. Apparently the French minister proved too ambitious with his agenda favoring businessmen and was dismissed in 1976. Hartling attempted to institute a firm savings program which brought on increased unemployment and ultimately toppled his government in January, 1975. The Social Democrats returned to power with Anker Jørgensen at the helm. During this period Ritt Bjerregaard was again appointed minister of education, a position she held until 1978. In 1979 she became minister of social affairs, remaining at that post until 1982. She was chairperson of the Parliamentary Group of the Social Democrat Party (1987-1992)

Years in politics did not alter her outspoken criticism of French policies of which she disapproved. When the French government began nuclear tests in the South Pacific, she publicly critized them.

She took an active role in bring Denmark into the European Economic community, becoming, in 1990, a member of the Parliamentary Assembly of the Countries of Europe. In 1992 she was elected vice president of that body. She also served as president of the Danish European Movement (1992-1994). She served on the Trilateral Commission of the Center for European Policy Studies. In 1995 Ritt Bjerregaard, the first female premier of Denmark, was sent to Brussels as the European Union environment commissioner. She has written several books on politics and women's role in politics.

Suggested Reading:

(1) *Marquis' Who's Who in the World 1997*. New Providence, NJ: Reed Elsevier, Inc., 1996. p. 149.
(2) *The Australian Magazine*. April 1996: 22.

Blanca, Doña (Blanche)

Queen of Navarre (1425-1441)

In the Middle Ages, from 1134 to 1458, Navarre was an independent kingdom in presentday northern Spain. Blanca was the daughter of Charles III the Noble of the House of Evreux (r. Navarre 1387-1425). In ca. 1420 Blanca married Juan II of Portugal, king of Aragon. They had a son, Carlos de Viana, and two daughters, Leonor (Eleanor of Navarre) and Blanche of Aragon. In 1425 Blanca succeeded her father, Capetian King Carlos III the Noble (r. 1387-1425) as queen of Navarre. She died in 1441, but the throne was not passed down to her heirs until after John's death 38 years later. He was succeeded by her son Don Carlos (d. 1461) and then by her daughter Eleanor (Leonor). John's second marriage produced a son, Ferdinand, who married Isabella of Castile, and who ultimately brought the southern part of the kingdom of Navarre under Aragonese control (1512).

Suggested Reading:

(1) Morby, John E. *Dynasties of the World*. Oxford: Oxford University Press, 1989. p. 114.
(2) McKendrick, Melveena, *Ferdinand and Isabella*. New York: American Heritage Publishing Co., 1968. pp. 22-23.
(3) Egan, Edward W. et. al., eds. *Kings, Rulers and Statesmen*. New York: Sterling Publishing Co., 1976. p. 430.

Blanche of Castile

Regent of France (1226-1236 and 1248-1252)

Blanche was born in 1188 in Palencia, Spain, to Alfonso VIII of Castile and Eleanor, daughter of Henry II of England. In 1199, when Blanche was only 11 years old, her grandmother, Eleanor of Aquitaine, arranged for her marriage to the future Louis VIII of France; in fact, the elderly Eleanor traveled from England to Spain to deliver Blanche to France herself, a gesture designed to emphasize the importance of the union for peace with both Spain and England. In 1214 Blanche and Louis had a son who would eventually become Louis IX. In 1216 when her uncle John of England died, Blanche tried to seize the English throne. Louis stormed England on her behalf but was defeated, and John's son was crowned Henry III. In 1223 Louis VIII succeeded to the throne of France but he died three years later. Blanche became regent of France and guardian for their son, Louis IX, who was 12 years old. She proved to be a strong and able ruler. To quell rebellious nobles, Blanche rode into battle at the head of her own troops. When the nobles tried to abduct her son, she expelled them and replaced them with commoners. It was Blanche who was responsible for the Treaty of Paris, which ushered in an era of peace and prosperity. When her son reached 21, Blanche was relieved of the regency, but she remained a large influence on his life and upon affairs of state. When Louis and his wife Margaret determined to embark on a crusade in 1248, Blanche, whose ability to rule had been proved during her son's minority, was once again made regent of France. There were foreign problems to solve: she had to persuade the English to keep the peace, and she had to maintain a delicate balance of relations with Holy Roman Emperor Frederick. Louis was captured by the Turks in 1250 and most of his troops were shot. He was ransomed and sent home, but Blanche died in 1252 while her son was still out of the country.

Suggested Reading:

(1) Runciman, Steven. *A History of the Crusades*. Cambridge: Cambridge University Press, 1987. vol. 3, *The Kingdom of Acre*. pp. 256, 274, 279-280.

(2) Heer, Friedrich. *The Medieval World*. tr. Janet Sondheimer. New York: Mentor/NAL, 1962. p. 319.

Bona of Savoy

Regent of Milan (1476-1479)

Bona was the wife of Galeazzo Maria Sforza, ruler of Milan from 1466 to 1476. They had a son, Gian Galeazzo. After her husband was assassinated in 1476, Bona served as regent, governing for her son. In 1478 she supported Florence against Naples after the Pazzi family conspiracy, an unsuccessful attempt to overthrow the Medici rulers of Florence. The Duchy of Milan was usurped in 1479 by Bona's brother-in-law, Ludovico il Moro.

Suggested Reading:

(1) Langer, William L., ed. *World History*. Boston: Houghton Mifflin, 1980. p. 322.

Bonaparte, Elisa

See Elisa Bonaparte

Boudicca (or Boadicea)

Queen of the Iceni (c. A.D. 60)

Born ca. A.D. 26 of a royal family, Boudicca was married to King Prasutagus, who ruled the Iceni in what is now Norfolk, England, by special arrangement under Roman suzerainty. Boudicca was tall and comanding, with tawny hair and what was described as a "harsh voice." She had produced two daughters but no male heirs when King Prasutagus died. Under terms of his will, he left his estate to his daughters and to Nero, Emperor of Rome, believing that he could count on the crown's protection of his family's holdings. However, the Romans immediately seized his kingdom, ousted his family, plundered his chief tribesmen and installed Suetonius Paulinus as provisional governor. Boudicca was publicly flogged and she watched her daughters, legendarily named Voada and Voadicia, being raped by the legionnaires. She immediately began organizing opposition and, while Paulinus was away, she initiated a determined revolt throughout East Anglia. During her brief reign of terror, her followers managed to sack Camulodunum (Colchester), Verulamium, Londinium (London), and various military installations, and reportedly took the lives of 70,000 Romans and Roman sympathizers. She left the Roman Ninth Legion in shambles. However, her victory was short-lived, for Paulinus retaliated with fresh troops and met the Britons at somewhere near Fenny Stratford on Watling. After a bloody standoff, the exhausted Britons were cut down and Roman rule was restored. Boudicca, unwilling to live under Roman rule and certain, at any rate, that she would be executed, took poison and died c. A.D. 60.

Suggested Reading:

(1) Duff, Charles. *England and the English*. New York: G.P. Putnam's Sons, 1955. pp. 51, 52, 63, 232.

(2) Markdale, Jean. *Women of the Celts.* tr. A. Mygind, et. al. Rochester, Vermont: Inner Traditions International, Ltd., 1986. pp. 27, 32, 253.
(3) Langer, William L., ed. *World History.* Boston: Houghton Mifflin, 1980. pp. 120, 179

Brigantia (or Brigit)

Legendary queen of the Brigantes (A.D. 51)

Brigantia is mentioned in inscriptions both in Britain and in Gaul. According to Cormac, she was the daughter of the Dagda (or lord of diverse talents, or good-at-everything god). She was the patron of poets and was called *banfile*, meaning "female poet." She is believed to be Christianized as St. Brigid.

Suggested Reading:

(1) Chadwick, Nora. *The Celts.* Harmondsworth, Middlesex: Penguin Books, Ltd. 1976. p. 169.
(2) Duff, Charles. *England and the English.* New York. G. P. Putnam's Sons, 1955. p. 42.

Brunhilde (or Brunichildis)

Queen Regent for Austrasia and Burgundy (575-581 and 595-613)

She was born ca. 550, the daughter of the Visigothic king, Athanagild, and Goiswinth. She was the sister of Galswintha, who became the second wife of the Merovingian king Chilperic I, ruler of an area which is presently Belgium. Brunhilde married Chilperic's half-brother, Sigebert I, king of the eastern kingdom of Austrasia from 561 to 575. Between them, the two brothers and their two sister wives controlled the whole Frankish world. However, when Galswintha was murdered at the instigation of Chilperic to please his mistress Fredegond, Brunhilde vowed revenge, and thus began a feud which lasted and escalated for 40 years amid plots and counter plots resulting in several murders. Sigebert was murdered by Fredegond's emissaries in 575 and Brunhilde's son Chilperic II was made king. During his minority, Brunhilde was made regent, and she soon married Merovech, Sigebert's nephew. In 581, Chilperic II was adopted by his uncle Chilperic I and Brunhilde was free to devote herself to venting her revenge upon Fredegond. When her son died in 595, Brunhilde was again made regent for her two grandsons: Theudoric II, King of Burgundy, and Theudebert II, King of Austrasia. She wielded tremendous power, and her only rival was Fredegond, who by that time was ruling Neustria for her young son, Clotaire II. On Fredegond's death in 598, Brunhilde seized Neustria as well, and so united under her dominion the entire Merovingian world. Her grandson Theudebert incurred her wrath in 612 and she persuaded his brother Theudoric to overthrow him. In 613, the Austrasian nobles who opposed her and favored Theudebert united under Clotaire II and were able to overthrow her government. Brunhilde was sentenced to death by being dragged behind a wild horse. Brunhilde probably inspired some of the ancient German heroic myths concerning a beautiful amazonian queen.

Suggested Reading:

(1) Gregory of Tours. *The History of the Franks*. tr. Lewis Thorpe. Harmondsworth, Middlesex: Penguin Books, Ltd., 1974. pp. 196, 221-222, 233, 247, 251, 254-256, 268, 272, 275, 279, 305, 370, 383, 401-402, 417, 426, 437, 453, 456-458, 480-481, 488-489, 491-492, 502-503, 505, 507, 514-515, 518, 524-526, 578.
(2) Sullivan, Richard E. *Heirs of the Roman Empire*. Ithaca: Cornell University Press, 1960. pp. 39-40.

Brundtland, Gro Harlem

Prime Minister of Norway (1981 and 1986-1989, 1990-1996)

She was born April 20, 1939 in Oslo, the daughter of Gundmund and Inga Brynolf Harlem. In 1960 she married Arne Olav Brundtland and had a daughter, Kaja, and three sons, Knut, Ivar, and Jorgen. She received her MD degree in 1963 from Oslo University, then attended Harvard University School of Public Health, where in 1965 she earned a Master's degree in Public Health. She returned to Oslo and served for two years as medical officer for the National Directorate of Public Health before becoming, in 1968, the assistant medical director for the School of Health Services in Oslo.

Dr. Brundtland entered political life in 1974 when she was appointed Minister of Environment for the Norwegian government, a post she held until 1979. She was elected Member of Parliament in 1974 from the

Europe Section C

Cartimandua

Queen, ruler of Brigantia (A.D. 41-60)

The Brigantes were a large northern British tribe during the time of Roman invasion of Britain. Cartimandua's consort and sometimes adversary was Venutius, who had ambitions to rule on his own. In A.D. 43, when the Romans invaded Britain, in a Celtic practice known as *celsine*, she signed a treaty placing herself under Roman protection. Her decision was very unpopular with the Brigantes, who launched a series of revolts against her. In A.D. 48 she was forced to call on her Roman protectors to quell a rebellion. When Caratacus, Welsh leader of an unsuccessful anti-Roman rebellion, approached Queen Cartimandua seeking asylum and an alliance, the queen, in a display of loyalty designed to buy Roman favor, had him arrested and turned him over to the Romans in chains. Her husband called her a traitor and began rallying support for her overthrow. In A.D. 57 he attempted to seize control of the government, but the Romans again intervened on her behalf. The couple eventually reconciled and ruled jointly for a while. Then Queen Cartimandua ran off with Vellocatus, the royal armor-bearer. Venutius and his troops gave chase, but again her Roman allies came to her rescue. Eventually in ca. A.D. 69, she abandoned the Brigantes altogether, and without her tie with the Romans, Vellocatus was powerless to prevent take-over. In 71, in a battle against the Roman general Venutius, Vellocatus and the Brigantes were defeated, and Rome annexed Brigantia.

Suggested Reading:

(1) Chadwick, Nora. *The Celts.* Harmondsworth, Middlesex: Penguin Books, Ltd., 1976. p. 65.
(2) Hubert, Henri. *The Greatness and Decline of the Celts.* New York: Arno Press, 1980. p. 159.

(3) Markdale, Jean. *Women of the Celts*. tr. A Mygind et. al. Rochester, VT: Inner Traditions International, 1986. p. 32.
(4) Rutherford, Ward. *Celtic Mythology*. Wellingborough, Northamptonshire: The Aquarian Press, 1987. p. 31.

Catalinda de Albret (or Catherine de Foix)

Queen of Navarre (1483-1484) co-ruler (1484-1516)

Catalinda was the grandaughter of Eleanor (Leonor, r. 1479) and Gaston IV of Foix. She succeeded her brother Fransesco Febo (Francis Febus, r. 1479-1483), who had married her mother Eleanor (Leonore), grandaughter of John II of Aragon and Dona Blanca of Navarre. She married Jean d'Albret c. 1502, and they had a son, Henry II, born in 1503. In 1512 King Ferdinand's troops succeeded in forcing southern Navarre to be annexed to Aragon and Castile, thus all but eliminating the throne of Navarre. She said to her husband at the time, "If we had been born you Catherine and I Don Jean, we would not have lost our kingdom." Catalinda died in 1516 and Henry became heir to the house of Albret claim. He gathered French forces and in 1521 invaded Navarre, intent on freeing it. He was defeated in his attempt; however, in 1530 Charles I of Spain, of his free will, ceded portions of Navarre back to Henry.

Suggested Reading:

(1) Morby, John E. *Dynasties of the World*. Oxford: Oxford University Press, 1989. p. 115.
(2) Carpenter, Clive. *The Guinness Book of Kings, Rulers & Statesmen*. Enfield, Middlesex: Guinness Superlatives Ltd., 1978. p. 222.

Caterina Sforza

Effective ruler of Forli and Imola (1488-1500)

She was born in 1462, the illegitimate daughter of Galeazza Maria Sforza, later duke of Milan, and his mistress. Reared by her grandmother, Cianca Vistonti-Sforza, she received an excellent education. Her father was assassinated in 1476. In 1477 Caterina was married by proxy to Girolamo

Riario of the Ordelaffi family, a nephew of Pope Sextus IV. When Venetian forces attempted to occupy her husband's lands in Forli, Caterina defended them in his absence (1483). When Sextus died, Caterina, seven months pregnant, held the fortress of Sant' Angelo until the new Pope could arrive to take possession. During her husband's illness, she ruled Forli for him. In 1488 her husband was killed by the Orsi family, but she made the Orsi pay dearly, in public executions, mutilations, dismemberings. While ruling on behalf of her son, she had to fight off neighbors, Papal claims and even the French. Her children were held hostage at one time, but she, being pregnant again, refused to yield the castle, explaining that she could always make more babies. Caterina took many lovers over the years. In 1489 her affair with Mario Ordelaffi so scandalized the Pope that he used her conduct as an excuse to attempt to award her lands to his own son, whose conduct was no better. One of her lovers, Giacomo Feo, of whom her legitimate son was jealous, had been speared to death and mutilated by a cohort of her son's. She had the killer, his wife and sons thrown down a well to drown (1495). Her second husband was Giovanni d'Medici (not the Pope), son of Pierofrancesco d'Medicis. In 1498 she had a son by Giovanni, Giovanni Della Banda Nera (John of the Black Bands), who became the greatest military leader of all the d'Medicis. In 1499, following the Treaty of Blois between France and Venice, the controversial and notorious Pope Alexander VI, citing a Papal bull designating Caterina as a "daughter of iniquity," decided that was grounds for giving her lands to his son, Cesare Borgia. Caterina did not plan to give up without a fight; Borgia was acting captain general of the Papal army and was aided by a large contingent of French troops, so she was aware that her chances of holding them off and surviving were slim. She wrote her uncle, "Should I perish, I want to perish like a man." Instead, she was captured in 1500 and repeatedly raped and sodomized for a year by Borgia's soldiers. She was released in 1501 and died in 1509.

Suggested Reading:

(1) Breisach, Ernst. *Caterina Sforza: A Renaissance Virago*. Chicago: University of Chicago Press, 1967.

(2) Hare, Christopher, *The Most Illustrious Ladies of the Italian Renaissance*. Williamstown, Mass.: Corner House Publishers, 1972. pp. 36, 135, 229-256.

Catherine

Countess, ruler of Vendome (1374-1412).

She was the daughter of Count Bouchard VI and Jeanne de Castile. When her father died in 1366, her mother and her brother, Count Bouchard VII, ruled Vendome jointly until his death in 1374. Catherine married Jean de Bourbon and bore a son, Louis I de Bourbon. She succeeded her brother and ruled until her death in 1412. Her son Louis I succeeded her.

Suggested Reading:

(1) Egan, Edward W. et. al., eds. *Kings, Rulers and Statesmen*. New York: Sterling Publishing Company, 1876. p. 162.

Catherine de Foix

See Catalinda de Albret

Catherine de Médicis

Regent of France (1552, 1560-1563, and 1574)

She was born in 1519, the daughter of Lorenzo de' Medici, duke of Urbino, and Madelaine de la Tour d'Auvergne, a Bourbon princess. She was the great-grandaughter of Lorenzo Il Magnifico, one of the greatest Italian leaders of all time. She was also the niece of Pope Clement VII. Her parents died when she was very young, and she was reared by nuns in Florence and Rome, who gave her an excellent education. In a pre-arranged marriage, she married Henry, duke d'Orleans in 1533, at the age of 14. Catherine had no children until she was 24, and Henry took a mistress, Diane de Poitiers, who had a great influence on him and his affairs for the rest of his life. Catherine remained in the background from that time onward until his death and only made her influence felt on the occasion of his absence when she received her first appointment as regent. In 1543, Catherine gave birth to a son who later became Frances II. She bore nine or ten children in all, seven of which lived. Three of her sons became kings of France, and two of her daughters became queens of Spain. In 1547 Henry became King Henry II, ruler of France. In 1552 he went off to continue his father's war against the Holy

Roman Emperor Charles V, and Catherine was appointed regent. In 1559 Henry was killed by the splinter of a broken lance while jousting. Frances II came to the throne, but ruled less than two years. He was succeeded by his brother, Charles IX, a boy of ten, in 1560. Catherine, a devout Catholic, became regent of France, to the despair of the Huguenots, the Protestants. Her greatest challenge was the animosity between Catholics and Protestants, which her Edict of Toleration was aimed at alleviating. In 1561 Jean Nicot brought back from Portugal an American import, a new herb for the queen's use in treating wounds and ulcers. Called the "Queen's herb," it was later called tobacco. In 1562 the first of the Wars of Religion erupted in France. Catherine presided over three civil wars in a decade. Charles was declared of age when he reached 13, but he remained under her domination for the rest of his life. She tried playing off the parties of the Protestant Condes against the Catholic Guises, entering into a plot with the Guises to rid the country completely of the Huguenots. She is credited with inducing Charles to order the Massacre of St. Bartholomew's Day in 1572 in which nearly all of the leading Huguenots in Paris were killed. All of Europe was scandalized by the bloodthirsty loss of life. Charles himself was guilt-ridden over the ghastly massacre and died within two years, the victim of tuberculosis. In 1572 Catherine had proposed her third and favorite son, Henry, for the throne of Poland, and in 1573 he had been crowned. After Charles' death in 1574, Catherine again assumed the regency for three months until Henry could be induced to return and be crowned Henry III. Henry was easily persuaded; he abandoned Poland at once. Catherine did not try to dominate her favorite son, who was considered a fop and a disgrace by the French people. She remained close and did his bidding, including making arduous diplomatic journeys on his behalf even in her later years. In 1589 he died as a result of a stab wound. Catherine died the same year at the age of 70.

Suggested Reading:

(1) Williamson, Hugh R. *Catherine de' Medici*. New York: Viking Press, 1973.
(2) Sédillot, René. *An Outline of French History*.tr. Gerard Hopkins. New York: Alfred A. Knopf, 1952, 1967. pp. 194, 199.

Catherine of Aragon

Regent of England (1512-1514)

She was born in 1485, the second daughter of King Ferdinand II of Aragon and Queen Isabella of Castile. She received an excellent education, particularly for a woman of her day, and was called a "miracle of learning." In 1501 she married Arthur, oldest son of King Henry VII of England, but he died a year later. In 1509 she became the first wife of Arthur's brother, Henry VIII. Unlike many royal couples of arranged marriages, the two appeared devoted on the many occasions when they entertained lavishly, and all might have gone well if Catherine had produced a male heir. During the next nine years she bore six children, but all died except Mary, who later became queen of England (1553-1558). Meanwhile, in 1512 Henry joined his father-in-law in a war against France, and Catherine served as regent in his absence. By 1527, since Catherine had produced no male heir, Henry appealed to Rome for an annulment on the grounds that she was his brother's widow. Catherine countered with an appeal arguing that her first marriage had never been consummated. The Pope delayed for years on making a decision. In 1531 Henry separated from his wife and two years later—after his marriage to Anne Boleyn—he had his own archbishop of Canterbury annul his first marriage. Parliament then passed the Act of Supremacy making the king, not the Pope, the head of the Church of England.

Suggested Reading:

(1) Mattingly, Garrett. *Catherine of Aragon*. Cambridge: Cambridge University Press, 1942.
(2) Myers, A.R. *England in the Late Middle Ages*. Harmondsworth, Middlesex: Penguin Books, Ltd., 1952. pp. 205, 237.
(3) Hudson, M. E. and Mary Clark. *Crown of a Thousand Years*. New York: Crown Publishing, 1978. pp. 77, 78.
(4) McKendrick, Melveena. *Ferdinand and Isabella*. New York: American Heritage Publishing Co., 1968. pp. 99, 100, 134, 140.

Catherine of Braganza

Regent of Portugal (1704-1705)

She was the daughter of King John IV and Luisa Maria de Guzman, who married her in 1662 to King Charles II of Great Britain. In the next two decades Catherine was frequently pregnant. She had a number of miscarriages but produced no heir, although Charles had 13 illegitimate offspring by a parade of mistresses. Catherine eventually returned to Portugal, ashamed of her own inadequacy and unable to tolerate his philandering. When he lay dying in 1685, he asked for his wife, but she sent a message asking that her absence be excused and "to beg his pardon if she had offended him all her life." He answered, "Alas, poor woman! She asks my pardon? I beg hers with all my heart; take her back that answer." Back in Portugal, Catherine made herself useful to the court: in 1704, while her brother was fighting in the War of Spanish Succession, she acted as regent on domestic matters.

Suggested Reading:

(1) Kenyon, J. P. *The Stuarts.* Glasgow: William Collins Sons and Co., 1970. pp. 100-143.
(2) Hudson, M. E. and Mary Clark. *Crown of a Thousand Years.* Harmondsworth, Middlesex: Penguin Books, 1952. p. 105.

Ceccoli, Edda

Co Captain Regent of San Marino (1991-1992) and (1998)

The Most Serene Republic of San Marino, which lays claim to being the oldest independent republic in Europe, is completely surrounded by Italy, with which it has had a treaty of friendship since 1862. The republic is governed by co-captains-regent who are elected from the parliamentary body for a term of six months only and cannot be re-elected in less than three year intervals.

Edda Ceccoli, elected to a five-year term in the Great and Good Council, the legislative branch of the government, was then elected by that body as Co-Captain-Regent in October 1991. In this position, for a period of six months, she presided over the ten-member Congress of State, the executive branch of the government. She was re-elected for another five-year term to the Great and Good Council, and in April 1998, that body again named her Co-Captain-Regent.

Suggested Reading:

(1) Delury, George, *The World Almanac and Book of Facts.* New York: Newspaper Enterprise Association, Inc., 1992. pp. 573-574.

(2) Famighetti, Robert, *The World Almanac and Book of Facts*. Mahwah, New Jersey: K-III Reference Corporation, 1998. p. 815.

Charlotte

Grand Duchess, ruler of Luxembourg (1919-1964)

She was born Josephine-Charlotte in 1896, the daughter of Duke William IV and the younger sister of Maríe-Adelaïde, whom she succeeded in 1919. Maríe-Adelaïde had been forced to abdicate during the German occupation of Luxembourg during World War I. In December of 1918 the Chamber voted to continue the existence of the grand duchy of Luxembourg, and Charlotte became its ruler, thwarting a coalition of Liberals and Socialists which attempted to bring an end to the dynasty and unite it with Belgium. Luxembourg then joined the League of Nations. Charlotte married Prince Felix of Bourbon, and in 1921 the future Grand Duke Jean was born. In 1922 Luxembourg concluded economic union with Belgium, but it was not until 1925 that French occupation troops were finally withdrawn from the land. In 1932, an agreement was made at the Ouchy Convention for the gradual reduction of economic barriers between Belgium, Luxembourg, and The Netherlands. Luxembourg enjoyed a period of relative prosperity under Charlotte until May, 1940, when the Germans again invaded and occupied it. Charlotte and her family fled to England and then to Canada, where they remained until American troops liberated their country in September, 1944. It was a more worldly Charlotte who returned to rule. In 1947 the grand duchy joined the Benelux union and the following year it officially abandoned its long held policy of "eternal neutrality." The country joined the North Atlantic Pact in 1949 and participated in the European Economic Community. On May 26, 1964, in one of her last official duties, she joined with President Charles de Gaulle of France and President Heinrich Luebke of Germany in opening the Moselle Canal. In 1964 she abdicated in favor of her son, Grand Duke Jean, who presided over a duchy now firmly committed to cooperation with the rest of the European community.

Suggested Reading:

(1) Newcomer, James. *The Grand Duchy of Luxembourg*. Lanham, Maryland: University Press of America, Inc., 1984. p. 16.

(2) Langer, William L., ed. *World Hisotry*. Boston: Houghton Mifflin, 1980. pp. 986, 1180, 1198.
(3) Carpenter, Clive. *The Guinness Book of Kings, Rulers & Statesmen.* Enfield, Middlesex: Guinness Superlatives Ltd. p. 165.

Christina

Queen of Sweden (1632-1654)

She was born in 1626 Stockholm, the daughter of King Gustavus Adolphus and Maria Eleonora of Brandenburg. She succeeded her father when she was only six years old, although she was not crowned until 1644. Her chief regent was Axel Oxenstierna. Witty and bright, she was particularly well-schooled: Descartes, for example, taught her philosophy. Under her reign education flourished, the first newspaper was established (1645), local rule was broadened, and industry was encouraged. Over the objection of Oxenstierna, she sought an end to the Thirty Years' War and was instrumental in concluding the Peace of Westphalia in 1648. She was easily persuaded to delegate her duties and give away crown lands. In 1654 she secretly became a convert to Roman Catholicism forbidden in Sweden—and shocked her constituents by abdicating in favor of her cousin Charles X Gustavus. She moved to Paris and immersed herself in the literate and scientific communities and became a popular patroness of the arts. In such a stimulating atmosphere, she began taking a belated interest in affairs of state. She made vain attempts to obtain the crowns of both Naples and Poland, and, when her cousin Charles X died in 1160, she vainly attempted to regain the Swedish throne. But the firmly entrenched state's ministers were set against her, primarily because of her Catholicism. She continued her associations with a brilliant entourage of friends and wrote a number of works, including her autobiography. She formed an intimate liason with Cardinal Decio Azzolino, even naming him her heir. She died in Rome in 1689 at the age of 63. Azzolino died only two months later.

Suggested Reading:

(1) Masson, Georgina. *Queen Christina*. New York: Farrar, Straus & Giroux, 1969.
(2) Derry, T.K. *A History of Scandinavia*. Minneapolis: University of Minnesota Press, 1979. pp. 120, 128-131.

(3) Egan, Edward W. et. al. *Kings, Rulers and Statesmen*. New York: Sterling Publishing Company, 1976. p. 449.

(4) Trevor-Roper, Hugh. *The Golden Age of Europe*. New York: Bonanza/ Crown, 1987. pp. 32, 126, 140, 144, 174.

Christine of France

Duchess, regent of Savoy (1638-1648)

She was the daughter of Henry IV, King of France from 1589 to 1610, and his second wife, Marie de' Medici. She married Victor Amadeus I of Savoy and bore three children: Francis Hyacinth, Henrietta, who married Ferdinand of Bavaria, and Charles Emmanuel II. Savoy was an independent state whose rulers also governed Piedmont. Victor Amadeus I ruled the two from 1630 to 1637. Following his death in 1637, their son Francis acceded to the throne, but civil war broke out. At the end of one year, Christine's younger son Charles Emmanuel came to the throne under her capable regency. Although the regency officially ended when he came of age in 1648, in reality, Christine continued to dominate him until her death in 1648.

Suggested Reading:

(1) Langer, William L., ed. *World History*. Boston: Houghton Mifflin, 1980. pp. 426, 473, 494.

Claude

Duchess of Brittany (1514-1524)

She was born in 1499, the daughter of Louis XII and Anne, duchess of Brittany (r. 1488-1514), from whom she inherited the duchy and became its last duchess. She married Francois III, who became Francois I, king of France. Upon her death in 1524, her husband annexed Brittany to France.

Suggested Reading:

(1) Carpenter, Clive. *The Guinness Book of Kings, Rulers & Statesmen*. Enfield, Middlesex: Guinness Superlatives Ltd., 1978. p. 90.

Claudine

Titular sovereign of Monaco (1457-1465)

She was born in 1451, the daughter of Catalan Grimaldi. In 1419 her grandfather John Grimaldi of the prominent Genoese family had succeeded in re-taking Monaco from the French for the final time. The title of prince or princess of Monaco was not assumed by a Grimaldi until 1659. Claudine became sovereign at the age of six, when Catalan died. In 1865, at the age of 14, she married Lambert, who became seigneur. In 1431 the couple had a son, John II, who inherited his mother's claim upon her death in 1514.

Suggested Reading:

(1) Carpenter, Clive. *The Guinness Book of Kings, Rulers & Statesmen.* Enfield, Middlesex: Guinness Superlatives Ltd., 1978. p. 173.

Constance

Duchess of Brittany, co-ruler (1171-1196)

She was the daughter of Conan IV (r. 1156-1171), from whom she inherited a weakened duchy of Brittany which Conan had allowed King Henry II of England to rule in part. Constance married King Henry's son Geoffroi II and ruled jointly with him. The couple had a son, Arthur I, born in 1187, who inherited the duchy upon her death in 1196.

Suggested Reading:

(1) Carpenter, Clive. *The Guinness Book of Kings, Rulers & Statesmen.* Enfield: Middlesex: Guinness Superlatives Ltd., 1978. p. 90.

Constance

Queen of Sicily (1189, 1194-1198) and regent of Germany (1197-1198)

She was born in 1154, the daughter of King Roger II (of Apulia) and his third wife Beatrice of Rethel. In 1186 she became the future empress of the Holy Roman empire by marrying the future Henry VI, the Lion, of the house of the Hohenstaufen (r. 1190-1197). When her nephew William II died in 1189, Constance, as legal heiress, claimed the throne of Sicily, but she was opposed by Count Roger and another of her nephews, Tancred of Lecce, son of her older brother Roger. The Sicilian people did not want Constance's husband, a German, for a ruler, and neither did the Papacy. Tancred grabbed the crown briefly in 1190, and while his enemies cried, "Behold, an ape is crowned!" Henry sent troops to unseat him. Tancred took his aunt Constance captive, but the Pope induced him to set her free. Tancred's death in 1194 cleared the way for Constance and Henry to assume the thrones of Sicily. Constance was installed as governor of the regno. That same year, their son Frederick II was born.

The people of Sicily hated the German Henry, who was a harsh ruler. Constance, and even Pope Celestine, may have been aware of a plot to assassinate him. When Henry discovered the plot, he took terrible vengeance, blinding all prisoners, even German ones. His death in 1197 of a fever was celebrated throughout the land. As regent ruler, Constance exercised particular political skill. She consolidated her power and secured the protection of Pope Innocent III in preserving her son's claim to the throne. She managed to have her son crowned king in April 1198 before he died in November of that same year.

Suggested Reading:

(1)   Smith, Denis Mack. *A History of Sicily*. New York: Dorset Press, 1968. vol. 1. *Medieval Sicily*. pp. 44-45, 47, 51, 55.

(2)   Painter, Sidney. *The Rise of the Feudal Monarchies*. Ithaca, NY: Cornell University Press, 1951. p. 114.

(3)   Runciman, Steven. *A History of the Crusades*. Cambridge: Cambridge University Press, 1952, 1987. vol. 2. *The Kingdom of Jerusalem and the Frankish East*. p. 428.

(4)   Previté-Orton, C. W. *The Shorter Cambridge Medieval History*. Cambridge: Cambridge University Press, 1952, 1987. vol. 1. *The Later Roman Empire to the Twelfth Century*. pp. 510, 605-615.

(5)   Ostrogorsky, George. *History of the Byzantine State*. New Brunswick, NJ: Rutgers University Press, 1969. pp. 411-412.

(6)   Langer, William L., ed. *World History*. Boston: Houghton Mifflin, 1980. pp. 224-225.

Constance

Queen of Sicily (1282-1302)

She was the daughter of King Manfred of Sicily, who ruled from 1258 to 1266, and his first wife Beatrix of Savoy. She was the grandaughter of Emperor Frederick II. She married Peter III, king of Aragon, who ruled from 1276 to 1285. Charles I of Anjou, son of Louis VIII of France, was out to create his own Mediterranean empire, and to that end he invaded Sicily, defeating King Manfred in 1266. The Papacy awarded Charles the kingdom of Sicily. In 1282, Constance's husband King Peter launched a long-planned campaign to recapture the throne in Constance's name, disguising his trip as an African crusade. He landed at Callo in 1282, defeated Charles, placed himself and Constance upon the throne of Sicily, and refused to do homage to the Pope. The Pope naturally opposed their rule and endeavored to have them deposed, and even the local nobility was opposed to the Argonese takeover. The struggle to maintain their family's right to ascendancy continued even after Peter's death. Constance acted as regent for their 11-year-old son James until he reached 18. The couple had four children: Alfonso III, who succeeded to the throne of Aragon; Isabella, who married Diniz, king of Portugal; James I, who succeeded to the throne of Sicily under his mother's regency and, as Jaime II, succeeded to the throne of Aragon in 1291; and Frederick III, who also ruled Sicily. James ruled for ten years, then exchanged Sicily for Corsica and Sardinia. He appointed his younger brother, then 17, as regent in 1291, when he took over Aragon from his brother. Four years later Frederick was elected king and eventually the Pope recognized him as such. Thus Constance's heirs were finally firmly established as rulers of Sicily.

Suggested Reading:

(1) Previté-Orton, C. W., *The Shorter Cambridge Medieval History.* Cambridge: Cambridge University Press, 1952, 1982. vol. 1. *The Later Roman Empire to the Twelfth Century.* pp. 510, 557.
(2) Langer, William L., ed. *World History.* Boston: Houghton Mifflin, 1940, 1980. pp. 228, 306, 313.

Crescentii

See Marozia Crescentii.

Cresson, Edith

Prime Minister of France (1991-1992)

She was born Edith Campion on January 27, 1934 in Boulogne-Billancourt, a suburb of Paris. She was raised with an English nurse, who taught her fluent English. Of her childhood, she later wrote, "One of the most obvious characteristics of the bourgeoisie is the boredom it produces." She attended a noted school of business, The School of Higher Commercial Studies, and earned a doctorate in demography. In 1959 she married a Peugeot executive, Jacques Cresson. At length her dissatisfaction with the bourgeois life led her to join the Socialist movement. Her enthusiasm and organizational abilities brought her to the attention of Francois Mitterrand during his 1965 failed presidential campaign. When he became head of the French Socialist Party in 1971, she remained his disciple. In 1975 the party asked her to run for parliament in a conservative district, and although she lost, her reputation as "la battante", "the fighter" was made. In 1977 she became Mayor of Thuré and in 1983, she became the only Socialist to defeat a sitting conservative Mayor when she was elected Mayor of Châtellerault.

After Mitterrand became president in 1981, Cresson became the first woman to serve as Minister of Agriculture, must to the disgust of French farmers, who referred to her as "La Parisienne." However, in that post, she raised their income by ten percent in 1982. In 1983 she was appointed Minister of Tourism and Trade, and in 1984, Minister of Trade and Industry. In 1988 she became Minister of European Affairs, but she resigned in October to enter the private sector; she joined Groupe Schneider, a French electrical manufacturer.

In less than three years the lure of politics had become too strong, and she returned to government service. She was chosen as France's first female Prime Minister in May of 1991. Her appointment marked a milestone for French women, who did not obtain the right to vote until 1946.

Cresson said that she planned to turn France into an industrial power rivaling Germany. But when she announced the members of her cabinet, which included many holdovers from her predecessor, opposition leaders predicted that her coalition could not last, and the headline in the newspaper *La Monde* read, "For How Long?"

In a magazine interview, Cresson said, "There are three places where women have always been excluded: the military, religion, and politics, I would say that today, it is still in politics where they have the least access."

Her outspoken statements on several occasions soon caused problems. She was hampered by "perceived political ineptitude", creating diplomatic uproars for criticizing British masculinity, for one, and the Japanese social order, for another. In regional elections held in March 1992, amid rising unemployment figures and strikes by workers in areas that were traditionally her supporters, her party suffered a stunning defeat, receiving only 18.3 per cent of the vote and losing a departmental council it had held since 1934. Cresson was forced to resign. President Francois Mitterrand replaced her with former Finance Minister Pierre Beregovoy.

Suggested Reading:

(1) Greenhouse, Steven. "'The Fighter' of France". *The New York Times.* 16 May 1991: A1, A31.
(2) Greenhouse, Steven. "French Prime Minister Quits; Woman Named to Post". *The New York Times.* 16 May 1991: A3.
(3) "A French First". *The New York Times.* 19 May 1991: E7.
(4) "Seasonal Work" *The New York Times.* 5 April 1992: 3A.

Cristina

Queen of Spain. See **María Cristina of Naples**

Europe Section D

Deidameia

Queen, ruler of Epirus (c. 235 B.C.)

She was the daughter of Alexandros II (r. 272-c. 240 B.C.) and the sister of Pyrrhus II (r. 240-c. 236 B.C.) and Ptolemaeus (r. c. 236-c. 235 B.C.). During a civil war, Ptolemaeus was killed, and Deidameia may be considered to have taken the throne briefly before she, too, was murdered. The Republican Party took over the government in 235 B.C.

Suggested Reading:

(1) Carpenter, Clive. *The Guinness Book of Kings, Rulers, & Statesmen.* Enfield, Middlesex: Guinness Superlatives Ltd., 1978. p. 75.

da Lourdes-Pintasilgo, María (or de Lurdes Pentassilgo)

Prime Minister of Portugal (1979-1980)

She was born in 1930 and trained as an industrial engineer. From 1965 to 1974 she was agent for the Co-operative Chamber. An avid spokesperson for women's causes, she was the author of several books addressing the problem of the Church's treatment of women, including: *The New Feminism, To Think the Church Anew,* and *Roads for Our Joint Effort.* She served as president of the Interministerial Commission dealing with the status of women.

The revolution of April 25, 1974, toppled Portugal's dictatorship of Antonio de Oliveira Salazar (1932-1968) and his successors, but in the aftermath the country was close to anarchy. From 1976 to 1983 sixteen provisional governments reigned over a Portugal in chaos. In 1976 Romalho Eanes (b. 1935) was elected president and re-elected in 1980. Maria da Lourdes-Pintasilgo was pressed into service in a number of cabinet posts.

She was Minister of Social Affairs and State Secretary for Social Security, for the Second and Third Provisional Governments. In 1979-1980 she served as Portugal's first woman Prime Minister, of the Fifth Constitutional Government.

Eames appointed her Amabassador to UNESCO, where she was a member of the Executive Countil and a part of the Portuguese Delegation to the General Assembly. She was a member of "The Graal", an international women's movement, and of the Women's Liason Group between the Catholic Church and the Ecumenical Council of Churches.

In 1986 she ran for the office of president, winning the primary, but losing in the general election. In 1987 she was elected Member of the European Parliament. She died in 2004.

Suggested Reading:

(1) WIC Biography, World Wide Web, 1997.
(2) "Nuno Moura Portugal", World Wide Web, April 1997.

Diane of Poitiers

Duchess, defacto co-ruler of France (1547-1559)

Diana, duchess of Valentinois, was born in 1499 and came to court as lady-in-waiting to Louise of Savoy and later to Queen Claude. She was married to Louis de Breze, comte de Maulevrier, who died in 1531. It was at that time that, even though she was 20 years his senior, she became the mistress of the future King Henry II, who ruled France from 1547 to 1559. She so completely dominated him that he gave her many of the crown jewels and kept her prominently at court, while his wife, Catherine de Médicis, was obliged to remain in relative obscurity, being brought out only to serve as regent in his absence and after his death. Although Diane had absolute power over Henry's decisions, she did not usually concern herself with the larger affairs of state but focused her interests upon arts and letters, becoming a patron of both. However, it is doubtful that she refrained from expressing her preferences and dislikes of Henry's advisors, or that she refused to express an opinion when Henry unburdened himself upon her. His complete enthrallment of and dependence upon a woman 20 years his senior suggests that she represented far more than a lover or companion; rather, that she was the mother authority which he never outgrew. Despite

69

the fact that she was so much older than he, she outlived him, because he died accidentally in 1559. She retired to the beautiful chateaux built for her by Philibert Delorme at Anet in Eure-et-Loir, where she died in 1566.

Suggested Reading:

(1) Langer, William L., ed. *World History*. Boston: Houghton Mifflin, 1980. p. 411.
(2) Harvey, Sir Paul and J. E. Heseltine. *The Oxford Companion to French Literature*. Oxford: Oxford University Press, 1959, 1993. p. 202.

Drahomira (or Dragomir)

Queen, regent of Bohemia (c. 926-928 or 921-924/5)

Drahomira was born Drahomira von Stoder and married Duke Rastislav I (Vradislav), ruler of Bohemia from c. 912 to 926. Rastislav's parents, Borivoj and Ludmila, were the first Czech rulers to adopt Christianity. The citizens of Bohemia were divided in their loyalty between their old pagan religions and the new Christianity. Drahomira and Rastislav had two sons, Wenceslas (b. 908) and Boleslav (The Cruel). Ludmila took it upon herself to educate Wenceslas, as heir to the throne, in the ways of Christianity, while Drahomira, a pagan, saw to Boleslav's upbringing. When her Rastislav died in c. 926, Wenceslas was only 14. His Christian grandmother became his regent, to the consternation of anti-Christian factions throughout the land. Drahomira, an ambitious and conniving woman, is said to have been behind the plot whereby anti-Christian agents broke into Tetin Castle and strangled Ludmila. Drahomira then assumed the regency herself. Wenceslas remained a Christian and Boleslav a heathen. Civil strife between Christians and non-Christians characterized Drahomira's regime, and her intrigues at court were so flagrant that Wenceslas chose to assume the reins of government in c. 930 when he was barely 18. Wencelas was a wise and beloved ruler who made the mistake of yielding to Henry the Fowler when the Germans threatened to invade, an action which further enraged the anti-Christian faction. In c. 935 he was murdered by his brother at the door of the church. (Some sources give his death as 929 and Drahomira's regency as 921-924/5.) King Wenceslas became Bohemia's patron saint, which would have been the last thing that Queen Drahomira would have wanted. The Christmas carol, "Good King Wencelas," refers to his deeds. Boleslav ascended to the throne as Boleslav I. After Wencelas' murder, Bohemia was incorporated into the Byzantine Empire under its own dynasty. Boleslav died in c. 935.

Suggested Reading:

(1) Langer, William L., ed. *World History*. Boston: Houghton Mifflin, 1980. p. 275.

(2) Kinder, Hermann and Werner Hilgemann. *Atlas of World History*. tr. Ernest A. Menze. Garden City, NY: Anchor/Doubleday, 1982. vol. 1. p. 169.

(3) Cooke, Jean, et. al. *History's Timeline*. New York: Crescent Books, 1981. pp. 47, 61.

(4) Morby, John. *Dynasties of the World*. Oxford: Oxford University Press, 1989. p. 155.

Dreifuss, Ruth

President of the Swiss Confederation (January 1, 1999-December 31, 1999), Member of the Federal Council (April 1, 1993-December 31, 2002)

She was born into a Jewish family on January 9, 1940 in St. Gallen in northeastern Switzerland. Her father, who worked in a textile importing company, volunteered with a group that helped Jewish refugees fleeing from the Holocaust. In 1945 he was caught helping falsify documents and lost his job, and the family moved to Geneva. She earned a Master of Economics at University of Geneva and worked as a left-leaning journalist at *Cooperation* 1961 to 1964. She was an assistant at the University of Geneva from 1970 to 1972, and then became scientific expert at the Federal Swiss Agency for Development and Cooperation between 1972 and 1981. From 1989 to 1992 she was a social democratic member of the Legislative Assembly for the City of Berne. From 1982 she was the Secretary of the Swiss Trade Union until 1992.

In 1992, representing the Canton of Geneva, she was elected to the Federal Cabinet, becoming the second woman and first Jew to hold the post. She served as Interior Minister during the investigation of Swiss wartime actions, and she took tough stands for reform of the nation's health insurance and for addressing the nation's drug problem. In August, 1998, Swiss banks agreed to a $1.25 billion settlement for money that Holocaust victims had deposited in Swiss banks. Ms. Dreifuss expressed relief that the banks had made a settlement, but she cautioned that the government's restitution work was not finished. In December, 1998, she was elected by Parliament to the one-year presidential post, which rotates among the seven-member Swiss Cabinet. Her election was a symbol of success in a country where women were not allowed to vote on the national level until 1971. She left the Federal Council on December 31, 2002.

Suggested Reading:

(1) Elizabeth Olson. "A First For Swiss: A Woman As President." *The New York Times International.* 27 December 1998: 7.

Europe Section E

Eleanor (or Leonor)

Queen of Navarre (1441-1481)

From 1285 to 1328 Navarre was a French province. Eleanor was the younger daughter of King John of Aragon and Queen Doña Blanca (Bianca, or Blanche) of Navarre, who ruled Navarre until her death in 1441. Eleanor's older brother Charles de Viana succeeded his mother. He and his father had serious disagreements; when Charles died suddenly in 1441 it was assumed that he had been poisoned. The next heir after Charles was his sister Blanche, the queen whom King Henry the Impotent of Castile had divorced. King John had Blanche imprisoned, where she died suddenly, possibly poisoned by Eleanor's orders. King John had his younger daugher Eleanor enthroned in Blanche's stead. Eleanor was married to Gaston IV, count of Foix (r. 1436-1470). Through their daughter, Catalina, they established a dynasty that was to be short-lived, because in 1512, Ferdinand of Aragon conquered the Spanish portion of Navarre. The French portion of Navarre would remain independent until 1610, when it was united with France. Eleanor's father continued to exercise dominion over her kingdom until his death in 1479. She died two years later, in 1481, and her grandson, Francis Phoebus, who had become count of Foix on his father's death in 1470, became king of Navarre.

Suggested Reading:

(1) Chapman, Charles E. *A History of Spain*. New York: The Free Press/ The Macmillan Company, 1965. p. 134.
(2) Morby, John E. *Dynasties of the World*. Oxford: Oxford University Press, 1989. p. 114.
(3) Langer, William L., ed. *World History*. Boston: Houghton Mifflin, 1980. p. 307.

(4) Egan, Edward W. et. al., eds. *Kings, Rulers and Statesmen*. New York: Sterling Publishing Company, 1976. pp. 157, 430.

Eleanor of Aquitaine

Duchess (of Aquitaine), Countess (of Pontiers), Queen (of both France and England), regent of England (1189-1199)

To cite only the regency of this remarkable woman is to disregard the tremendous and far-reaching impact she had on the affairs of Europe during her lifetime. She was born ca. 1122, the daughter of William X, duke of Aquitaine and count of Poitiers. Upon her father's death in 1137, she inherited Aquitaine and Poitiers and married Louis VII the Young, who became king of France that year. She and Louis had two daughters: Marie, who married Henry of Champagne; and Alice, who married Thibault of Blois. Eleanor was considered far more intelligent than Louis. In 1148 she and her retinue, dressed in battle garb, accompanied him on the Second Crusade. They went first to Antioch, where Eleanor's uncle Raymond of Tripoli sought Louis' help in recovering Montferrand from the Turks. Louis was not quite ready to fight, or perhaps Raymond's proposal did not sound prestigious enough; at any rate, he said that he wanted to make a pilgrimmage to Jerusalem before he began any military campaigns. Eleanor, the more sensible of the two, pleaded her uncle's cause; in fact, she and Raymond were in each other's company so much that tongues began to wag and Louis, growing jealous, announced that he would set off for Jerusalem at once. Unwilling to be bullied, Eleanor announced that she would stay in Antioch and get a divorce, whereupon Louis dragged her by force from her uncle's palace. Historian William of Tyre assessed Eleanor as a "fatuous woman," but in the light of her long and illustrious career, his assessment would appear to be short-sighted and biased. Kinder historians have described her as possessing good looks, charm, courage, passion, self-will, hot temper, sound sense, and a taste for poetry and romance. Louis lost all in the crusade: honor, the battle, even, for all practical purposes, his wife. He returned home in 1149, a temporarily chastened man. After a brief attempt at reconciliation, the couple separated and the marriage was annulled (1152)—no male heir had, after all, been produced. Eleanor saw to it that her lands were returned to her and then promptly married Henry, duke of Normandy, who in 1154 became Henry I, king of England. During her marriage to the English king, she continued to administer her own lands, Aquitaine consisting of Guienne and Gascony. The couple had eight children: William; Henry; Richard I the

Lionhearted ("ruled" 1189-1199); Geoffrey; John Lackland (r. 1199-1216); Matilda, who married Henry the Lion; Eleanor, who married King Alfonso VIII of Castile; Joan, who married both King William II of Sicily and Count Raymond VI of Toulouse. In 1168 Queen Eleanor gave her favorite son Richard the duchy of Aquitaine and in 1172 made him duke of Poitiers. In 1173 her sons revolted against their father, with not only Eleanor's blessing, but her military support. The sons were defeated in 1174, but it was Eleanor whom her husband sent to prison, for 15 years. She was released upon her husband's death in 1189. Richard became king, but he left in a few months on the Third Crusade. Eleanor was given vice-regal powers, but she would much rather have sailed with her son. However, rules of the Third Crusade specifically barred the participation of women. After three years away from his throne, Richard was on the way home when he was captured by Duke Leopold of Austria and held for ransom of 150,000 marks, an astronomical sum, even for Eleanor to raise. She rounded up the money and traveled in person to escort her son home in 1194. He had been gone five years. The queen arranged for him to be crowned again, but a month following his coronation, he left again for Normandy, leaving the Archbishop of Canterbury in charge, never going to England again. When he died in 1199, the great Richard the Lionhearted had actually served six months as king of England. Eleanor, to solidify relations between England and France, quickly arranged a marriage between her grandaughter, Blanche of Castile, and the Dauphine of France; in fact, to ensure its success, in 1200, at almost 80 years of age, she traveled to Castile to fetch Blanche and deliver her personally to France. Then she returned to Aquitaine, which her son John had inherited from his brother, and defended it against her grandson Arthur of Brittany, who tried to claim it for France. She continued to be on hand to thwart Arthur during the campaign at Mirebeau in 1202, when at last John could take him prisoner. Triumphant but exhausted, she retired to the monastery at Fontevrault, Anjou, where she died in 1204.

Suggested Reading:

(1) Kibler, William W., ed. *Eleanor of Aquitaine: Patron and Politician.* Austin: The University of Texas Press, 1976.

Eleanor of Arborea

Ruler of Arborea (1383-1404)

Arborea, located in the center of Sardinia, was one of the four territorial divisions of that island, one of the largest in the western Mediterranean. Eleanor succeeded her father as queen, or "judge," of Arborea and is famous as a warrior queen. Her small realm had been invaded first by Pisans and then by Alfonso IV of Aragon, who drove out the Pisans. Eleanor fought valiantly in an effort to push the invaders out but she did not succeed. She died in 1404 without securing her realm from invaders. However, another of her endeavors was more successful: it was due to her efforts at codifying the laws, completing work begun by her father, that in 1421 her Carta de Logu was adopted by the Sard Parliament, to be effective for the entire island. It remained in effect until the Treaty of Utrect in 1713.

Suggested Reading:

(1)   Delane, Mary. *Sardinia, The Undefeated Island.* 1968.

Elisa Bonaparte (or Elisa Lucca)

Duchess of Tuscany, princess of Piombino and ruler of the principality of Lucca (1805/9-1814)

She was born Marie Anne (Elisa) Bonapart in 1777 on the island of Corsica, the oldest daughter and one of eight surviving children of Carlo Maria Bonapart, a lawyer, and Maria Laelitia Ramolini. Her father's family, of ancient Tuscan nobility, had emigrated to Corsica in the sixteenth century. She was the younger sister of Napoleon, who was born in 1782. She married Felix Bacciochi. Napoleon was generous with his brothers and sisters; he first made Elisa the duchess of Tuscany. In 1905 he made her ruler of the principality of Lucca, in the Tuscany region of north-central Italy, and princess of Piombino. Elisa, like her famous brother, demonstrated remarkable administrative abilities. A woman of strong convictions, she occasionally found herself at odds with her family, even with Napoleon. At one point near the end of Napoleon's life he noted that all but Elisa had disappointed him. In 1815, following Napoleon's defeat, the Congress of Vienna assigned Lucca to the Spanish infanta Queen Maria Luisa of Etruria. Elisa withdrew to Bologna and later to Trieste, where she died in 1820, a year before her exiled brother.

Suggested Reading:

(1) Morby, John. *Dynasties of the World*. Oxford: Oxford University Press, 1989. p. 108.
(2) Egan, Edward W. et. al., eds. *Kings, Rulers and Statesmen*. New York; Sterling Publishing Company, 1976. p. 277.
(3) Putnam, John J., "Napoleon". *National Geographic 161* February 1982: 142-189, particularly p. 168.

Elizabeth

Queen, regent of Hungary and Croatia (1382-1385 and 1386)

She was the daughter of Croatian *Ban* Sjepan Kotromanic and the wife of Ljudevit I (r. 1342-1382), who also inherited the Polish throne when his uncle, King Kazimir died. They had two daughters, Marija and Jadviga, both minors when Ljudevit died in 1386. Marija was betrothed as a child to Sigismund of Luxembourg, Prince of Bohemia and son of Charles IV, Emperor of the Holy Roman Empire and King of Bohemia. Jadviga inherited the Polish throne and later married Ladislav Jagielo, Grand Duke of Lithuania. Marija, at age twelve, inherited the Hungarian and Croatian thrones, with Elizabeth assuming the regency with the aid of Nikola Gorjanski, Paladin of Hungary. But Croatian nobles resented the rule of the two queens, and Ivan Palizna, Templar Prior of Vrana, led a plot to invite Stjepan Tvrdko, King of Bosnia, to become King of Croatia. Gorjanski learned of the plot and brought both queens, with a strong army, from Hungary to Croatia to confront the rebels. The conspiracy collapsed, and the queens were welcomed royally in the capital, Zadar, where Marija presided over a session of the Croatian *Sabor* (parliament) before returning to Hungary. Soon, however, a new movement, spearheaded by the Horvat brothers, Ivaniz, *Ban* of Macva, and Pavao, Bishop of Zagreb, sought to install Marija's cousin, Prince Charles of Durazzo, on the throne. Charles accepted the invitation and traveled to Croatia to assume the throne. After a year, he went on to Hungary to oust Marija there as well. Marija abdicated, and Charles assumed that throne. However, Elizabeth, Gorjanski, and Forgacs instigated a plot to assassinate Charles, and Marija was installed as Queen of Hungary and Croatia for a second time (r. 1386-1395). Now Palizna, who had fled to Bosnia when his own plot failed, joined forces with the

Horvat brothers and began another uprising. Gorjanski again set out for Croatia with an army and both queens, but this time, the army was routed by the Horvats. Gorjanski and Forgacs were executed, and both queens were imprisoned in Palizna's palace, Novigrad on the Sea. On demand of Charles' widow, Elizabeth was put to death (1386). Marija was freed by her betrothed, Sigismund of Luxembourg, who had entered the breach and taken the Hungarian crown for himself in behalf of his wife.

Suggested Reading:

(1)   Gazi, Stephen. *A History of Croatia*. New York: Barnes & Noble Books, 1993. pp. 58, 60-62.

Elizabeth

Queen, ruler of Hungary (1439-1440)

Elizabeth was the daughter of Holy Roman Emperor Sigismund, king of Hungary from 1387 to 1437, and his first wife Barbara of Cilli. She married Albert V, duke of Austria, who became King Albert II of Hungary upon her father's death. As Albert was also crowned king of Germany and Bohemia, Elizabeth became queen of those realms as well. The couple had a daughter, Elizabeth. Albert II had the makings of a strong leader and immediately set about ending territorial feuds by appointing arbiters. He also divided Germany into governable administrative districts. However, he died after only two years (May, 1439) while on an unsuccessful campaign against the Turks. Elizabeth was pregnant at the time. In 1440 she gave birth to their son, whom she named Ladeslov V Posthumus. In May 1440, to prevent Hungary from falling permanently under Polish rule, she compelled the primate to crown her baby king, exactly one year after her husband had died. She then made her cousin Frederick V of Styria (later Emperor Frederick II) his guardian. However, from 1440 to 1444 Hungary was nominally ruled by Vladislav Vi of Poland. Elizabeth was supported in her struggle to win her son's throne by some influential Croatian magnates and by the Serbian despot, George Brankovic, who had been granted large estates in Hungary. Elizabeth's forces met Vladislav's General Hunyadi in 1442 and were defeated. All might have been lost but for Vladislav's death in 1440, which cleared the way for Elizabeth's baby son to "rule." Her daughter Elizabeth married Casimir IV, king of Portugal, Vladislav's brother.

Suggested Reading:

(1) Dvornik, Francis. *The Slavs in European History and Civilization.* New Brunswick, NJ: Rutgers University Press, 1962. pp. 234, 349, 436.

(2) Langer, William L., ed. *World History.* Boston: Houghton Mifflin, 1980. pp. 337-339.

(3) Egan, Edward W. et. al., eds. *Kings, Rulers and Statesmen.* New York: Sterling Publishing Company, 1976. p. 229.

Elizabeth I

Queen of England (1558-1603)

She was born in 1533, the daughter of Henry VIII and his second wife Anne Boleyn. Her childhood and early adulthood were fraught with danger and disaster. Her mother was beheaded when she was three years old. During the reign of her brother Edward VI, his protector, Edward Seymour had his own brother Thomas tried for treason and executed, accused of plotting to marry Elizabeth and usurp the throne. Elizabeth, a nominal Protestant, was considered a constant threat to her Catholic sister Mary, who ruled from 1553 to 1558. For a while during Mary's reign, Elizabeth was imprisoned in the Tower of London, suspected of having aided Sir Thomas Wyatt in a rebellion against the queen. These early experiences, whereby she was often saved by cautious circumspection, helped her perfect a technique which was to hold her in good stead throughout her reign: the technique of giving "answerless answers." Elizabeth schooled herself particularly well; during her teens she could already speak six languages. In later years this facility with languages would place her at an advantage with foreign dignitaries, with whom she often conversed in their own languages. Elizabeth came to the throne in 1558, at the age of 25, when her sister Mary died. In later years of her 45-year reign, she would become known as the Virgin Queen and still later as Good Queen Bess. The greatest threat to her throne was posed by her cousin Mary Stuart, queen of Scots, a threat which Elizabeth ended by consenting to Mary's beheading once her involvement in an assassination plot by Anthony Bolington was clearly proved. In 1588 she raised a fleet and force to defend against the Spanish Armada. She rode out to the mouth of the Thames to address her troops, saying in part, " . . . I am come amongst you . . . not for my recreation and disport, but being resolved, in the midst and heat of the battle, to live or die amongst you all . . . ." Her presence and her speech so inspired Drake's pitifully small fleet that the Spanish Armada was routed and forced to retreat to the North Sea, where it was destroyed by storms. Elizabeth dabbled more frequently in foreign affairs after that, endeavoring to undermine, wherever possible, the Catholic influence. She assisted The Netherlands in gaining independence from Spain, and she helped the Protestants gain a foothold in France. The trait of hers which exasperated her ministers and foreign rulers alike, which they considered a terrible womanly weakness, was perhaps her greatest strength. That trait was what they considered to be indecisiveness. It was, instead, caution and circumspection. Elizabeth seemed to rule by instinct, knowing just when to withhold a decision, often until the need for decisive action had passed and a crisis had thus been averted. For years she used this trait to keep the nations of Europe guessing concerning her marriage plans. Half the monarchs of Europe curried her favor, hoping for a beneficial union. In her innate wisdom, she kept her plans to herself, neither rejecting nor accepting overtures. This technique was her special ploy to manipulate affairs of state. When it became apparent that she would not marry, would not produce an heir, she kept the world guessing, until she lay on her deathbed, about whom she would name as her successor. At the end of her reign, England was poised to become a major world power and a colonial giant. During the latter years of her reign, literature flowered, as did, to a lesser degree, art and architecture. She personally attended the premier of the new playwright Shakespeare's *Twelfth Night*. Even today, Elizabeth is generally considered to be one of England's greatest monarchs. In 1603, almost 70 years old, she named from her deathbed James VI of Scotland, the Protestant son of her cousin Mary, queen of Scots, as James I of England, first of the Stuart line.

Suggested Reading:

(1) Johnson, Paul. *Elizabeth I*. New York: Holt, Rinehart and Winston, 1974.
(2) Luke, Mary M. *Gloriana: The Years of Elizabeth I*. New York: Coward McCann & Geoghegan, 1973.
(3) Smith, Lacey Baldwin. *Elizabeth Tudor: Portrait of a Queen*. Boston: Little Brown & Co, 1975.

Elizabeth I (or Elisaveta Petrovna)

Tzarina of Russia (1741-1762)

Elizabeth was born in 1709, the daughter of Peter the Great, who ruled Russia from 1682 to 1725, and Catherine I, who ruled from 1725 to 1727. When her mother was on her deathbed, she named her late husband's grandson, Peter II, to succeed her. Elizabeth was 18 at the time, a beautiful, vivacious, and popular young woman at court. When Peter died in 1730, the throne was offered to Anna, a niece of Peter the Great. Anna ruled for ten years and on her deathbed named her grand-nephew Ivan as her successor and her niece Anna Leopoldovna as regent. By this time Elizabeth was 31, still very popular at court, particularly among the guards. Anna Leopoldovna, believing that Elizabeth's popularity would make it more difficult for her to conduct her regency, had decided to banish Elizabeth to a convent, but the French ambassador and other anti-German factions in the court learned of the plan and approached Elizabeth with the idea of staging a *coup d'Etat*. On a night late in 1741, Elizabeth dressed as a palace guard, stole into the palace with the other guards, and arrested the infant emperor, his regent-mother, and her advisers. Elizabeth was then proclaimed empress of Russia. She immediately reinstated the Senate which had been created by her father but abolished by his successors. She then left control of most state affairs to her ministers while she turned her attention to westernizing her country. She established Russia's first university in Moscow and founded the Academy of Arts in St. Petersburg, now Leningrad. The privileged classes prospered in her reign while the lot of the serfs grew worse. The government's financial base deteriorated, although the country itself grew in stature as a European power. Russia fought a war with Sweden and gained a portion of Finland. She joined with France and Austria in the Seven Years' War against Prussia's Frederick the Great, but by choosing her nephew Peter III as her successor, she was paving the way for Peter to undo all the gains made against Prussia. She realized he was not a strong choice, so she chose with extra care a wife for him and groomed her for her future role herself. That young girl would become Catherine the Great. Elizabeth died in 1762.

Suggested Reading:

(1) Coughlan, Robert, *Elizabeth and Catherine*. New York: G. P. Putnam's Sons, 1974.
(2) Riasanovsky, Nicholas V., *A History of Russia*. Fifth Edition. New York and Oxford: Oxford University Press, 1993. pp. 242-243, 246-253 *passim*, 263, 258f.

Elizabeth II

Queen of Great Britain (1952-)

Elizabeth Alexandra Mary was born in 1926, the elder daughter of Prince Albert, duke of York (later to become King George V who ruled 1936-1952) and Lady Elizabeth, daughter of Claude Bowes—Lyon. She and her younger sister Margaret Rose spent early childhood never expecting to be thrust into the limelight. In 1936 her uncle Edward VIII abdicated and her father became king. Elizabeth suddenly found herself next in line for the throne. At age 13 she first met her distant cousin, Lieutenant Philip Mountbatten, prince of Greece and prince of Denmark. Eight years later they were married. Their first son, Charles, was born the following year, 1948. Subsequently the couple had a daughter, Anne, and two more sons, Andrew and Edward. Elizabeth acceded to the ostensively symbolic position of queen in 1952. However, as queen, she has exercised more than ceremonial power, according to the London *Economist*: "Any prime minister who thinks that the weekly audition is a mere formality is in for a shock. The queen's experience tells . . . . She has seen every cabinet paper and important Foreign Office dispatch of the past 35 years and has held weekly meetings with eight consecutive prime ministers. She has met most foreign heads of state and has complained to the Foreign Office that its briefings are too simple. The queen is not only powerful but also popular . . . ." Both Winston Churchill and Harold Wilson were embarrassed to find that the queen was sometimes more up to date than her prime ministers. Wilson said when he retired, "I shall certainly advise my successor to do his homework before his audience." It has been speculated that the queen has performed her job so well that she would be unlikely to abdicate at age 65. The queen lives in 600-room Buckingham Palace in London, a dozen rooms of which are the royal apartment. Although the palace and its 51 1/2-acre grounds require a staff of 346 employees, the queen is thrifty at that. One authority, Robert Lacey, says the apartment is "visibly frayed at the edges." Yet the government allowance of 6.3 million dollars for maintneance is usually inadequate and the queen must make up the shortfall from her private funds. The queen is one of the wealthiest women in the world. She owns 52000 acres of prime land. As alternate residences she has at her disposal Windsor Castle on the Thames near London and Holyroodhouse in Scotland. She also has estates at Sandringham in Norfolk and Balmoral in Scotland, both of which she maintains at her own expense. The British people regard the queen as a symbol of unity, stability, and tradition, and although liberal British press occasionally critizes the wealth of some of the royal family, the queen herself remained largely above criticism until the untimely death of her ex-daughter-in-law, Diana.

In 1994 her son Prince Charles had become increasingly unpopular when he announced that he never loved his estranged wife, Lady Diana Spencer. Liberal sources wrote that the best hope to save the monarchy was for Elizabeth to reign as long as Queen Victoria—for 63 years, until 2015. At that time, Charles and Diana's older son William would be 21 and could ascend the throne, bypassing his father entirely. In 1997 the divorced princess was killed in an automobile accident in Paris, occasioning an outpouring of grief of monumental proportions around the world. As England and the world mourned Diana's death, the queen remained in seclusion until public criticism compelled her to make an appearance to express the family's and the nation's grief.

Suggested Reading:

(1) "The Sleaze Factor" *World Press Review* December 1994, p. 27.
(2) Hudson, M. E. and Mary Clark. *Crown of a Thousand Years*. New York: Crown Publishing, 1978. pp. 148 150.
(3) "Throne Power". *World Press Review* February 1988: 38.
(4) "Life in the Grand Style for Europe's Leaders". *U.S. News & World Report*. 21 June 1982.

Elizabeth of Görlitz (or Elizabeth of Luxembourg)

Co-ruler of Luxembourg (1412-1415), ruled alone (1415-1419 and 1425-1444)

Elizabeth was the second wife of Antoine of Burgundy, duke of Brabant, who in 1406 had been named successor to Limburg and Brabant by the childless Duchess Joanna, his great aunt. Elizabeth and Antoine had two sons, John IV, later duke of Brabant (1415-1427), and Philip, later duke of Brabant (1427-1430). During the reign of Holy Roman Emperor Wenceslas IV (also king of Bohemia), the ruler spent so much attending peace conferences in Prague trying to bring an end to the many internal conflicts that plagued his realm, that the various princes of Germany began to demand some degree of separate rule for Germany. Anarchy reigned in much of the outlying areas of his realm. Wenceslas was eventually imprisoned as a heretic and Antoine and Elizabeth, as heirs of the house of Limburg, saw opportunity to become pretenders to the duchy of Luxembourg. Wenceslas managed to get out of prison and restore himself briefly in ca. 1411, but in 1412 he returned to prison and Antoine and Elizabeth claimed the throne of Luxembourg. Wenceslas was executed in 1415, but Antoine also died the same year. Although Wenceslas' brother Sigismund became king of Germany, Elizabeth managed to hold onto Luxembourg. She ruled alone for five years while her son John IV became duke of Brabant. In 1419 Duke Johann of Bavaria assumed rule of the duchy until he died in 1425. Elizabeth then ruled alone again from 1425 until 1443 or 1444. In the meantime, her son John had died in 1427 and her younger son Philip became duke of Brabant until 1420, when he also died. Elizabeth, having outlived her heirs, continued as sole ruler of Luxembourg until c. 1443, when she ceded it to Philip the Good, her husband's nephew. Luxembourg then joined the house of Burgundy.

Suggested Reading:

(1) Langer, William L., ed. *World History*. Boston: Houghton Mifflin, 1980. pp. 406-407.
(2) Egan, Edward W. et. al., eds. *Kings, Rulers and Statesmen*. New York: Sterling Publishing Company, 1976. p. 297.

Elizabeth of Luxembourg

See Elizabeth of Görlitz

Elizabeth of Poland

Queen (of Hungary), regent of Poland (1370-c. 1377)

She was the daughter of King Vladislav IV, king of Poland from 1305 to 1333. In 1320 she married Charles Robert of Anjou, king of Hungary (1310-1342), and they had two sons: Andrew, who married Joanna I, queen of Naples, and Louis I, king of Hungary (1342-1382) and king of Poland (1370-1382). Her brother, Casimir III succeeded their father as king of Poland in 1333 but died in 1370 leaving no male heir, so Elizabeth's son Louis I was named king of Poland. Louis had no interest in governing Poland and appointed his mother Elizabeth as regent. She ruled Poland until she died c. 1377.

Suggested Reading:

(1)   Dvornik, Francis. *The Slavs in European History and Civilization*. New Brunswick, NJ: Rutgers University Press, 1962. pp. 48, 82.

(2)   Egan, Edward W. et. al., eds. *Kings, Rulers and Statesmen*. New York: Sterling Publishing Company, 1976. pp. 338-339.

Emma

Queen, regent of The Netherlands (1889-1898)

She was born Emma of Waldeck Pyrmont and became the second wife of King William III, ruler of The Netherlands from 1849 to 1890. In 1880 they had a daughter, Wilhelmina, who became second in the line of succession, the king's elder son by his first wife Sophia having died the previous year. In 1884 his other son, Alexander, died, making Wilhelmina heir apparent. During King William's final illness, Queen Emma served as regent. William died in 1890, and Emma continued as regent for ten-year-old Wilhelmina until she reached the age of 18. During her rule, Emma was faced with putting down two serious revolts in the Dutch East Indies (1894 and 1896). The Liberal party, in power at the time, passed a new electoral law in 1896 which more than doubled the number of citizens allowed to participate in the electoral process, but workers would not satisfied with anything less than universal suffrage. The Liberal ministry continued to pass social legislation for the next five years. Queen Emma retired at the time of her daughter's majority.

Suggested Reading:

(1)   Langer, William L. *World History*. Boston: Houghton Mifflin, 1980. pp. 475, 674.

Ermengarde

Countess, ruler of Carcassonne (1067-1070)

Carcassonne was located in the southwestern section of presentday France. Ermengarde was the daughter of Count Roger II who ruled Carcassonne until his death in 1060. Her brother, Roger III, succeeded his father but died in

1067. Ermengarde married Raimond Bernard, vicomte d'Alby. She inherited the realm in 1067 from her brother and ruled until her death in 1070.

Suggested Reading:

(1) Egan, Edward W. et. al., eds. *Kings, Rulers and Statesmen*. New York: Sterling Publishing Company, 1976. p. 156.

Ermengarde

Viscountess, ruler of Narbonne (1143-1192)

Narbonne was located in the southeastern section of presentday France. Ermengarde was the daughter of Aimery II who ruled from 1105 to 1134. When he died, he was succeeded by her brother, Alfonse Jourdain, count of Toulouse, who ruled from 1134 until he died in 1143. Ermengarde then presided over Narbonne for almost 50 years. She was the leader of the French royalist party in the south of France which was in opposition to the English. She has been described as a nobly-born Joan of Arc. She was married several times, but her husbands took no part in the government of Narbonne. Ermengarde fought numerous wars defending her domain, was a patron of troubadours and protector of the Church. She gained renown as an arbitor and judge in complex cases of feudal law. She had no children, so when she died in 1192 she named as her heir her nephew, Pierre de Lara.

Suggested Reading:

(1) Heer, Friedrich. *The Medieval World*. tr. Janet Sondheimer. New York: Menton/NAL, 1962. p. 318.
(2) Egan, Edward W. et. al., eds. *Kings, Rulers and Statesmen*. New York: Sterling Publishing Company. p. 159.

Ermensinde (or Ermensind)

Countess, ruler of Luxembourg (1196-1247)

Due to the fact that her grandmother, Ermensinde I, a daughter of Conrad I (r. 1059-1086), had married Godfrey, count of Namur, Ermensinde II was of the house of Namur, originally a medieval county in presentday southeastern Belgium. Around the year 1100 the low-country territories began to expand and form principalities, weakening the hold of the German kings, so far away. With the decline of the power of German kings, emperors could do little to enforce their influence in the lowlands. Ermensinde inherited rule of the principality of Luxembourg in 1196 from her father, Count Henry IV the Blind, who ruled from 1136 to 1196. She married Walram III, duke of Limburg, and had a son, Count Henry V, born in 1217, who inherited the rule when Ermensinde died in 1247.

Suggested Reading:

(1) Egan, Edward W. et. al., eds. *Kings, Rulers and Statesmen.* New York: Sterling Publishing Company, 1976. p. 297.
(2) Morby, John E. *Dynasties of the World.* Oxford: Oxford University Press, 1986. p. 92.

Eugenie-Marie

Countess (of Teba), Empress, regent of France (1859, 1865, 1870)

Maria Eugenia Ignacia Augustina de Montijo de Guzman was born in a tent, to escape falling ceilings, during an earthquake in 1826. She was the daughter of a Spanish grandee, Don Cipriano de Guzman y Palafox y Portocarrero, count of Teba, and Doña María Manuela. Her uncle Eugenio was the count of Montijo, and her father was his heir if he died childless. In 1853 she married Louis Napoleon who had been elected president of the French republic, but who the year before had become Emperor Napoleon III when the monarchy was reestablished. The new red-haired empress was strikingly beautiful, brilliant, and charming, but pious, naive, and unschooled in affairs of state. Two events altered the degree of her involvement in political life: an assassination attempt against her husband in 1855 and the birth of their son Napoleon—Eugene-Louis in 1856, whom she hoped to see become the next emperor. Eugenie-Marie, a devout Catholic, became intent in fostering her faith. While her husband attempted to liberalize domestic policy, she worked for conservative causes, becoming the leader of the Clerical Party at the palace. Napoleon III concentrated much of his energies on war with Austria and on the Franco-Prussian War. In addition, he was afflicted with bouts of ill health throughout his reign. On at least three occasions, 1859,

1865, and 1870, possibly more, Eugenie-Marie served as regent while he was out of the country. She was first appointed regent in 1859 during the war against Italy. In 1861 she was instrumental in the decision to create a Mexican Empire and to make Austrian Archduke Maximilian its Emperor. In 1862 Eugenie, believing that a united Italy was a threat to French security, suggested that Victor Emanuel's kingdom be broken up into four states of an Italian federation. But she was determined that Victor not take Rome, insisting that French troops stay there, for fear that the Pope might excommunicate her and Napoleon if the French abandoned Rome. In 1869 she officially opened the Suez Canal with the Turkish Khedive and Franz Joseph. In a time when entrance into medical school was denied women, she interceded in behalf of promising women applicants to gain them admittance. In 1870 she was appointed regent while Napoleon took supreme command of the army against the Prussians in the Franco-Prussian War. Napoleon's defeat and surrender following the Battle of Sedan (1870) left him a prisoner of war. Eugenie as regent refused to negotiate with the Prussians, who wanted her to cede them Alsace and Lorraine. She wrote a personal letter to King William of Prussia asking him not to annex those territories. In a courteous reply the king wrote that Prussia's security required their possession. Napoleon's defeat made the likelihood of his reassuming his reign slim, so Eugenie-Marie sought exile in England. The deposed emperor died in 1873 following an operation for bladder stones, but Eugenie continued to play a part in politics, because her son was immediately proclaimed Napoleon IV by the Bonapartists. In 1879, hoping that her son would capture the imagination of the French people and return to claim the crown much as her husband had done, Eugenie encouraged him to mount an expedition to Africa to gain notoriety and military experience. But he was killed by Zulus, and Eugenie's aspirations died with him. She was not completely out of politics, however; she was 88 at the outbreak of World War I. She offered her yacht to the British Admiralty; it became a mine sweeper. She contacted the British War Office and offered to convert a wing of her 41-room mansion, Farnborough Hill, into a hospital. She continued to live in exile, becoming a well-loved celebrity wherever she went. She died at age 94 in 1920 while on a visit to Madrid.

Suggested Reading:

(1)   Ridley, Jasper. *Napoleon III and Eugenie* New York: The Viking Press, 1980.

(2) Weber, Eugen. *France*. Cambridge: The Belknap Press of Harvard University, 1986. pp. 95, 97, 181.

(3) Langer, William L., ed. *World History*. Boston: Houghton Mifflin, 1980. p. 683.

Euphrosine

Countess, ruler of Vendome (1085-1102)

She was the sister of Bouchard III who began his rule with the help of his guardian uncle, Giu de Nevers, and ruled from 1066 to 1085. She married Geoffroi Jourdain, sire de Previlly. When Count Bouchard III died in 1085, Euphrosine became countess and ruler. When she died in 1102, she was succeeded by Count Geoffroi Grisegonella.

Suggested Reading:

(1) Egan, Edward W. et. al., eds. *Kings, Rulers and Statesmen*. New York: Sterling Publishing Company, 1976. p. 162.

Europe Section F

Finnebogadottir, Vigdis

President of Iceland (August 1, 1980-August 1, 1996)

In Iceland surnames are a combination of the father's first name and the suffix dottir (daughter) or sson (son). People are called by their first names, since surnames are usually lengthy and complex. A woman does not take her spouse's name when she marries but is known by her maiden name all her life. Vigdis was born April 15, 1930 in Reykjavik to Finnbogi Ruter Thorvaldsson, a civil engineer and professor at the University of Iceland, and Sigridur Eriksdottir, a nurse, chairman of the Icelandic Nurses Association for 36 years. Vigdis was interested in the theater. She attended junior college in Reykjavik, then in 1949 went abroad to study at the University of Grenoble and at the Sorbonne. She also attended the University of Copenhagen where she studied theater history. In 1953 she married but divorced after nine years; she returned to Iceland where she taught French both in college and on television. At age 42, she became the first single, divorced woman in her country to adopt a child: a daughter, Astridur. In 1972 she became director of the Reykjavik Theater Company, which flourished under her direction. She became interested in politics in 1974 when she helped organize a petition campaign for the removal of the U.S. naval base at Keflavik. According to Washington columnist Betty Beale, Vigdis first ran for president in 1980 on a dare. Her opponents were three men. She was elected, the first popularly elected woman president in history, and she easily won reelections in 1984, 1988, and 1992. Although the post of president is largely ceremonial, with governing power vested in the prime minister, Vigdis did have some authority in the government. She signed all bills passed by the Althing, or parliament. If she vetoed a bill, it went before the people in a national referendum. In times of crisis, i.e., the death of the prime minister, the president of Iceland would oversee the forming of a new government. As cultural ambassador for her country, the Nordic blond made state visits to other countries to educate the world to the fact that Iceland is not a place of snow and ice. On a five-city U.S. tour in 1987 called the "Scandinavia Today" celebration, she took along the "gourmet ambassador", founder of Iceland's only gourmet magazine, Hilmar Jonsson, to prepare typical Icelandic foods to illustrate how far Icelanders have come from the days of eating large chunks of raw cod fish. Although she encouraged the modernization of her country, and was particularly interested in bettering the status of women, there are some areas of Icelandic life which are sacred, which she hoped progress will not alter. She was proud of the Norse heritage of her people, and she was unwilling to see Iceland become too worldly. The state-run television did not operate on Thursday night, for example, because that is traditionally family night. Until 1989, the manufacture and sale of beer were prohibited on the island. Vigdis described her position in an interview: "The role of the president is to be a symbol for the nation of unity and identity." In 1990 the Women's International Center presented President Finnbogadottir with the International Leadership Living Legacy Award. When she stepped down from her post in 1996, she held the record as having the longest time in a democratically elected presidential office in the world.

Suggested Reading:

(1) Moritz, Charles, ed. *Current Biography Yearbook, 1987*. New York: H. W. Wilson Co., 1987. pp. 169-172.
(2) Beale, Betty, "Word From Washington: Iceland's President Kicks off Scandinavian Culture Extravaganza." *Houston Chronicle*. 5 September 1982: 7:11.
(3) Young, John Edward, "Iceland's 'Chef of State' Needs Plenty of Cod and Imagination." *The Christian Science Monitor*. 8 July 8 1987: 25.
(4) "Exercising Patience". *World Press Review* September 1990: 55.

Fischer, Andrea

German Politician, Cabinet Minister (1998-2001)

She was born on January 14, 1869 in Arnsberg/Westfalen. She was a member of the German Green Party and served as a member of the German Bundestag. She became Federal Minister for Health from 1998 to 2001. In 2002 she dropped out of the Bundestag. She became an apprentice printer and worked in an offset print shop before going to school to study economics.

Suggested Reading:

(1) *http://www.andrea-fischer.de*

Fredegund (or Fredegond)

Queen, regent of Neustria (584-597)

A study of the life of Fredegund should put to rest for all time the argument that if women ruled, peace would reign. She was at least the third wife of Merovingian King Chilperic I, who ruled the western Frankish kingdom of Soissons, from 561 to 584. Soissons was located in present day western Belgium. The area has been called by several names. When the Frankish kingdom was divided among Chlotar I's four sons at the time of his death in 561, Chilperic's part, the smallest part, was called Tournai, or the kingdom of Soissons. When Chilperic's half-brother died in 567, Chilperic received a large portion to the south, and later this entire area was designated as Neustria. Chilperic was possibly the most barbaric king of the Franks. Gregory of Tours claims that he had many wives, but the first of record were Audovera and Galswintha, sister of Queen Brunhilde. Fredegund, a former servant and Chilperic's mistress, induced him to repudiate Audoveda and to garrot Galswintha. This murder began a 40-year feud between Brunhilde and Fredegund. Fredegund and Chilperic married, and if the account of Gregory of Tours is accurate, she became one of the most bloodthirsty queens in history. She and Chilperic had many children, at least six known ones, most of whom died, and it was their deaths which motivated many of her bloodthirsty acts. Another motivation was the desire to rid the Frankish world of Brunhilde and her husband Sigebert. She sent two emissaries to assassinate Sigebert, who was also planning an attack on Chilperic, his brother. The entire Frankish world was infected with an epidemic of dysentery during Chilperic's reign. When her young son Samson became ill, Fredegund rejected him and wanted to have him put to death. She failed in her attempt, but he died anyway. When two more of her children were near death, she decided the disease was God's punishment because Chilperic had amassed so much wealth by taxing paupers. She ordered him to burn the tax demands. Chilperic sent messages to the people promising never to make such assessments again, but the children died anyway. She attempted to have two of her step-sons killed. She had her step-son Clovis's girl-friend and the girl's mother tortured before she had him stabbed for making "unforgivable remarks" about her. When she lost a fourth child to dysentery, she tortured and killed a number of Parisian housewives as alleged witches, charging that they had caused his death. She and Chilperic had Leudast, count of Tours, tortured to death for scurrilous behavior and perfidious talk. She had at least one daughter left, Rigunth, who in 584 was sent off to Toulouse with 50 carts of wealth as her dowery, which she claimed was not from the country's treasury.

That same year, their baby Lothar was born, and shortly afterward, Chilperic was assassinated. Fredegund knew that she must preserve the child's life at all cost, as it was her last tie to power—although she did claim to be pregnant again at the time of Chilperic's death, just as a precaution. She took her wealth and took refuge in a cathedral, but she and the chief advisors of Chilperic's reign were removed to the manor of Rucil so that a new regime could be formed around the baby Lothar. But Fredegund was far from finished. She sent a cleric from her household to gain Queen Brunhilde's confidence and then assassinate her. When he failed, she murdered him. She then sent two priests to assassinate King Childebert II and his mother, Queen Brunhilde, but they were intercepted and executed. In 586, after she had had a bitter argument with Bishop Praetextatus, he was stabbed, apparently at her instigation. She came around to his room to watch him slowly die. She then poisoned a man who dared to berate her for murdering the bishop. She tried, but failed, to murder the bishop of Bayeux for investigating her part in the bishop's murder. Her daughter Rigunth, back home after all her wealth was plundered, often insulted her mother, and they frequently exchanged slaps and punches. After a particularly vexing exchange, Fredegund tried to murder her daughter by closing the lid of a chest on her throat. She sent twelve assassins to murder King Childebert II, but they were all caught. She had three men decapitated with axes at a supper she gave for that specific purpose, because their constant family quarreling was causing a public nuisance. Other members of the victims' families wanted the queen arrested and executed, but she escaped and found refuge elsewhere. Later, in Paris, she sent word to King Guntram of Burgundy that was more a command than a request: "Will my lord the King please come to Paris? My son is his nephew. He should have the boy taken there and arrange for him to be baptised . . . and he should deign to treat him as his own son." The king took Fredegund, as regent, and Lothar

(Clothar II) under his protection, but he had to be convinced by a large body of sworn depositions that the boy was Chilperic's legitimate son, since Fredegund had taken a few lovers in her time. King Guntram died in 592, and Brunhilde's son King Childebert II of Austrasia tried to take both Burgundy and Neustria, since he did not think that Fredegund and Lothar would be strong enough to resist an attack. This kind of attack and counter-attack continued until Childebert's death three years later, and then the struggle was left to the two aging women, Fredegund and Brunhilde, who kept it up until Fredegund's death in Paris in 597.

Suggested Reading:

(1) Gregory of Tours. *The History of the Franks*. tr. Lewis Thorpe. Hamondsworth, Middlesex: Penguin Books, Ltd., 1986. pp. 222-587.
(2) Previté-Orton, C. W. *The Shorter Cambridge Medieval History*. Cambridge: Cambridge University Press, 1952, 1982. Vol. 1. *The Later Roman Empire to the Twelfth Century*. pp. 156-157.

Europe Section G

Galla Placidia

See Placidia, Galla

Grey, Lady Jane

Queen of England for nine days (1553)

Jane was born in 1537, the daughter of Henry Grey, marques of Dorset, later duke of Suffolk, and Lady Frances Brandon, sister of Henry VIII. Jane was the great-granddaughter of Henry VII. She led a short and unhappy life. At the age of 16, at the instigation of the duke of Northumberland, she was married to his son, Lord Guildford Dudley, and went to live with Dudley's parents, whom she found disagreeable. A few weeks later, the duke, an ambitious man who had plans to make his son the king, persuaded the dying King Edward VI to name Lady Jane as heir to the throne, by-passing the legal heirs, Edward's sister Mary Tudor, daughter of Henry VIII, and after her, his sister Elizabeth, then his cousin Mary of Scots. When Jane first learned of the scheme to name her queen, she fainted. Nevertheless, when Edward Vi died in July of 1553, she allowed herself to become a pawn in the political intrigues against Mary Tudor. She and Guildford were escorted to the Tower of London where she was proclaimed queen on July 10, 1553. But Mary had gained great popular support, and the duke of Northumberland, realizing this, left town, leaving his son and daughter-in-law to their own devices. The mayor of London announced Mary as queen, and the duke of Suffolk, Jane's father, convinced her to step down. She left the Tower in relief, saying that she never wanted to be queen in the first place. Northumberland was executed, but Queen Mary "could not find it in her heart to put to death her unfortunate kinswoman, who had not even been an accomplice of Northumberland but merely an unresisting instrument in his hands." But in 1554, when Jane's father was involved in an insurrection led by Sir

Thomas Wyatt, Queen Mary became convinced that her throne would be threatened so long as Jane lived. Jane, her father, and her husband were all executed in 1554.

Suggested Reading:

(1) Plowden, Alison. *Lady Jane Grey and the House of Suffolk*. New York: Franklin Watts, 1986.
(2) Hudson, M.E. and Mary Clark. *Crown of a Thousand Years*. New York: Crown Publishing, 1978. pp. 82-85.

Guendolena

Legendary ruler, briefly, of Loegria (England) (c. pre 9th c.)

She was the daughter of Corineus, who was given Cornwall as his province as a reward for accompanying Brutus, great grandson of Aeneas, as leader of the second group of Trojans. She married Brutus' oldest son, Locrinus, who ruled over England. His name is the root for the name of England used in modern Welsh. The couple had at least one son and heir. Locrinus fell in love with Estrildis, daughter of the King of Germany, and forsook Guendolena. Later she drowned Estrildis and killed her husband in battle. Guendolena ruled briefly before turning the throne over to her son.

Suggested Reading:

(1) Geoffrey of Monmouth, trans. L. Thorpe. *History of the Kings of Britain*. Harmondsworth: Penguin, 1966.

Gyda

Queen of English jarldom (c. 988-c. 995)

She was the daughter of a Viking king—by Snorre's account, of Ireland—and the younger sister, or more likely half-sister, of Anlaf Curaran (Olaf Kvaran, d. 992, or Amlaibh, who ruled Dublin 857-871), the King of Dublin in Ireland. During the era of numerous petty kingdoms, Gyda, described as "young and beautiful", first married a mighty jarl (chieftain) in England.

It might be noted in passing that King Svein Forkbeard had a daughter, Gyda, who married the exiled son of Jarl Hakon of Norway, Eirik Hakonarson; however, Gyda was the name of other early queens, among them, Gyda, the wife of Edward the Confessor and her mother, also named Gyda, or Githa, the mother of Harold, king of England.

When Gyda's husband died, she ruled the land in her own right. A warrior and duelist named Alvini wooed her, but she said that she would choose her husband from among the men of her own country. The prospective husbands gathered dressed in their finery all except Olav Trygvason, a Norwegian harrier who called himself Ali, later to become the great sea king. She chose Olav, but Alvini challenged him to a duel. Olav defeated Alvini, banished him from England, and married Gyda. They had a son who became Viking King Trygvi. For a while, Olav divided his time between England and Ireland, making raids. Later he returned to Norway to claim his heritage as Olav I, king of Norway (A. D. 995). Presumably he left Queen Gyda behind. He had several wives, both before and after Gyda, but she is not mentioned again.

Suggested Reading:

(1) Sturlason, Snorre. *Heimskringla, or The Lives of Norse Kings.* tr. A. H. Smith, ed. notes by Erling Monsen. New York: Dover Publications, Inc., 1990. pp. 137-138, 471.

(2) Jones, Gwyn. *A History of the Vikings.* Oxford: Oxford University Press, 1984. p. 137.

Europe Section H

Halonen, Tarja Kaarina

President of Finland (1999-)

Tarja Halonen was born in Helsinki on December 24, 1943, the daughter of working-class parents Lyyli Elina Loimola and Vieno Olavi Halonen. The couple divorced after World War II, and in 1950 Lyyli Halonen married Thure Forss, an electrician. Tarja attended Kallio Elementary School and Kallio Gymnasium, graduating in 1962. She attended the University of Helsinki in 1962 to study Art History, but switched to Law the next year, receiving a Master of Laws degree in 1968. Her specialty was criminal law.

In the 1960s she quit the Evangelical Lutheran Church of Finland in protest of its policy of taxing church members, and its stance against female priests at the time—now the church accepts women priests. From 1969 to 1970 she was Social Affairs Secretary and Organization Secretary for the National Union of Students. She joined the Social Democratic Party in 1971, working as a lawyer in the Central Organisation of Finnish Trade Unions until her election to Parliament in 1979. She continued as a Member of Parliament until her election as the 11th President in 2000.

That same year she married her partner of fifteen years, Dr. Pentti Arajärvi. At the time the couple had two grown children who acted as attendants: Halonen's daughter Anna Halonen, and Dr. Arajärvi's son Esko.

She is the first female to hold the high office in Finland's history and has been extremely popular among Finns. She was reelected for a second term in 2006. She is particularly known for her interest in human rights, women's rights, and the problems of globalization. In 2006 she was rumored to be a potential candidate for the UN Secretary General, but she denied an interest at that time, saying that she wanted to finish her term as President before examining other options.

Suggested Reading:

(1) "Halonen criticised as global do-gooder; PM Vanhanen comes to President's defence." *Helsingin Sanomat Magazine*, April 26, 2004.

(2) "The President of the Republic of Finland" official website.

Hart, Judith

British Labour Party MP (1951-1987)

She was born Constance Mary Judith Ridehalgh on September 8, 1924. She was educated at Clitheroe Royal Grammar School, the London School of Economics, and the University of London, becoming a lecturer at a teacher training college. In 1946 she married Anthony Bernard Hart.

In 1951 she entered political life with an unsuccessful bid for a Labour Party seat in Parliament from Bournemouth West. In 1955 she tried unsuccessfully for a seat from Aberdeen South. Finally, in 1959, she was elected as a member for Lanark, a seat she held for 24 years. During that time, she held ministerial office as joint Parliamentary Under Secretary of State for Scotland (1964-1966), Minister of State, Commonwealth Office (1966-1967). She was appointed a Privy Counsellor in 1967 and was Minister of Social Security (1967-1968), Paymaster-General, with a seat in the Cabinet (1968-1969), Minister for Overseas Development (1969-1970, 1974-1975, and 1977-1979). In opposition, she was front bench spokesperson for overseas (1979-1980). She was awarded a DBE.

When her constituency was abolished in 1983, she sat for Clydesdale until 1987.

In 1988 she was awarded a DBE and created a Life peer, as Baroness Hart of South Lanark. She died on December 8, 1991.

Suggested Reading:

(1) www.wikipedia.org.

Hedwig, Saint

Duchess of Silesia (c. 1236, 1241-1243)

She was the daughter of Bertold III of Andrechs, marquis of Meran, count of Tirol and prince (or duke) of Carinthis and Istria. Her mother was Agnes, daughter of the count of Rotletchs. At a very young age, Hedwig's parents placed her in a monastary. At the age of 12, she became the wife of Henry I, duke of Silesia from 1201 to 1238. The couple had six children: Henry II the Pious, Conrad, Boleslas, Agnes, Sophia and Gertrude. After the birth of their sixth child, at Hedwig's suggestion, the couple agreed not to cohabit, so as to remain pure, and never to meet except in public places. At her persuasion, and with her dower, Henry built the monastary of Cistercian nuns at Tretnitz, the construction of which took 16 years. In 1163 Silesia (now mostly in Poland) was divided into Upper and Lower Silesia, each ruled by a Piast prince. Henry and his son tried without success to reunite the territory, while Hedwig ruled Silesia. When her husband was taken prisoner by the duke of Kirne, her son Conrad raised an army to rescue him but Hedwig, who had great faith in her own prayers, dissuaded him from attempting the rescue, saying that she was sure that in due time he would be released. In 1238 Henry I died, but Hedwig remained duchess of Silesia, although she concerned herself only with matters of the Church. In 1241 Henry II was killed in the battle of Liegnitz, which pitted the Silesian Knights of the Teutonic Order against the Mongol army under the command of Baider, son of Jagatai. Hedwig died in 1243 and was cannonized in 1266.

Suggested Reading:

(1) Butler, Alban. *The Lives of the Fathers, Martyrs and Other Principal Saints*. Chicago: The Catholic Press, Inc., 1961. vol. 4. pp. 1290-1295.

(2) Löwenstein, Prince Hubertus Zu. *A Basic History of Germany*. Bonn: Inter Nationes, 1964. p. 38.

Henriette de Cleves

Duchess, ruler of Nevers (1564-1601)

Henriette was the daughter of Francois II, duke of Nevers from 1562 to 1563, and the sister of Jacques, duke of Nevers from 1563 to 1564. As was frequently the case with minor rulers, Henriette inherited the financial problems of several of the men in her family. By the time of her grandfather, Francois I, the concept of provincial governors had been well established (although actually the term "governor" had come into usage for royal provincial agents as early as 1330). Governors were originally appointed when there was no male heir. Four of the 142 major governors of the period from 1515 to 1560 were dukes of Nevers, the first being Henriette's grandfather, Francois I, who was appointed governor of Champagne. He dissipated much of his fortune in the discharge of his duties, particularly on military campaigns. When he died early in 1562, he left Henriette's father Francois II, the new governor of Champagne, bankrupt. Francois II died in battle only ten months later, leaving the guardian of Henriette's young brother Jacques de Cleves the job of liquidating the debts. Henriette's dowery was lowered, and to protect her jewels from creditors, she hid them at the Paris townhouse of the president of the *parlement*, Pierre de Seguier. Seguier's wife eventually filed a protest: "Since the day that the said lady left her family jewels (with us) . . . a merchant has not ceased to bother us . . . . We plead to be freed from the charge of keeping the jewels." Before the liquidation process had begun, Jacques also died, in 1564. Since there was no male heir in the Cleves line, the property could have been dispersed among others as was often the case. But in 1565 King Charles IX issued extraordinary permission for the family property and titles to pass to Henriette, and a marriage was arranged for her with the prospective heir of some large estates, Ludovico Gonzaga, or Louis de Gonzague. The two succeeded to the duchy and guided it for 37 years. The marriage did not solve Henriette's financial problems completely, for Garzague had debts of his own, and his inheritance wasn't as large as that of the Cleves'. In addition, Henriette had to provide doweries for her two sisters. Each received 700,000 pounds worth of land and doweries totalling another 600,000 pounds. Louis sold many properties, but much of the estate administration fell to Henriette. Louis was in the prime of his military career, serving as mobile army commander and courtier. He was wounded in 1568 and in 1573, and he was forced to borrow money to pay his men. Despite this, the Nevers' were the chief creditors of the monarchy during this period. Henriette had at least one daughter and, in 1581, a son, Charles II, (Charles de Gonzague) who succeeded upon her death in 1601, but who actually had become co-governor of Champagne with his father in 1589 and who succeeded as duke when his father died in 1595.

Suggested Reading:

(1) Harding, Robert R. *Anatomy of a Power Elite*. New Haven: Yale University Press, 1978. pp. 21, 143-149.

(2)   Egan, Edward W. et. al, eds. *Kings, Rulers and Statesmen*. New York: Sterling Publishing Company, 1976. p. 159.

Hilda, Abbess, of Whitby and Hartlepool (U.K.)

Presided over the Synod of Whitby (664-680)

Hilda was born in 614 in Ireland, the daughter of Prince Hereric of Deira, and entered the convent at an early age. In 657 she founded a monastery for both monks and nuns at Whitby. At the Synod of Whitby, the church authorities decreed that the Northunbrian Church would follow the teachings of the Roman Catholic Church rather than those of the Celtic Irish Iona. Although Abbess Hilda was not disposed to the teachings of Roman Catholicism, she bowed to the council's ruling. She was a sought-after teacher and patroness of the arts. Kings, noblemen and churchmen all sought her counsel. The poet Caedmon came to her attention and under her influence, he became a monk. She was known for her wisdom and, because of her generosity, was called "mother of the poor." After a six-year illness, she died in 680. Soon miracles were reported at her tomb, and in time she was named a Saint and her bones were enshrined. Her Feast Day is November 17. A tradition claims that she rid Eskdale of serpents by driving them off a cliff and cutting off their heads with a whip. The ammonites whose fossils can be found at Whitby are said to be these serpents.

Suggested Reading:

(1)   Matthews, John & Caitlin. *British & Irish Mythology*. London: Diamond Books, 1995. p. 94.

Hiltrude, Dowager Princess

Regent of Bavaria (748-754)

She was the daughter of Charles Martel, Major Domus in Austrasia (719-741) and Duke of Franks (737-741). She married Odila I of Bavaria, who died in 748. Thereafter, Hiltrude assumed the Regency for their son, Tassilo, until her death in 754.

Himnechildis

Queen, guardian/ regent of Austrasia (662-675)

She was the wife of Sigibert III, king of the eastern Frankish kingdom of Austrasia from 632 to 656. She had at least one child, a son, Dagobert II. When her husband died, their son Dagobert was shorn of his long royal hair and sent to an Irish monastary by Grimoald, father of the pretender Childebert. Sigibert's nephew Childeric II, age 13, was then proclaimed ruler of Austrasia under the joint guardianship of Queen Himnechildis and the Major Domus (mayor of the palace), Ebroin. Childeric II was assassinated in 675 and Himnechildis and the Austrasian mayor Vulfoald (Wulfoald), with the help of Wilfrid, bishop of York, traced her son Dagobert, age 26 by that time, and restored him to his throne.

Suggested Reading:

(1) Previté-Orton, C.W. *The Shorter Cambridge Medieval History.* Cambridge: Cambridge University Press, 1952, 1982. vol. 1. *The Later Roman Empire and the Frankish East.* p. 158.

Hortense de Beauharnais

Queen, regent of Holland (1810)

She was born in 1783, the daughter of Alexander, vicomte de Beauharnais, and Josephine Tascher de la Pagerie of Martinique. Reared in Paris, she spent the years from age five to ten on Martinique when her parents separated. When her father died, Josephine married Napoleon I (1797), and that marriage was to change Hortense's future. Attractive, intelligent and cultured, she later wrote in her memoirs, "My life has been so brilliant and so full of misfortune that the world has been forced to take notice of it." She was a gifted pianist and composer of popular songs, at least two of which were sung by French troops. In 1802 she married Louis Bonaparte, Napoleon's brother, and became, so to speak, sister-in-law to her step-father Napoleon. She bore three sons: Charles Napoleon (b.1802, d.1807), Napoleon Louis, (b. 1804), Louis Napoleon, later Napoleon III, (b. 1808, possibly to someone other than Louis). She became queen of Holland in 1806 when Napoleon gave her husband Louis the crown. In 1809 she took a lover, the Comte de Flahault. In 1810 Louis abdicated in favor of his elder son and appointed Hortense as regent of Holland. In 1811, nearly a year after her husband had gone into exile at Teplitz, she became pregnant. She went into hiding and gave birth to a son who was placed into the charge of his paternal grandmother, the novelist Madame de Souza. However, word of the pregnancy may have reached her husband because the two separated when he returned. After the surrender of Napoleon, Hortense received 400,000 franks per year and the title of duchesse de Saint-Leu, although she lost the rank of queen. Her husband received a lower title, the Comte de Saint-Leu, which annoyed him. In 1814 her husband sued for separation demanding custody of their older son. The principle of paternal authority was enshrined in French law, and her lawyers told her it was pointless to contest, but she did. Although her lawyer made a brilliant impassioned appeal for the right of a mother against the archaic laws which considered only the rights of the father, the court ruled in favor of the father. Although he did not comply immediately, Napoleon Louis eventually went to live with his father. During the restoration and the Hundred Days, Napoleon stayed in Hortense's home for four days. She once received protection of Alexander I, tzar of Russia, but after she had accepted the pension and title from King Louis XVIII and the friendship of the tsar, her support of Napoleon during the Hundred Days seemed traitorous. The tzar said of her, "She is the cause of all the troubles which have befallen France." Napoleon Louis married his cousin Charlotte, daughter of King Joseph, and opened a paper factory, designing the machinery himself. He experimented with mechanical flight as well. Hortense and her younger son Louis Napoleon sought exile in England. Louis Napoleon joined the Bonapartists and after an unsuccessful attempt or two, gained the election as president of France. Later, the republic reverted briefly to an empire, and Louis became Napoleon III. Hortense died of cancer in 1837 with her son at her side.

Suggested Reading:

(1) Ridley, Jasper. *Napoleon III and Eugenie*. New York: Viking Press, 1980. pp. 3-13.

Europe Section I

Ide d'Alsace

Countess of Boulogne (1173-1216)

Ide was the daughter of Countess Marie of Boulogne (Countess from 1159-1173) and Matthieu d'Alsace. When her mother died in 1173, Ide became ruler of Boulogne. She married four times. When she died in 1216, she was succeeded by Mauhaut de Dammartin.

Suggested Reading:

(1) Egan, Edward W. et al., eds., *Kings, Rulers, and Statesmen*. New York: Sterling Publishing Company, 1976. p. 152.

Indzhova, Renata

Interim prime minister of Bulgaria (1994-1995)

Late in 1989, Premier Todor Zivkov, who had been head of state since 1971 and had held power for 35 years, was ousted and also expelled from the Communist party. He was replaced as general secretary by Peter T. Mladenov, who went on to become president. Mladenov instituted some reforms, such as restoring civil rights of the Bulgarian Turks and instituting a multiparty system. In 1990, parliament voted to revoke the constitutionally guaranteed dominant position of the Communist party. In the nation's first democratic parliamentary elections since World War II held in 1990, Mladenov's party lost, and he resigned shortly afterward. The opposition leader, Khelyu Khelev, was chosen to replace him. A new constitution was put in place in 1991 that provided for the direct election of a president, and in the election held in 1992, Khelev again won the presidency. The post of prime minister, long held by longtime Communist leader Andrei Lukanov, was now chosen freely from among members of parliament. In 1994, as economic conditions and accompanying strikes worsened in Bulgaria, threatening to topple the government, Renata Indzhova, a member of parliament from her district, was selected as a coalition candidate to fill the post of prime minister until the next general election could be held and unpopular austerity measures could be instituted.

Suggested Reading:

(1) Famighetti, Robert, ed. *The World Almanac*. Mahwah, NJ: K-III Reference Corporation, 1997. p. 747.

Irene Godunova (or Irina)

Tsaritsa, ruler of Russia (7-17 January 1598)

She was the widow of Fyodor I Ivanovich (Theodore, r. 1584-1598) and sister of Boris Godunov (r. 1598-1605). She took the throne for ten days after the death of her husband, then retired to a convent and became a nun. After a brief interregnum, her brother Boris was elected to succeed her. She died in 1603.

Suggested Reading:

(1) Riasnovsky, Nicolas V. *A History of Russia*. Oxford: Oxford University Press, 1993. p. 156.
(2) Carpenter, Clive. *The Guinness Book of Kings, Rulers, & Statesmen*. Enfield, Middlesex: Guinness Superlatives Ltd., 1978. p. 245.

Isabella

Countess, ruler of Foix (1398-1412)

She was the daughter of Gaston III Phebus, who ruled Foix from 1343 to 1391, and the sister of Matthieu de Castelbon, who succeeded his father upon his death in 1391 and ruled until 1398. She married Archambaud de Graille, and they had at least one son, Jean de Graille. She acceded upon her brother's death in 1398 and ruled until her own death in 1412. Her son Jean then became count of Foix.

Suggested Reading:

(1)   Egan, Edward W. et. al., eds. *Kings, Rulers, and Statesmen.* New York: Sterling Publishing Company, 1976. p. 157.

Isabella I the Catholic

Queen of Castile (1474-1504)

She was born in 1451, the only daughter of Juan II, ruler of Castile from 1406 to 1454, and his second wife Isabella of Portugal. Her half-brother was Enrique IV (Henry IV), who ruled Castile when his father died, from 1454 to 1474. Because Isabella was Enrique's heir, he had plans for her marriage to which she violently objected, for Isabella had larger ideas for a political match with the possibility of uniting Spain. In a furtive ceremony in 1469, Isabella married her second cousin Ferdinand II, heir of the king of Aragon. This secret union would prove to be one of the most important events in Spanish history, for their heir would inherit both the kingdom of Aragon and the kingdom of Castile, thus forming Spain as we know it. And although theirs was not a love match, they grew to be the most devoted of couples, even insisting on being buried together at death. The couple had five children: John, Isabella, Juana, Maria and Catherine. In 1474 Enrique died and Isabella became queen of Castile. Enrique's daughter Juana contested the claim and a civil war followed. When it ended in 1479, Isabella was the undisputed queen. That same year King Juan II of Aragon had died, and Ferdinand had become King of Aragon. The two countries were administered separately during the lifetimes of the couple.

Following a flagrant breach of the truce between the Moors in Granada and Castile, Isabella became determined to drive the Moors from her land. The battle lasted a decade (1482-1492). When she was well into her fourth pregnancy and prepared to join her husband in Cordoba, she was warned that it was foolish to travel so close to the Moorish capital, but she told her advisers, "Glory is not to be won without danger." Throughout the campaign, the king rode at the head of her army and Isabella became quartermaster and financier. She also visited camps to encourage the soldiers and established field hospitals and front line emergency tent-hospitals. The latter became known as Queen's Hospitals. The truce in 1492 made Spain an all-Christian nation again after 781 years.

In 1486 Christopher Colombus, seeking financial backing for his search for a shorter route to Asia, knew that he stood a better chance of impressing the intuitive and enthusiastic Isabella than her cautious husband. However, although Colombus' proposition excited her imagination, all her funds were being funneled into the war with Granada. It was not until 1492, when Santangel, Ferdinand's Keeper of the Privy Purse, reminded Isabella that her goal had been to make her country preeminent in Europe, that she summoned Colombus to return to make a contract. During the next ten years she funded four voyages to the new world. Isabella is remembered for her support for Columbus, but she also was a great patron of literature, the arts and the church. She died in 1504, shortly before Columbus returned from his fourth voyage.

Suggested Reading:

(1) McKendrick, Melveena. *Ferdinand and Isabella*. New York: American Heritage Publishing Co., 1968.

(2) Chapman, Charles E. *A History of Spain*. New York; Free Press/ Macmillan, 1965. pp. 111, 123-124, 133-134, 139, 154, 202-230, 292-294.

(3) Langer, William L., ed. *World History*. Boston: Houghton Mifflin, 1980. pp. 304-305.

Isabella II

Queen of Spain (1833-1868)

She was born in 1830, the elder daughter of King Ferdinand VII, who ruled Spain from 1814 to 1833, and his fourth wife, Maria Christina of Naples. Three months before he died, at the urging of his wife, Ferdinand set aside the Salic Law, or male succession law, to assure the succession of his infant daughter and depriving his brother, Don Carlos, of the throne. Isabella was proclaimed queen at age three with her mother as regent. Don Carlos' dispute of her claim culminated in the first Carlist War (1834-1839). In 1840 General Baldomero Espartero, a Progressist, seized power, forced Maria Christina to leave the country, assumed the regency himself, and became a virtual dictator. In 1843 he was deposed by the military and Isabella was declared of age to rule, although she was only 13. In 1846 she married her cousin, Francisco de Asiz de Borbon, the duke of Cadiz. She had four children: Isabella, Maria de la Paz, Eulalia, and Alfonso XII. In 1847 the second Carlist War and republican uprising weakened the liberal system that was in place. A new prime minister, O'Donnell, engaged the country in war against Morocco from 1859 to 1860. Isabella was separated from her husband, and it was rumored that she took lovers, including an actor, son of a cook, Carlos Marfori, whom she made minister of state. Her reign continued to be plagued by political unrest and uprisings. In 1868 a revolution forced her to flee to France and she was declared deposed. However, in 1870 she took the formal step of abdicating in favor of her son, Alfonso XII, who, after much shuffling of leadership in Spain, declared for a constitutional monarchy when he came of age in 1874. Isabella died in Paris in 1904.

Suggested Reading:

(1) Chapman, Charles E. *A History of Spain*. New York; Free Press/ Macmillan, 1965. pp. 498-503, 506.

(2) Langer, William L., ed. *World History*. Boston: Houghton Mifflin, 1980. pp. 694-697.

(3) Ridley, Jasper. *Napoleon III and Eugénie*. New York: Viking Press, 1980 pp. 144, 154, 158, 162, 167-168, 205, 246, 323, 492, 539.

Isabella Clara Eugenia of Austria

Co-ruler of the Spanish Netherlands (1598-1621), sole governor (1621-1633)

She was born in 1566, the daughter of King Philip II, who ruled Spain from 1556 to 1598, and his third wife Elizabeth of Valois. Philip unsuccessfully proposed Isabella as successor, in 1587, to the English throne after the execution of Mary Queen of Scots, and, in 1598, to the throne of France after the assassination of her uncle Henry III. She married Albert, archduke of Austria, and received as dowery the ten southern Spanish Netherlands provinces to rule (1598). The rule of Isabella and Albert signaled a change in policy: Flemish Catholics were treated in a consiliatory manner rather than driven to hostility. Under their rule the Southern Netherlands regained part of its earlier prosperity. The seven provinces of the Northern Netherlands had a measure of autonomy, and Isabella and Albert attempted to reunite the provinces, first by diplomacy and later by force, but they failed. Albert died in 1621, and the Netherlands became a Spanish sovereignty, but Isabella remained and ruled as governor for her nephew the king (Philip IV) until her death in Brussels in 1633.

Suggested Reading:

(1) Geye, Pieter. *The Revolt of The Netherlands 1555-1609*. London: Ernest Benn Ltd., 1958. pp. 218, 223, 227, 232, 239-243.
(2) Trevor-Roper, Hugh et. al., *The Golden Age of Europe*. New York: Bonanza/Crown Publishers, 1987. pp. 53, 84-85, 89, 101.

Isabella d'Este

Marquessa, regent of Mantua (1495 and 1509)

Isabella received the kind of education usually reserved for a noble boy. At 16 she married Francesco II Gonzaga, the Marquis of Mantua. She administered his lands during his absence leading Venetian forces against Charles VIII in 1495. They had a son, Federico, born in 1500. In 1509, when her husband was taken prisoner by the Venetians, she ruled Mantua and held it against the threatening forces of the Venetians. Her husband Gonzaga was released by intervention of the Pope. As a reward for his support of Emperor Maximilian I against Venice, their son was named duke of Mantua. Isabella, a great patron of the arts and letters, presided with her husband over a splendid and impressive court.

Suggested Reading:

(1) Mee, Charles L., Jr. *Daily Life in Renaissance Italy*. New York: American Heritage Publishing Co., Inc., 1975. pp. 70-72.

Isabella (or Isabel) Farnesio (or Elizabeth Farnese) of Parma

Queen and defacto co-ruler of Spain (1714-1746)

She was born in 1692 in Parma, Italy, the niece and step-daughter of the duke of Parma. In 1714 she married Philip V of Spain after the death of his first wife, the popular Maria Louisa Gabriela of Savoy. Maria had been influenced by Madame des Ursins, sent to be her maid of honor by King Louis XIV because she was familiar with the customs of Spain, having been married to and widowed by the Duke of Braciano, a Spanish grandee. After Maria's death, a young Italian abbot had suggested to Madame des Ursins that Isabella, being sweet and gentle of nature, would be a suitable wife for King Philip, and her pliable character would enable Madame des Ursins to retain her own power at court. After the marriage, Isabella, a handsome, ambitious woman, immediately dismissed Madame des Ursins on their first meeting and took complete control of her husband. Philip was so besotted by her that he sometimes struck her in a fit of jealous rage. However, Isabella was willing to overlook his capricious behavior in order to maintain her control over him. Early in 1715 she managed the elevation of the young Italian abbot, Alberoni, to head affairs of state. Eventually he would be made cardinal. Her chief ambitions were to break France's influence over the Spanish crown and the recovery of Italian possessions by exiling Austrians from Italy. The couple had seven children: Charles, Francisco, Philip, Luis Antonio, Mariana, Teresa, and Antonia. Since Philip had two sons by his first wife, Isabella had not much hope that her children would reign on the Spanish throne, so she spent much of her reign attempting to supplant Austrian power in Italy, securing Italian principalities for her children to govern. She was shrewd in her choice of ministers, selecting those who would carry out her foreign policy to the ends that Spain's imperialistic gains in Italy were significant. Isabella made improvements in the country's economy and enacted reforms in the military and administrative branches of the government. Her husband abdicated briefly in 1724 in favor of his oldest son Luis but returned when Luis died of smallpox that same year. Her husband died in 1746 and was succeeded by his son Ferdinand VI by his first wife. Isabella then retired from court. She died in 1766.

Suggested Reading:

(1) Chapman, Charles E. *A History of Spain*. New York: Free Press/ Macmillan, 1965. pp. 374-375.
(2) Langer, William L., ed. *World History*. Boston: Houghton Mifflin, 1980. pp. 487-489.

Isabella of Bavaria

Regent of France by reason of her husband's insanity (1392-1422)

Isabella was born in 1371, the daughter of Stephen III, duke of Bavaria-Ingolstadt. In 1385 she married Charles VI, king of France, who ruled from 1380 to 1422. Her husband's first attack of insanity occurred in 1392. The following year the first of their six children was born. In the ensuing years she was frequently regent as Charles' seizures of insanity grew worse and more protracted. She chose Philip of Burgundy as an advisor, and later the king's brother Louis, duke of Orleans, became her constant advisor. When he was killed in 1407, she turned to John the Fearless, the new duke of Burgundy as of 1404. In 1415 Henry V of England invaded France and defeated the French at Agincourt, reconquering Normandy for the English. In 1417 her son Charles, who would rule later as Charles VII (1422-1461), determined to gain control, had his mother imprisoned. She was rescued by John the Fearless, who assisted her in establishing a new seat of government, first at Chartres and then at Troyes. In 1419, as the English continued to advance, John the Fearless was assassinated. The following year King Charles, with Isabella's support, accepted the Treaty of Troyes, in which he repudiated the dauphin as illegitimate and adopted Henry V as heir. Henry V continued his steady conquest of France until his death in 1422. Isabella's husband died the same year. She faded from the political arena as the dauphin schemed to regain his rightful throne. She died in 1435 in Paris.

Suggested Reading:

(1)   Langer, WIlliam L., ed. *World History*. Boston: Houghton Mifflin, 1980. pp. 299-301.
(2)   Runciman, Steven. *A History of the Crusades*. Cambridge: Cambridge University Press, 1952, 1987. vol. 3. *The Kingdom of Acre*. p. 456.

Isabelle

Princess, co-ruler of Achaea (1289-1297, 1301-1307)

Achaea was a Frankish Crusader principality in the area of Attica in Greece. Isabelle was the daughter of Guillaume II (r. 1246-1278). In 1276 Guillaume became a vassal of Carlos I, king of Sicily and Naples (r. 1278-1285), who passed the principality on to his son, Carlos II of Naples (r. 1285-1289) In 1289 Carlo II waived his rights and Isabelle, with her first husband, Florent of Hainaut, assumed the throne. When Florent died in 1297, Carlos II again took the throne until Isabelle's remarriage in 1301. She and her second husband, Philippe I of Savoy, ruled until 1307, when she was deposed in favor of Philippe II, son of Carlos II of Naples. Isabelle had a daughter, Mathilde, who assumed the throne in 1313.

Suggested Reading:

(1) Carpenter, Clive. *The Guinness Book of Kings, Rulers, & Statesmen.* Enfield, Middlesex: Guinness Superlatives Ltd., 1978. p. 1.

Isabelle

Duchess, co-ruler of Lorraine (1431-1453)

She was the daughter of Charles II the Bold (r. 1391-1431), who married her to the heir to Bar, René I (also Rinaldo, king of Naples) and thus consolidated the two parcels into a much strengthened duchy of Lorraine. She had two sons who ruled after her, Jean II (r. 1453-1470) and Nicolas (r. 1470-1473).

Suggested Reading:

Carpenter, Clive. *The Guinness Book of Kings, Rulers & Statesmen.* Enfield, Middlesex: Guinness Superlatives, Ltd., 1978. p. 92.

Europe Section J

Jacqueline (or Jacoba)

Countess, ruler of Holland, Zeeland, and Hainault (1417-1433), duchess of Bavaria and countess of Ostrevant (1433-1436)

The daughter of William IV of the house of Bavaria (r. Holland 1404-1417), Jacqueline assumed the throne upon his death. In 1415 she married John of Touraine, dauphin of France, who died two years later. The German king Sigismund refused to recognize Jacqueline's right to rule, so in 1418 she married her cousin John IV, duke of Brabant. When John mortgaged Holland and Zeeland the following year, Jacqueline repudiated their marriage and, in 1421, went to England and married Humphrey, duke of Gloucester. In 1424 the couple returned to Holland with an army to retake her lands; however, when the forces against them seemed overwhelming, Humphrey deserted and retreated to England the following year. Jacqueline was taken prisoner by Philip the Good, duke of Burgundy, who had his own designs on Holland. In 1425 she escaped and marshalled her English forces to combat Philip; however, in 1428 the Pope intervened, declaring her English marriage null. She was forced to make peace with Philip and to promise not to marry without his consent. In 1430 she secretly married Francis, lord of Zulen and St. Maartensdijk, with an eye to overthrowing Philip. But Francis was taken prisoner in 1432 and Jacqueline was forced to abdicate the following year. Thereafter Holland and Hainault were united with Burgundy. Jacqueline was made duchess of Bavaria and countess of Ostrevant in 1434. She died two years later.

Suggested Reading:

(1) Morby, John. *Dynasties of the World.* Oxford: Oxford University Press, 1989. p. 91.
(2) Langer, William L. *World History.* Boston: Houghton Mifflin, 1980. p. 406.

Jadwiga (or Hedwig)

"Maiden king" of Poland (1384-1399)

Jadwiga was born ca. 1373, the third daughter of Louis I of Anjou, king of Poland (1370-1382) and king of Hungary (1342-1382), and Elizabeth of Bosnia. Polish nobility had made a special agreement to accept any one of Louis' daughters as their next ruler. Louis did not have serious concerns about Poland, which he governed through his regent-mother Elizabeth until her death, and thereafter through a council of regents. But he was concerned that the succession to the Hungarian throne should be secure. He had appointed Jadwiga as his successor and had betrothed her and formally celebrated her marriage at the age of five to William of Habsburg, anticipating by such a union a closer relationship between Hungary and Austria. But after Louis died in 1382, the Hungarian nobles elected her sister Maria as "king of Hungary." Maria, who had been married to Sigismund, son of Emperor Charles IV, had been designated by Louis to inherit the throne of Poland after the oldest sister Catherine died in 1378. But Polish nobles, who did not want the Holy Roman emperor to have a hand in their future, urged Queen Elizabeth to name her younger daughter Jadwiga as successor to the Polish throne. However, they did not approve of Jadwiga's Austrian husband and decided that she should marry the new grand duke of Lithuania. Jagiello hoped that he would reclaim their territory lost to Hungary. During the interregnum following Louis' death (1382-1384) Poland suffered through civil wars and upheavals, while Polish nobles vied to increase their own power and privileges. In 1384 Jadwiga was formally elected and crowned "king." William of Hapsburg, Jadwiga's former "husband," after trying in vain to defend his right by attempting to occupy Wawel castle in Cracow, returned to Vienna. Jadwiga, who had been genuinely fond of him, had to content herself with marrying the 35-year-old Jagiello "for the good of her country." In 1386 at age 12, she was married to Jagiello, who had converted to Catholicism and taken the name Wladyslaw II. Jagiello never intended merely to play the role of prince consort, but the young Jadwiga, being the hereditary claimant, had the right to rule on her own if she wished; therefore the ruling class of Poland did not wholeheartedly accept his attempts to rule. Frustrated in his ambitions, he was nevertheless able to unite his dukedom of Lithuania, three times the size of Poland, with Poland and to convert the country to Catholicism. Jadwiga remained somewhat intimidated by her older husband. She bore no children and died at the age of 29 in 1399.

Only then did Jagiello become ruler of Poland in his own right. He married again three times. His last wife, Sonia of Kiev, bore two sons who became kings of Poland.

Suggested Reading:

(1) Dvornik, Francis. *The Slavs in European History and Civilization.* New Brunswick: Rutgers University Press, 1962. pp. 83-84, 129-130, 169, 222, 224, 436.
(2) Langer, William L., ed. *World History.* Boston: Houghton Mifflin, 1980. pp. 337-340.
(3) Egan, Edward W. et. al., eds. *Kings, Rulers, and Statesmen.* New York: Sterling Publishing Company, 1976. p. 361.

Jane

Queen of England. See Grey, Lady Jane

Jane

Queen of Naples. See Joanna I

Jeanne I

Countess, ruler of Dreux (1345-1346)

Jeanne was the daughter of Count Robert, who ruled Dreux from 1309 to 1329. She succeeded her brothers, Jean II, who ruled from 1329, when their father died, to 1331, and Pierre, who ruled from 1331, when his brother died, to 1345. When she died a year later, her aunt, Jeanne II, succeeded her.

Suggested Reading:

(1) Egan, Edward W. et. al., eds. *Kings, Rulers, and Statesmen.* New York: Sterling Publishing Company, 1976. p. 157.

Jeanne I

Countess of Champagne (1274-1304) See Juana I, queen of Navarre

Jeanne II

Countess, ruler of Dreux (1346-1355)

Jeanne was the second daughter of Count Jean II, who ruled Dreux from 1282 to 1309, and the sister of Count Robert, who ruled from their father's death in 1309 to 1329. She married Louis, vicomte de Thouars, and bore a son, Simon. When her niece, Countess Jeanne I died in 1346, she succeeded to the reign. Her son Simon succeeded her in 1355.

Suggested Reading:

(1)   Egan, Edward W. et. al., eds. *Kings, Rulers, and Statesmen.* New York: Sterling Publishing Company, 1976. p. 157.

Jeanne d'Albret (also Joan III or Juana III)

Queen of Navarre (1555-1572)

Jeanne was born ca. 1528, the daughter of Henry II, king of Navarre (1517-1555), and his second wife, Margaret of Angouleme. From 1521 until he died, Henry warred with France for the return of his Navarre territories lost by his parents in 1514. In 1548 Jeanne married Antoine de Bourbon, duke of Vendome. They had a son, Henry, born in 1553, who had scant prospects of becoming King Henry IV of France because there were so many in the line of succession ahead of him. In 1555, Jeanne became queen of Navarre when her father died. In a series of religious wars in France, Antoine, first a leader of the Protestant faction, eventually changed his mind and became a champion of the Catholics. Queen Jeanne, however, publicly announced her Calvinism on Christmas in 1560. In 1562 her estranged husband Antoine was killed fighting the Calvinists. In 1568 Queen Jeanne, who had remained neutral during the first two religious wars, entered the third war. When her brother-in-law Louis I, head of the army, was killed in Jarnac, she hurried to the scene and proclaimed her son Henry, age 15, the head of the army. When the war ended in 1570, Jeanne and Catherine de Medicis began arrangements for a marriage between Henry and Catherine's daughter, Margaret of Valois. The marriage occurred two years later. Queen Jeanne traveled to Paris to prepare for the event but died of a respiratory infection two months before the ceremony took place. Henry not only became king of Navarre, but also, in 1589, King Henry IV of France, and Navarre became a part of France.

Suggested Reading:

(1) Tuchman, Barbara W. *A Distant Mirror, The Calamitous 14th Century.* New York: Ballantine Books, 1978. p. 595.
(2) Trevor-Roper, Hugh. *The Golden Age of Europe.* New York: Bonanza/ Crown, 1987. p. 162.
(3) Harding, Robert R. *Anatomy of a Power Elite.* New Haven, CT: Yale University Press, 1978. pp. 39, 176, 188.
(4) Langer, William L., ed. *World History.* Boston: Houghton Mifflin, 1980. pp. 410, 411.
(5) Egan, Edward W. et. al., eds. *Kings, Rulers and Statesmen.* New York: Sterling Publishing Co., 1976. p. 162.
(6) Morby, John E. *Dynasties of the World.* Oxford: Oxford University Press, 1989. p. 115.

Jeanne de Castile

Co-ruler of Vendome (1366-1374)

Jeanne was married to Count Jean VI who ruled Vendome from 1336 to 1366. They had two children, Catherine and Bouchard VII. When her husband died in 1366, Jeanne served as co-ruler with her son, for whom she was guardian. Bouchard died in 1374, and her daughter assumed the reign.

Suggested Reading:

(1) Egan, Edward W. et. al., eds., *Kings, Rulers, and Statesmen.* New York: Sterling Publishing Company, 1976. p. 162.

Jeanne de Chatillon

Countess, ruler of Blois (1279-1292)

She was the daughter of Jean de Chatillon, count of Blois and Chartres, who ruled from 1241 to 1279. She married Pierre, count of Alencon. She succeeded to the rule of Blois on her father's death. She died in 1292, leaving no offspring, and was succeeded by her German cousin, Hugues de Chatillon.

Suggested Reading:

(1) Egan, Edward W. et. al., eds. *Kings, Rulers, and Statesmen.* New York: Sterling Publishing Company, 1976. p. 152.

Jeanne de Nemours (or Marie de Savoie-Nemours)

Duchess, regent of Savoy (1675-1684)

Savoy, located between France, Austria, and Italy (and now a part of Italy), had once been occupied by French forces, and although it had long since regained its sovereignty and had even expanded its holdings, it had constantly to play diplomatic dodgeball between the two powers, France and the Hapsburg Empire. Jeanne was the wife of Charles Emmanuel II, ruler of Savoy from 1638 to 1675. In 1666 they had a son, Victor Amadeus II, who succeeded as ruler when his father died in 1675. Jeanne acted as regent not only until he attained majority, but until 1684. Jeanne inherited a Francophile orientation of Savoy's policy, which she thought it wisest to continue. After Savoy had acquired Sicily and following the Treaty of Utrecht in 1713, Jeanne encouraged her son to trade, through diplomatic maneuvering, his title of duke of Savoy by exchanging Sicily for Sardinia. He then became the king of Sardinia-Piedmont in 1720, but he abdicated in 1730. Jeanne did not live to see his abdication; she died in 1724.

Suggested Reading:

(1) Langer, William L., ed. *World History.* Boston: Houghton Mifflin, 1980. pp. 494-495.
(2) Morby, John E. *Dynasties of the World.* Oxford: Oxford University Press, 1989. p. 110.

Jeanne de Penthièvre

Duchess, ruler of Brittany (1341-1365)

She was born in 1319, the daughter of Jean III (r. 1312-1341), whose death occasioned a dispute over the right of succession.

Her uncle, Jean IV de Montfort, the younger brother of Jean III, also claimed hereditary right, and for the first four years she fought for control of Brittany. In 1365 she was forced to cede her rights to her cousin, Jeane V de Montfort (r. 1365-1399). She died in 1384.

Suggested Reading:

(1)   Carpenter, Clive. *The Guinness Book of Kings, Rulers, & Statesmen.* Enfield: Middlesex: Guinness Superlatives Ltd., 1978. p. 90.

Joan (or Jeanne, Juana I)

Countess of Champagne (1274-1305). See Juana I, queen of Navarre

Joan (or Jeanne)

Countess, Capetian ruler of Artois (1329-1330)

Artois was located in northern France. Joan was the daughter of Mahaut (r. 1302-1329) and Otto IV, count of Burgundy, not to be confused with the duchy of Burgundy, of which Eudes IV, her future son-in-law, was duke at the time (r. 1315-1349) Joan married Philip V of France (r. 1316-1322) and had at least two daughters, Joan II (r. 1330-1346) and Margaret (r. 1361-1382). In 1329 Joan I succeeded her mother Mahaut but ruled only one year before she died. Her daughter Joan II succeeded her.

Suggested Reading:

(1)   Morby, John E. *Dynasties of the World.* Oxford: Oxford University Press, 1980. p. 94.

Joan II (or Jeanne)

Countess, Capetian ruler of Artois (1330-1347).

Artois was located in northern France. Joan II was the daughter of Joan I (r. 1329-1330) and Philip V (r. France 1316-1322). She married Eudes IV, duke of Burgundy (r. 1315-1349) and inherited the rule of Artois at the death of her mother. Joan II and Eudes IV had a son, Philip, whose son Philip of Rouvres (r. 1347-1361) succeeded his grandmother. After 1349 Philip also ruled Burgundy.

Suggested Reading:

(1)   Morby, John E. *Dynasties of the World*. Oxford: Oxford University Press, 1989. pp. 94-95.

Joanna I (or Jane, Joan I, Giovanna I or Giovanni I)

Countess of Provence (1343-1382), queen of Naples (1343-1381)

She was born in 1326, the daughter of Charles of Calabria and Maria of Valois, and the grandaughter of Robert the Wise, king of Naples from 1309 to 1343, whom she succeeded upon his death, becoming the first queen of Naples. Queen Joanna, intelligent and politically astute as well as beautiful, married her cousin, Andrew of Hungary, brother of Hungarian King Louis I (or Lewis), as a political ploy to reconcile Hungarian claims upon Naples. The influx of Hungarians brought by Andrew into Naples angered many, including Joanna, who feared that the Hungarians intended to take over Naples. Andrew was assassinated in 1845, if not by her instigation, at least with her consent. In 1347 she married Louis of Taranto but was forced to take exile in Avignon when her former brother-in-law, King Louis I, invaded Naples to avenge his brother's death, accusing her of strangling him. During her five-year exile, she sold Avignon to Pope Innocent VI in return for a declaration by him of her innocence of the assassination. Her second husband died ten years after her return, and she took as her third. In 1862 she married King James of Majorca. He died in 1875, and the following year she married Otto of Brunswick, a military man. At one time she named her niece's husband, Charles III of Durazzo, as her heir, but later she repudiated him and adopted Louis, duke of Anjou, brother of France's King Charles V. Durazzo appealed to Pope Urban VI, who in 1381 crowned him king of Naples in Rome. Durazzo then invaded Naples, imprisoned Joanna and, a year later, had her murdered by suffocation (1382).

Suggested Reading:

(1) Tuchman, Barbara W. *A Distant Mirror, The Calamatous 14th Century.* New York: Ballantine Books, 1978. pp. 201, 330, 333, 334, 337, 399, 409.
(2) Gibbon, Edward. *The Decline and Fall of the Roman Empire.* Chicago: Encyclopedia Britannica, 1952. vol. 2. pp. 509, 577.
(3) Morby, John E. *Dynasties of the World.* Oxford: Oxford University Press, 1989. pp. 87, 102.

Joanna II (or Joan II, Giovanna II, or Giovanni II)

Queen of Naples (1414-1435)

She was born in 1371, the daughter of Margaret of Durazzo and Charles III, who ruled Naples from 1382 to 1386 and Hungary from 1385 to 1386. She was the sister of Ladislas I, who succeeded as king of Naples after their father was murdered in 1386. She first married William of Austria, but after he died in 1406, her amorous escapades kept Italian diplomacy in an uproar. When her brother Ladislas I died in 1414, Joanna succeeded to the throne and appointed her current lover Pandolfello Alopo grand chamberlain. The following year she married Jacques de Bourbon, Comte de la Marche, who had her lover executed and then attempted to wrest the throne from her. But Italian barons, not wanting a French takeover, ousted him and sent him back to France. Joanna used the succession unmercifully as a maneuvering device. She adopted, then renounced, Alfonso V of Aragon (the Magnanimous) as her heir; adopted, then disinherited, Louis III of Anjou as her heir; readopted, then redisinherited, Louis and, when Louis died, finally named his son Renè as her heir. She died in 1435, leaving Alfonso and Renè to fight it out. Alfonso was the victor and became the next king of Naples.

Suggested Reading:

(1) Langer, William L. *World History.* Boston; Houghton Mifflin, 1980. p. 314-315.
(2) Carpenter, Clive. *The Guinness Book of Kings, Rulers, & Statesmen.* Enfield, Middlesex: Guinness SuperlativesLtd., 1978. p. 147.

Joanna III (or Giovanna III)

Queen of Naples (1516-1555). See Juana la Loca

Joanna of Austria

Regent of Portugal (1557-1562)

She was the daughter of Charles V, Holy Roman Emperor, and Isabella, daughter of King Manuel I of Portugal. She married John of Portugal, second son of King John III (the Pious) of Portugal, who ruled Portugal from 1521 to 1557. In 1554, months before their son was born, John died. The boy, Sebastian I, succeeded to the throne three years later when his grandfather died. Joanna served as regent for five years. During her regency Portugal's overseas dominions frequently erupted in rebellions. In 1562 King John's brother, Cardinal Henry was appointed to replace her for the remaining six years of the regency.

Suggested Reading:

(1) Langer, William L., ed. *World History*. Boston: Houghton Mifflin, 1980. pp. 418-419.

Johanna (or Joanna)

Countess, ruler of Flanders (1205-1244)

She was the daughter of Baldwin IX, emperor of Constantinople (1171-1195), and Maria of Champagne. She became sole ruler from the House of Hainault of Flanders in 1205. In 1212 she married Ferdinand of Portugal, who served as co-regent until 1233, when he died. She then ruled alone during a difficult period of Belgian history, when the country was devastated by war. Upon her death in 1244, she was succeeded by her sister Margaret II. Flanders, a great center of economic activity and a much fought-over territory, was ruled by women for 65 years.

Suggested Reading:

(1)   Heer, Friedrich. *The Medieval World*. tr. Janet Sondheimer. New York: Mentor/NAL, 1962. p. 318.
(2)   Morby, John E. *Dynasties of the World*. Oxford: Oxford University Press, 1989. p. 90.
(3)   Egan, Edward W. et. al., eds. *Kings, Rulers, and Statesmen*. New York: Sterling Publishing Company, 1976. p. 52.

Johanna

Duchess, ruler of Brabant (1355-1404/6)

Johanna, of the House of Burgundy, was the daughter of John III, who ruled Brabant from 1312 to 1355, and she succeeded him at his death in 1355. She married Wenceslas, duke of Luxembourg. On a ceremonial visit to Brabant in 1356, she tendered upon her subjects a new constitution, called *Joyeuse Entree*, which conferred broad liberties to her subjects. Johanna had no children. Due to ill health, she abdicated in 1204, but no successor was named. On her deathbed she named as successor her great-nephew Antoine of Burgundy (r. 1406-1415), grandson of her sister, Margaret, and son of Philip the Bold. She died in 1406.

Suggested Reading:

(1)   Morby, John E. *Dynasties of the World*. Oxford: Oxford University Press, 1989. p. 94.
(2)   Langer, William L., ed. *World History*. Boston: Houghton Mifflin, 1980. p. 406-407.

Jolanthe

Duchess, co-ruler of Lorraine (1473-1480)

She was a kinswoman of Jean II (r. 1453-1470) and Nicolas (r. 1470-1473). When Nicolas died, she inherited the duchy. She was married to René II, grandson of René I (co-ruled 1431-1453). René II ruled with her until her death in 1480, whereupon he became sold duke of Bar and Lorraine.

Suggested Reading:

(1)   Carpenter, Clive. *The Guinnes Book of Kings, Rulers, & Statesmen.* Enfield, Middlesex: Guinness Superlatives Ltd., 1978. p. 92.

Juana I (or Joan I)

Queen of Navarre (1274-1305)

She was born in 1273, the daughter of Henry I (Enrique) the Fat (r. Navarre 1270-1274). She succeeded from the House of France to the rule of Navarre and Champagne upon his death when she was only an infant. From the mid-thirteenth century onward, the counts or countesses of Champagne were also kings or queens of Navarre. In 1284, she was married to Philip IV the Fair of France (r. France 1285-1314), considered by his detractors as a cruel and greedy tyrant. Juana inherited the rule of Champagne after the death of her father. During Philip's reign of France, the French feudal monarchy was at its apex. He forbade private feudal wars, decreeing as illegal the practice of nobles to ride about carrying arms. He effectively weakened the Church's influence in politics. One of Juana's sons, Louis, ruled Champagne following her death in 1305 and, upon the death of his father in 1314, became king of France as Louis X. Thereafter Champagne was a part of France. Louis also inherited Navarre but when he became king of France, he passed Navarre to his brother Philip, later Philip V (r. France 1316-1322). As Louis had died leaving a male heir, the question had arisen whether the crown of France should pass to his granddaughter or to Philip's second son. Although everywhere else in Europe except in the Empire and the Holy See, women could ascend the throne; however, France chose to continue the Roman tradition, thus electing Philip. When Philip died, a third son, Charles IV, succeeded his brother (r. 1322-1328). Juana's daughter Isabella married Edward II of England (r. England 1307-1327). In 1304 Queen Juana founded the College of Navarre. She died in 1305.

Suggested Reading:

(1)   Heer, Friedrich. *The Medieval World.* tr. Janet Sondheimer. New York: Mentor/NAL, 1962. p. 251.
(2)   Morby, John E. *Dynasties of the World.* Oxford: Oxford University Press, 1989. pp. 70, 85, 114.

(3)   Painter, Sidney, *The Rise of the Feudal Monarchies*. Ithaca: Cornell University Press, 1951. pp. 37, 39-41.
(4)   Sédillot, René. *An Outline of French History*. tr. Gerard Hopkins. New York: Alfred A. Knopf, 1967. pp. 115-116, 126-127, 152-153, 160.
(5)   Langer, William L., ed. *World History*. Boston: Houghton Mifflin, 1980. p. 298.

Juana II (or Joan II)

Queen of Navarre (1328-1349)

She was born in 1311/12, the daughter of Margaret of Burgundy and King Louis X, who (r. France 1314-1316). She inherited the kingdom of Navarre at the death of her uncle, King Charles I (r. 1322-1328), who was also Charles IV, king of France. She married Count Philip of Evreux (Philippe III). Under Jeanne, Navarre became an independent nation again. Philip died in 1343. Their son, Charles II the Bad (Carlos), inherited her throne when she died in 1349.

Suggested Reading:

(1)   Morby, John E. *Dynasties of the World*. Oxford: Oxford University Press, 1989. p. 114.

Juana la Loca (the Mad)

Queen of Castile (1504-1506/55), queen of Aragon (1516-1555),

She was born in 1479, the daughter of Isabella I of Castile and Ferdinand II of Aragon. She was married to Philip (the Handsome) of Burgundy and became archduccess of Burgundy. Philip became Philip I in 1504 when, upon Isabella's death, Juana inherited her mother's throne. Juana bore two sons: Charles, who first became Charles I, king of Spain, then Charles V, Holy Roman emperor; and Ferdinand, who succeeded his brother as Holy Roman emperor. She had four daughters: Eleanor, who married King Manuel I of Portugal; Isabella, who married King Christian II of Denmark; Maria, who married King Louis II of Hungary; and Catherine who married King John III of Portugal. When Philip died in 1506, Juana lost her sanity completely. She toured the country with his coffin and finally retired three years later to Tordesillas, still accompanied by his embalmed corpse.

Suggested Reading:

(1) McKendrick, Malveena. *Ferdinand and Isabella*. New York: American Heritage Publishing Company, 1968. pp. 99, 130-136, 140, 141, 144, 146-147.
(?) Chapman, Charles E. *A History of Spain*. New York: The Free Press/ Macmillan, 1965. pp. 207-209, 235, 233.
(3) Langer, William L., ed. *World History*. Boston: Houghton Mifflin, 1980. pp. 406, 415, 428.

Julia Avita Mammaea

Augusta, regent of the Roman Empire (222-235)

Commonly referred to as Mammaea, she was the daughter of Julia Maesa and Julius Avitas and the sister of Julia Soaemias. She married Gessius Marcianus, and in 208 they had a son, Severus Alexander, a personable and intelligent child. Julia's mother persuaded her grandson Emperor Elagabalus to adopt Alexander as his heir. When Elagabalus was murdered, Julia Mammaea's son Alexander, age 14, became emperor. His mother acted as regent with a senatorial advisory council. After the death of her mother in 226, Julia Mammaea emerged as the real power, totally dominating the young emperor. In 232 she even accompanied the army on the Persian campaign, the failure of which was then ascribed to her interference. While on campaign in 235, she and her son were slain at Mainz by mutinous Roman soldiers led by Maximus Julius Verus.

Suggested Reading:

(1) Gibbon, Edward. *The Decline and Fall of the Roman Empire*. Chicago: Encyclopedia Britannica Press, 1952. vol. 1. pp. 271-272.
(2) Rawlinson, George. *Ancient History*. New York: Barnes & Noble Books, 1993. pp. 431-433.
(3) Peters, F. E. *The Harvest of Hellenism*. New York: Barnes & Noble Books, 1996. pp. 559-560, 579.

Julia Domna

Empress, regent of the Roman Empire (211-217 intermittently)

She was born in Emesa, Syria, the daughter of the prominent high priest Bassianus. Renowned for her intelligence and beauty, she was the elder sister of the famous and equally well endowed Julia Maesa. In A.D. 187 she married the governor of Gallia Lugdunansis, Lucius Septimius Severes, who became Roman Emperor in 193. She had two children in Gaul: Caracella (born in 188) and Geta (born in 189). Devoutly religious, she introduced the Semitic goddess Tanit (as Caelestis Dea) into the Roman world. In 203 she began gathering about her in Rome a group of philisophers and other literary figures. Her life was to change drastically in 207, when Severus mounted an expedition to Britain, taking Julia and their sons with him. He died in 211 while in Britain, and his sons became co-emperors and bitter antagonists. In 212 Caracella persuaded Julia to act as intermediary to bring the two together for reconciliation. When Geta appeared, Caracella had his brother stabbed to death in his mother's arms. Caracella then ruled alone and was frequently gone on military campaigns, leaving Julia in charge of the administration of civil affairs. In 217 he was murdered by his praetorian prefect Macrinus, who was then proclaimed emperor. On news of her son's death, Julia committed suicide (217), allegedly by starvation, either voluntarily or upon Macrinus' orders.

Suggested Reading:

(1) Peters, F. E., *The Harvest of Hellenism*. New York: Barnes & Noble Books, 1996. pp. 430, 547, 557, 558.
(2) Gibbon, Edward. *The Decline and Fall of the Roman Empire*. Chicago; Encyclopedia Britannica Press, 1952. vol. 1, pp. 48, 52, 54-55, 58.
(3) Bowder, Diana. *Who Was Who in the Roman World*. Ithaca, NY: Cornell University Press, 1980. pp. 89-90, 226-227, 270-271, 491-494.

Julia Maesa

Augusta, defacto regent of Roman Empire (217-226)

She was born in Emesa, Syria, the daughter of the high priest Bassianus and the younger sister of Empress Julia Domna. She married a Roman senator,

Julius Avitus. They had two daughters: Julia Soaemias, mother of Emperor Elagabalus (r. 218-222); and Julia Mammaea, mother of Emperor Severus Alexander (r. 222-235). Elagabalus resembled his kinsman Caracella, so after Caracella had been murdered by Macrinus, Julia Maesa plotted the overthrow of Macrinus by having Syrian troops pass off Elagabalus as Caracellas' bastard son, proclaiming him emperor. Elagabalus succeeded to the throne, but his grandmother held the real power. She introduced the Syrian cult of Bael at Rome. Elagabalus was bisexual and had a tendency toward transvestism. He took three different wives and many casual sexual encounters with various other partners. His conduct so disgusted his soldiers that by 221 it was clear to Julia Maesa that he would soon be murdered. She persuaded him to adopt his cousin Alexander, age 14, as his son and Caesar. Alexander was so popular that Elagabalus became jealous and tried to have him killed. The outraged soldiers murdered Elagabalus and his mother Julia Soaemias in 222. Julia Maesa continued to exercise her power until her death in c. 226.

Suggested Reading:

(1) Rawlinson, Georg. *Ancient History*. New York: Barnes & Noble Books, 1993. pp.431-433.
(2) Peters, F. E. *The Harvest of Hellenism*. New York: Barnes & Noble Books, 1996. pp. 558, 559.
(3) Bowder, Diana. *Who Was Who in the Roman World*. Ithaca, NY: Cornell University Press, 1980. pp. 180-181, 271, 272.
(4) Gibbon, Edward. *The Decline and Fall of the Roman Empire*. Chicago: Encyclopedia Britannica Press, 1952. vol. 1, pp. 58, 60-61.

Juliana

Queen of The Netherlands (1948-1980)

Juliana Louise Emma Marie Wilhelmina was born in The Hague in 1909, the only child of Queen Wilhelmina and Prince Henry of Mecklenburg-Schwerin. As a teenage princess, she met her cousin Edward, Prince of Wales (the late duke of Windsor), and it was hoped in some circles that the two would be attracted to each other. Instead, the prince said, "Juliana, you have heavy legs," to which she retorted, "If the House of Windsor had been standing as long as the House of Orange, your legs wouldn't be so skinny." She studied at the University of Leiden from 1927 to 1930. In 1937 she married Prince

Bernhard of Lippe-Biesterfeld. The couple had four daughters: Beatrice (1938), Irene (1939), Margaret (1943), and Marijke (1947). During World War II, she and her children took refuge in Ottowa, Canada, returning to The Netherlands in 1945. In 1947 and 1948 she acted as regent during her mother's illness and became queen in September, 1948, following her mother's abdication. She was not crowned because in Holland the crown belongs to the people. The ceremony installing a new ruler is called inauguration. In 1947 she freed from Dutch rule all The Netherlands East Indies except New Guinea, which later became the Republic of Indonesia. In the 1950's Juliana became interested in faith healing, and the news that she had put a faith healer on the payroll was met with public indignation. The marriage of her daughter Princess Irene to a Spanish Carlist and of Princess Beatrix to a German ex-nazi aroused political controversy, as did the prince consort's acceptance of a large sum of money from Lockheed Aircraft Corporation in 1976. Juliana abdicated in 1980 in favor of her daughter Beatrix.

Suggested Reading:

(1) Hoffman, William. *Queen Juliana: The Story of the Richest Woman in the World*. New York: Harcourt Brace Jovanovich, 1979.

(2) Langer, William L., ed. *World History*. Boston: Houghton Mifflin, 1980. p. 475.

(3) Gunther, John. *Inside Europe Today*. New York: Harper & Bros., 1961. pp. 114-115.

(4) Clark, Sydney. *All the Best in Holland*. New York: Dodd Mead & Co., 1963. p. 76.

(5) Uglow, Jennifer S., ed. *International Dictionary of Women's Biography*. New York: Continuum, 1982. p. 250.

Europe Section K

Kazimiera-Daniute Prunskiene

See Prunskiene, Kazimiera-Daniute

Kelly, Ruth

Secretary of Education in Great Britain (2007)

She was accused of hypocrisy for taking her dyslexic son out of a state school and sending him to a L15,000 a year boarding school.

Suggested Reading:

(1) "News in Brief" *Guardian Weekly* January 12-18, 2007. p. 14.

Europe Section L

Leonora Telles (or Leonor Teles de Meneses)

Queen, regent of Portugal (1383-1384)

Kings usually married for political gain and seldom for love. Leonora's marriage to King Ferdinand I the Handsome, who ruled Portugal from 1367 to 1383, followed the love-smitten Ferdinand's repudiation of a previous betrothal to a Castilian princess and precipitated a war between Portugal and Castile. Leonora and Ferdinand had a daughter, Beatrice, who was later married to John I of Castile. When Ferdinand died in 1383, Queen Leonora became regent for her daughter for the Portuguese throne. This arrangement led to strong opposition among the people, who detested both the regent and her Galician lover-adviser, João Fernandes Andeiro, count of Ourém. An illegitimate brother of Pedro I, John of Aviz, led a successful revolt and murdered Andeiro. Queen Leonora fled the country and appealed to the king of Castile for help. The Castilian army marched upon Lisbon in May, 1384, but an outbreak of plague forced it to retreat four months later. John I was proclaimed king in 1385, becoming the first ruler of the Avis dynasty. Leonora was imprisoned in a convent at Tordesillas. She died in 1386.

Suggested Reading:

(1) Langer, William L., ed. *World History*. Boston: Houghton Mifflin, 1980. pp. 306-307, 309.

Lestor, Joan (Baroness Lestor of Eccles)

British Member of Parliament (1966-1983 and 1987-1997)

She was born on November 13, 1931 and educated at Blaenavon Secondary School, Monmouth; William Morris High School, Walthamstow, and

London University. Thereafter, she worked as a teacher in a nursery school.

In 1958 she entered local politics, becoming a councillor on the Metropolitan Borough of Wandsworth and later the London Borough of Wandsworth. During that time she co-founded the anti-fascist magazine, *Searchlight Magazine*. She served on the London County Council from 1962 to 1964, and in 1964 as a member of the Labour Party she contested Lewisham West. She was elected a Member of Parliament for Eton and Slough in 1966 and held this seat until the boundary changes of 1983, when she contested the new constituency of Slough but lost to Conservative candidate John Watts. She returned in 1987 representing Eccles and held this seat until 1997.

On June 4, 1997, she was created a life peer as Baroness Lestor of Eccles, of Tooting Bec in the London Borough of Wandsworth.

Joan Lestor died on March 27, 1998.

Suggested Reading:

(1)   www. Leigh Rayment's Peerage Page.
(2)   www. wikipedia.org.

von der Leyen, Ursula Gertrud

German Minister in Angela Merkel's Cabinet (2005-)

She was born October 8, 1958 in Brussels, Belgium to Heidi Adele and Ernst Albrecht. He worked at the Council of the European Union. In 1971 the family moved to Lehrte, in Lower Saxony. She studied medicine and economics at the universities of Göttingen, Münster, London School of Economics, Hannover, and Stanford University. She was employed as assistant doctor at the medical school at Hannover from 1987 to 1992. During that time, in 1990, she joined the conservative Christian Democrat Union. She married Heiko von der Leyen, a professor of medicine, and the couple had seven children.

From 2003 to 2005 she served as a minister in the state government of Lower Saxony. In 2005 she was appointed by Chancellor Angela Merkel to her Coalition Cabinet. She was named Federal Minister for Family, Senior Citizens, Women and Youth. She is best noted for advocating a mandatory censorship of child pornography on the Internet.

Suggested Reading:

(1) *Who's Who in the World.*

Libuše Vyšehrad

Legendary Princess Regnant of Bohemia (ca. 710-734)

She was the daughter of King Krok, ruler of the Czech tribes prior to ca. 710. After his death, Libuše became ruler from Vysehrad and "highest court of appeal" for tribal disputes. She married Premysl Orac (Przemysl Ploughman) and they established the Przemyslid Dunasty, which governed the Czechs until the 14ᵗʰ Century.

Louise Hippolyte

Princess, titular ruler of Monaco (1731)

She was born in 1697, the daughter of Prince Atoine I of the house of Grimaldi. She married James, duke of Estouteville, who then became Prince James I. She bore a son, Honore III. Her father died in 1731. Princess Louise, heir to the throne, died the same year, and the prince consort ruled for two years. He abdicated in 1733 in favor of their son and died in 1751.

Suggested Reading:

(1) Morby, John E. *Dynasties of the World.* Oxford; Oxford University Press, 1989. p. 89.
(2) Egan, Edward W. et. al., eds. *Kings, Rulers, and Statesmen.* New York: Sterling Publishing Company, 1976. p. 316.

Louise de Savoy

Duchess, regent of France (1515-1516 and 1525-1526)

She was born in 1476, the daughter of Philip II, duke of Savoy, and Marguerite de Bourbon. She married Charles de Valois-Orleans, count (later duke) of Angouleme, and had two children: Margaret, who became queen of Navarre; and Francis, who married Claude, daughter of King Louis XII, and became King Francis I in 1515. A strong and ambitious woman with great diplomatic skills, Louise, who was never a queen, was appointed regent during both her son's expeditions to Italy. When Holy Roman Emperor Charles V captured Francis I and held him prisoner, Louise kept the country running, negotiated Francis' release, and was able to convince England's King Henry VIII to sign a treaty of alliance with France, Venice, and Pope Clement VII against Charles V. When the wars between Francis and Charles threatened to bankrupt both, they were forced, in 1529, to negotiate. Again Louise was called upon, this time to negotiate the peace with Charles' aunt, Margaret of Austria. The two arranged the Treaty of Cambrai, called the "Ladies' Peace." She died in 1531.

Suggested Reading:

(1)   Langer, William L., ed. *World History*. Boston; Houghton Mifflin, 1980. pp. 410, 422, 429.

Lourdes-Pintasilgo

See da Lourdes-Pintasilgo, María

Ludmila

Regent of Bohemia (c. A.D. 921)

She was born ca. A.D. 820 in what is now Czechoslovakia. She married Prince Borivoj, ruler of Bohemia. They converted to Christianity, becoming the first Czech sovereigns to do so. They built Bohemia's first Christian church, near Prague. They had a son, Ratislav, who married Drahomira, a pagan. Ludmila's grandsons from this union were Wenceslas and Boleslav. Ludmila reared Wenceslas as a Christian, while her daughter-in-law reared Boleslav as a pagan. When Ratislav died in 920, the anti-Christian faction attempted to seize control of the government, but Ludmila urged Wenceslas, age about 13, to take over the reigns of government in the name of Christianity. Ludmila acted as regent when Wenceslas became ruler of Bohemia in ca. 921. However, at Drahomira's instigation, agents stole into Tetin Castle and strangled Ludmila in 921. She became a martyr and a saint, as did Wenceslas some eight years later. The carol "Good King Wenceslas" sings his virtues.

Suggested Reading:

(1) Cooke, Jean et. al. *History's Timeline*. New York: Crescent Books, 1981. pp. 46, 61.
(2) Kinder, Hermann and Werner Hilgemann. *Atlas of World History*. tr. Ernest A. Menze. Garden City, NY: Anchor/Doubleday, 1982. vol. 1, p. 169.
(3) Langer, William L., ed. *World History*. Boston: Houghton Mifflin, 1980. p. 255.

Luisa

Regent of Etruria (1803-1807), duchess of Lucca (1815-1824)

Etruria was a kingdom which only existed from 1901 to 1807 by terms of the Treaty of Luneville between Austria and Napoleon. Located in Tuscany in presentday Italy, it was created especially for the house of Bourbon-Parma by Napoleon Bonaparte. Luisa was born in 1782, the daughter of Charles IV, who ruled Spain from 1788 to 1808, and Maria Luisa of Parma. Luisa married Louis, ruler of Etruria from 1801 to his death in 1803. They had two children, Luisa and Charles, king of Etruria (1803-1807), for whom she served as regent. After the fall of Napoleon, Luisa was awarded the duchy of Lucca (1815), which she ruled until her death in 1824.

Suggested Reading:

(1) Langer, William L., ed. *World History*. Boston: Houghton Mifflin, 1980. p. 700.

Luisa María de Guzmán

Regent of Portugal (1656-1662)

She was the wife of John IV of the house of Braganza, king of Portugal from 1640 to 1656. They had three children: Catherine, who married Charles II of England; Alfonso IV, who ruled as king of Portugal from 1656 to 1667, and Pedro II; who ruled as regent from 1667 to 1683 and as king from 1683 to 1706. When John IV died in 1656, Alfonso, age 13, ascended to the throne with Luisa María serving as regent during his minority. Alfonso proved to be both frivolous and vicious. Some also characterized him as feeble-minded. His outrageous conduct prompted his brother Pedro, considered to be wise and just, to imprison him and set himself up as regent in 1667. When Alfonso died in 1683, Pedro II could legally ascend to the throne.

Suggested Reading:

(1) Langer. William L., ed. *World History*. Boston: Houghton Mifflin, 1980. pp. 490, 491.

Luise-Marie (or Louise of Bourbon-Berry)

Duchess, regent of Parma and Piacenza (1854-1859)

Luise Marie was born in 1819, the daughter of Ferdinand, the last duke of Berry, and Caroline of the Two Sicilies. She married Duke Charles III, ruler of Parma from 1849 to 1854. Within five years they had four children: Margarita, Robert, Alicia, and Enrico. When Duke Charles was assassinated in 1854, their son, Robert, age six, became duke of Parma. Luise-Marie served as regent until 1859, when she transferred her powers to a provisional government. Robert, age ten, was deposed. Parma was incorporated in Piedmont Sardinia in 1860 and into Italy in 1861. Luise-Marie died in 1864; Robert died in 1907.

Suggested Reading:

(1) Egan, Edward W. et. al., eds. *Kings, Rulers, and Statesmen*. New York: Sterling Publishing Company, 1976. p. 270.
(2) Morby, John E. *Dynasties of the World*. Oxford: Oxford University Press, 1989. p. 109.

Europe Section M

McAleese, Mary

President of Ireland (1997-)

She was born in 1951 in Belfast, the first of nine children in a Catholic family. Her father owned a pub in the Falls area of Belfast, but the family lost both business and home during sectarian violence in the 1970s. At that time the family moved to Rostrevo in County Down.

She studied law at Queen's University in Belfast, receiving LLB (1973), MA, MIL, and FRSA degrees. After studying to be a barrister, in 1974 she began practice in Belfast, primarily criminal and family law. In 1975, at age 24, she moved to Dublin to accept the post as Reid Professor of Criminal Law, Criminology, and Penology at Trinity College.

In 1976 she married Martin McAleese, a former athlete who trained as an accountant in Dublin. In 1980 he went back to Trinity College to study dentistry. The couple had three children: Emma (1982), and twins Sara Mai and Justin (1985). In 1987, when Martin set up practice in County Armagh, the family moved to Rostrevor, County Down. In 1987 Mary McAleese was appointed Director of the Institute of Professional Legal Studies, a department of Queen's University. In 1994 she was made Pro Vice-Chancellor of Queen's. She was the first female in history to hold one of the three Pro-Vice Chancellor positions.

In 1997 popular President Mary Robinson announced that she would not seek re-election but would accept a post as the United Nation Commissioner on Human Rights. Among the candidates to replace her were Mary McAleese, a professed devout Roman Catholic and nationalist, and Mary Banotti, a member of the European Parliament, Fianna Fail. Despite a smear campaign suggesting pro-Sinn Fein leanings, with a surprising show of voter strength, she was elected the eighth president of Ireland, the first native of Northern Ireland ever to win an election in the Irish Republic.

Following her sweeping win, McAleese declared the dawn of "the true age of the Irish" and said she hoped her victory would help banish guerilla strife from Ireland. Promising that hers would be a bridge-building presidency, to help end the sectarian conflict between Catholics and Protestants, she said, "I hope we may find our way back to a spirit of mutual generosity." However, one of her first gestures of religious healing, which she described as an attempt to improve Catholic-Protestant relations, was to receive Communion at a Protestant service in Dublin. A Northern Ireland Catholic priest and an archbishop declared that she had violated church law, and the Papal Nuncio in Dublin was reported to have informed the Vatican.

Suggested Reading:

(1) "Presidential Election Home Page" www.Ireland.gov, December 1997

(2) "McAleese Triumphs over Rivals to Take Presidency" by William Graham. *Irish News*, October 16, 1997: 1.

(3) "Battle Lines Begin to Fade across Northern Ireland" by Carl Honore. *The Houston Chronicle*, 16 November 1997: 25A.

(4) "President Defies Media Stereotypes" by Patricia Casey. *The Irish Times* "Opinion", 16 December 1997: 1.

(5) "In Ireland, Gesture of Religious Healing Inflames the Faithful" by James F. Clarity. *The New York Times*. 21 December 1997: 10Y.

Mahaut I

Dame, ruler of Bourbon (1215-1242)

She was the heir of Archambaud V, ruler of Bourbon from 1116 to 1171. She first married Gautier de Vienne, who ruled Bourbon upon Archambaud's death in 1171 until his own death in 1215. Mahaut then ruled in her own right from 1215 to 1242. She then married Gui II de Dampierre and had two daughters, Mahaut II de Dampierre and Agnes. She was succeeded by Archambaud VII in 1242.

Suggested Reading:

(1) Egan, Edward W. et. al. *Kings, Rulers, and Statesmen*. New York: Sterling Publishing Company, 1976. p. 153.

Mahaut

Countess, Capetian ruler of Artois (1302-1329)

She was the daughter of Robert II, the Noble (r. 1250-1302) from whom she inherited the county of Artois. She married Otto IV, count of Burgundy. At the time, there were two Burgundies: a county and a duchy. The couple had a daughter, Johanna (Joan I), who succeeded her upon her death. Mahaut's grandaughter, Johanna II, married the duke of Burgundy, thus reuniting the two Burgundys for a short period.

Suggested Reading:

(1)   Morby, John E. *Dynasties of the World.* Oxford: Oxford University Press, 1989. p. 94.

Mahaut (or Matilda) de Boulogne

Countess, ruler of Boulogne (1125-1150)

Her father, Eustache III, who ruled Boulogne from 1095 to 1125, retired to a Cluniac monastary in 1125, leaving Boulogne to his daughter to rule. She married Etienne de Blois, who in 1135 became, by usurpation from his cousin, also named Matilda (and called Empress Maud), King Stephen of England (1135-1154). Mahaut, who was also sometimes called Empress Maud by the British, was much more popular with the English people than Empress Maud, the other Matilda, who, to further confuse matters, was also Mahaut's cousin on the other side of the family. Thus Mahaut and Etienne were both cousins to England's Empress Maud, but not to each other. Mahaut and Etienne had five children, three of whom succeeded her sequentially as rulers of Boulogne: Eustache IV, Guillaume and Marie. Eustache IV succeeded her upon her death in 1150.

Suggested Reading:

(1)   Egan, Edward W. et. al. *Kings, Rulers, and Statesmen.* New York: Sterling Publishing Company, 1976. p. 152.

Mahaut de Courtenay

Countess, ruler of Nevers (1192-1257)

She was the daughter of Pierre de Courtenay and Countess Agnes de Nevers, who ruled from 1181 to 1182, and whom she succeeded in 1192. In 1199 she married Count Herve de Donzy, who died. In 1226 she took a second husband, Guy de Forez. Upon her death in 1257 her grandaughter Mahaut II de Bourbon succeeded her. In 1259 Guy de Forez sold all his French property to Cardinal Mazarin.

Suggested Reading:

(1) Egan, Edward W. et. al. *Kings, Rulers, and Statesmen*. New York: Sterling Publishing Company, 1976. p. 159.

Mahaut de Dammartin

Countess, ruler of Boulogne (1216-1269)

She succeeded upon the death of Countess Ide d'Alsace, who ruled Boulogne from 1173 to 1216. She married Philippe Hurepel, the son of Philip Augustus. She died in 1260.

Suggested Reading:

(1) Egan, Edward W. et. al. *Kings, Rulers, and Statesmen*. New York: Sterling Publishing Company, 1976. p. 152.

Mahaut II de Dampierre

Countess, ruler of Bourbon (1249-1262), ruler of Nevers (1257-1266)

She was the daughter of Gui II de Dampierre and Dame Mahaut I, who ruled Bourbon from 1215 to 1242. She succeeded Baron Archambaud VII, who ruled from 1242 to 1249. She married Eudes de Bourgogne, and they had a daughter, Yolande de Bourgogne. Mahaut II was the grandaughter of Countess Mahaut de Courtenay, who ruled Nevers for over a half-century, from 1182 to 1257, and whom she succeeded as ruler of Nevers upon her grandmother's death in 1257. In 1262 she was succeeded by her sister Agness as ruler of Bourbon, but she ruled Nevers until her death in 1266. She was succeeded in Nevers by her daughter Yolande.

Suggested Reading:

(1) Kemp-Welch, Alice. *Six Medieval Women*. London: Macmillan Co., Ltd., 1913. pp. 93, 102.
(2) Egan, Edward W. et. al., eds. *Kings, Rulers, and Statesmen*. New York: Sterling Publishing Company, 1976. p. 153.

Manning-Buller, Dame Eliza

Director General of MI5 in Great Britain (2006-)

She told senior MPs there was no imminent terrorist threat to London or the rest of the country less than 24 hours before the July 2006 suicide bombings.

Suggested Reading:

(1) "News in Brief" *Guardian Weekly*. January 12-18, 2007. p. 14)

Margaret II (or Black Meg)

Countess, ruler of Flanders (1244-1278), ruler of Hainault (1244-1280)

She was born c. 1200, the daughter of Maria of Champagne and Baldwin IX, Count of Flanders and Hainault, who in 1204 was crowned Baldwin I, first Latin Emperor of Constantinople. She was the sister of Johanna, who ruled Belgium from 1206 to 1244. Margaret was first married to Buchard of Avenes, who had been pledged to serve the Church. His marriage led to his excommunication and his imprisonment by his sister-in-law, Countess Johanna. Although she had borne him a son, Margaret was persuaded to seek a divorce or an annulment. She later married William of Dampierre and bore another son, Guy. When her sister died in 1244, Margaret acceded to the throne. In 1278 she abdicated, naming as her successor her younger son, Guy. However, her first son resorted to force in protesting her decision.

The civil war which followed was resolved by a compromise by which each son would rule a portion of the land. However, in the end Margaret outlived them both. She died in 1280.

Suggested Reading:

(1) Morby, John E. *Dynasties of the World.* Oxford: Oxford University Press, 1989. p. 90.
(2) Egan, Edward W. *Kings, Rulers, and Statesmen.* New York: Sterling Publishing Company, 1976. p. 52.

Margaret

Duchess of Carinthia, countess of Tirol (1335-1362)

She was born Margaretha Maultasch in 1318, the daughter of the duke of Carinthia and count of Tirol. In 1330 she was married to John Henry of Luxembourg, age nine. When her father died in 1335, she inherited Tirol but was forced to cede Carinthia, which had been given to her family by Rudolph I in 1286, back to Germany. Margaret's marriage, after 11 years, was still childless. She acted in collusion with the Tirolese to expel John Henry, whose brother Charles (later Emperor Charles IV) had stepped in to rule. In 1342 Holy Roman Emperor Louis IV the Bavarian annulled Margaret's previous marriage and married her to his son Louis, margrave of Brandenburg. This marriage displeased not only the Pope and the Luxembourgians, but the Tirolese as well, who did not want to be ruled by the Germans. An uprising against Margaret and her new husband had to be suppressed, and there was serious doubt that she would be able to maintain control. But after Louis IV was deposed in 1346, the successor Charles IV favored the status quo for Tirol's rulers, who would remain in control as long as there was an heir. If Margaret produced no heir, she would cede Tirol to the Hapsburgs. Margaret bore one son, Meinhard, and the lineage of Tirol seemed secure. However, her husband died in 1361, and after she had passed child-bearing years, her only son died in 1363. Holy Roman Emperor Rudolph IV persuaded her to cede Tirol to him, and she retired to Vienna, where she died in 1369 at age 51.

Suggested Reading:

(1)   Dvornik, Francis. *The Slavs in European History and Civilization*. New Brunswick, NJ: Rutgers University Press, 1962. pp. 44, 52, 53, 54.

Margaret (Margaret of Brabant)

Countess, Burgundian ruler of Artois (1361-1382)

She was the daughter of Joan I (Jeanne, r. 1329-1330) and Philip V (r. France 1316-1322). She married Louis of Nevers (Louis II of Crecy), count of Flanders (r. 1322-1346). They had a son, Louis III of Mâle (r. Flanders 1346-1384), and a daughter, Margaret II (r. Flanders 1384-1405). Margaret succeeded her mother as ruler of Artois in 1362. Upon her death, Artois was united with Flanders under first her son's and then her daughter's rule.

Suggested Reading:

(1)   Morby, John E. *Dynasties of the World*. Oxford: Oxford University Press, 1989. p. 94.

Margaret III (or Margaret of Flanders or Margaret of Mâle)

Countess, ruler of Belgium (1384-1405)

She was born in 1350, the daughter of Margaret of Brabant (r. Artois 1362-1382) and Louis II de Mâle (of Nevers). In 1369 she married Philip le Hardi, duke of Burgundy (1384-1404). She was heiress to the county of Burgundy, Artois, Nevers, and Rethel. The couple had four children: John, duke of Burgundy, Philip, count of Nevers, Margaret and Antoine, duke of Brabant. Belgium had been under Burgundy rule from 1334 to 1377, so Louis II de Mâle actually ruled Flanders from 1377 to 1384. Margaret died in 1405. At that time Flanders became unified with Burgundy.

Suggested Reading:

(1)   Morby, John E. *Dynasties of the World*. Oxford: Oxford University Press, 1989. p. 90.

(2) Egan, Edward W. et. al., eds. *Kings, Rulers and Statesmen*. New York: Sterling Publishing Co., 1976. pp. 52, 160.

(3) Langer, William L., ed. *World History*. Boston: Houghton Mifflin, 1980. pp. 299, 300, 406-407.

Margaret (or Margrete or Margarethe)

Queen of Denmark and Norway (1375-1412), regent of Sweden (1389-1412)

She was born in Denmark in 1353, the daughter of King Valdemar IV Atterdag, ruler of Denmark from 1340 to 1375, and Helvig, sister of the duke of Schleswig When she was six years old, she was married to King Haakon VI, ruler of Norway from 1343 to 1380. She spent her youth in the court in Norway. In 1370 she bore a son, Olaf V, and began to take an active interest in government soon afterward. After her father's death in 1375, she succeeded in getting her five-year-old son Olaf elected to the Danish throne with herself as regent. After her husband's death in 1380, she also ruled Norway for her son. When Olaf died in 1387, Margaret adopted her six-year-old nephew, Erik of Pomerania, as heir to the throne She was asked by Swedish nobles to assist in an uprising against Swedish King Albert. The nobles proclaimed her queen of Sweden in 1388 and granted her a large domain consisting of lands belonging to former chancellor Bo Jonsson Grip. Her forces captured Albert in 1389 and held him prisoner for six years until peace was concluded. In 1397 she united the three Scandinavian countries in the Union of Kalmar, which lasted unchanged until 1523. Despite her heir's coronation in 1397, Margaret remained the sole ruler for the rest of her life. She strengthened her influence over the church and kept the ambitious German princes at bay, primarily through diplomacy. However, she was obliged to use force against Holstein in 1412, and during the conflict, she died suddenly.

Suggested Reading:

(1) Dahmus, Joseph. *Seven Medieval Queens*. Garden City, NY: Doubleday, 1972. pp. 233-275.

(2) Morby, John E. *Dynasties of the World*. Oxford: Oxford University Press, 1989. p. 149.

(3) Egan, Edward W. et. al., eds. *Kings, Rulers, and Statesmen*. New York: Sterling Publishing Company, 1976. pp. 112-113, 447.

(4) Langer, William L., ed. *World History*. Boston: Houghton Mifflin, 1980. pp. 334-336.

Margaret of Anjou

Queen, Lancastrian leader (1455-1485), acting regent of England (1460-1461)

She was born in 1430, the daughter of René I of Anjou, titular king of Naples (1435-1442), and Isabella, duchess of Lorraine from 1431 to 1453. In a 1445 marriage arranged as part of a two-year truce in the Hundred Years' War, she became the wife of King Henry VI, who ruled England from 1422 to 1461. The couple had one son, Edward, born in 1453. Margaret was not popular with her English subjects. Her husband suffered bouts of insanity and was never declared fit to rule. Richard, duke of York, served as lord protector. In 1455 a civil war (the War of the Roses) broke out between the houses of Lancaster and York. Richard of York asserted his hereditary claim to the throne, and the lords decided that he should be next in the line of succession, excluding Margaret's son Edward. He actually gained control of the government until Margaret ousted him in 1456. Here the qualities with which Shakespeare described her became evident: "stern, obdurant, flinty, rough, remorseless." (Henry VI, Part III, Act 1, scene iv) She was more than capable of acting in the interests of the king: both her mother and her grandmother had ruled their lands. In 1459 the second round of hostilities erupted. During the Battle of Northampton in 1460, Henry VI was taken prisoner, and Margaret refused to accept the terms for his release which would exclude her son as Henry's heir. Instead, she raised an army in the north and defeated Richard of York, who died on the field in Wakefield, Yorkshire. But southern England had not forgotten The Hundred Years' War with France, had not forgotten that Margaret was French. Londoners rallied around York's son, also named Edward, defeated Margaret's army, and proclaimed Edward of York king in 1461. She and her son fled to Scotland with Henry VI. In 1464 a fresh Lancastrian uprising brought them back to England. Henry VI was again captured in 1465 and imprisoned in the Tower of London. In 1470 Margaret, then in France, entered into collusion with Richard, duke of Warwick, in a plot to restore Henry VI to the throne. However, Warwick was killed in battle on the day that she returned to England in 1471. Margaret and her son headed the forces at Tewksbury which attempted to hold off Edward of York, but they were defeated for the final time. Margaret's son Edward was killed, and she was taken prisoner. Henry VI was murdered in prison. In 1475 King Louis XI of France ransomed Margaret. She returned to France where she died in poverty in 1482.

Suggested Reading:

(1) Myers, A. R. *England in the Late Middle Ages*. Harmondsworth, Middlesex: Penguin Books, Ltd., 1976. pp. 126-130, 193.

(2) Dahmus, Joseph. *Seven Medieval Queens*. Garden City, NY: Doubleday, 1972. pp. 276-327.

Margaret of Austria (Marguerite d'Autriche)

Duchess of Savoy, regent of The Netherlands (1507-1515 and 1519-1530)

She was born in 1480, the daughter of the future emperor Maximilian I (r. 1486-1519) and Mary, duchess of Burgundy (r. 1477-1482). She was the sister of Philip the Handsome. In 1483 she was betrothed to the future Charles VI, who later repudiated her. She then married the infante John of Spain who died shortly after the marriage (1497). In 1501, she married Philbert II, duke of Savoy, who died in 1504. In his memory, she built the beautiful church of Brou near Lyons. In 1507 her father appointed her successor to her late brother Philip as regent of The Netherlands for her nephew Charles. In 1508 she also represented another young nephew, Ferdinand of Aragon (Holy Roman Emperor Ferdinand I) and her father in negotiating a settlement of the French claims in the Burgundian Netherlands. Her nephew Charles was declared of age in 1515, but he reappointed her in 1519 while he was occupied in securing the Hapsburg throne. He ruled as Charles V from 1519 to 1556. In 1529 Margaret negotiated the Treaty of Cambrai, "The Ladies' Peace," with Louise of Savoy, settling claims of France upon Italy, Flanders, and Artois, and claims of Germany upon Burgundy. Margaret continued to rule The Netherlands until she died in 1530.

Suggested Reading:

(1) Harvey, Sir Paul, and J. E. Heseltine, comps. *The Oxford Companion to French Literature*. Oxford: Oxford University Press, 1959. p. 452.

(2) Langer, William L., ed. *World History*. Boston: Houghton Mifflin, 1980. pp. 422, 429.

Margaret of Austria

Duchess of Parma, governor general of The Netherlands (1559-1567)

She was born in 1522, the illegitimate daughter of Holy Roman Empire Charles V (Charles I of Spain), who ruled Spain from 1516 to 1556 and the empire from 1510 to 1556, and Johanna van der Gheenst. In 1536 Margaret married Alesssandro de' Medici, duke of Florence, but she was widowed in less than a year. In 1538 she married Ottavio Farnese, who became duke of Parma in 1547. They had a son, Alessandro Farnese. Her half-brother, King Philip II of Spain, appointed her governor general of The Netherlands in 1559. Under her regency the provinces prospered, despite heavy taxation. She presided over the three governing councils: Privy, State and Finances, which were to see to it that the Protestants (Calvinists) were suppressed and that King Philip's demands for funds were met. She was saddled with carrying out a highly unpopular program without military backing, for her subjects had no desire to pay for a foreigner's military campaigns. The northern part of her territory (Holland) had embraced Calvinism while the southern part (Belgium) was still Catholic. Both segments opposed Spanish rule, the Spanish garrison, the introduction of the Spanish inquisition, the penal edicts against heretics. She rejected a petition submitted to her by 300 nobles objecting to religious persecution. An advisor referred to the signers as "beggars," and soon all those opposed to Spanish rule took as their appellation, "Beggars." In 1566 Calvinist riots led Margaret, who still had no troops from King Philip, to call in German mercenary troops. In 1567 she dealt with religious uprisings by mass executions. Philip II eventually sent in the duke of Alva with 10,000 troops to replace Margaret and to repress the uprisings. In 1580 she returned to The Netherlands as head of the civil administration under her son Alessandro. She retured to Italy in 1583, where she died in 1586.

Suggested Reading:

(1) Geye, Pieter. *The Revolt of the Netherlands, 1555-1609*. London: Ernest Benn, 1958. pp. 70, 75, 78, 79, 87-92, 98, 100, 101, 154.
(2) Masselman, George. *The Cradle of Colonialism*. New Haven: Yale University Press, 1963. p. 27.

(3) Clough, Shepard B. et. al. *European History in a World Perspective*. Lexington, MA: D.C. Heath and Co., 1975. vol 2, pp. 638, 713-715.

(4) Trevor-Roper, Hugh. *The Golden Age of Europe*. New York: Bonanza/Crown, 1987. pp. 66, 80, 82.

(5) Langer, William L., ed. *World History*. Boston: Houghton Mifflin, 1980. pp. 407-408.

Margaret of Navarre

Queen, regent of Sicily (1166-1168)

She was the wife of William I, ruler of Norman Sicily from 1154 to 1166. It was claimed that she took as her lover the chief minister, Maio of Bari. In 1153 she had a son, William II, who succeeded his father at the age of 13. Margaret, as regent, first ruled through her favorite, Peter, a Saracen eunuch, a former slave who had been freed by her husband. But barons who had earlier been exiled by William I saw the chance to regain their estates under the regency of a woman, and they began to return and rebuild their castles. Peter decided to escape to Morocco to avoid the inevitable conflict building between the barons and Queen Margaret. In 1167 she appointed her cousin Stephen of Le Perche chief minister and Peter of Blois as her son's tutor. But Stephen's harsh manner made him unpopular. When rumor spread that he was siphoning money to France, a riot quickly spread at Messina. Stephen fled to Jerusalem, and Peter went back to France. Into the void stepped an Englishman, Walter Offamillo, who seized power and used the Palermo mob to help him become archbishop. He remained the center of power for 20 years. In effect, Margaret's influence was at an end. Even after William came of age in 1172, he did not openly cross the archbishop. Offamillo effectively ended Margaret's attempt to rule.

Suggested Reading:

(1) Smith, Denis Mack. *A History of Sicily*, New York: Dorset Press, 1968. vol. 1, *Medieval Sicily*. pp. 38-40.

Margaret of Norway (or the Maid of Norway)

Child queen of Scotland (1286-1290)

She was born ca. 1282, the daughter of King Eric II Magnusson, who ruled Norway from 1280 to 1299, and Margaret, daughter of King Alexander III of Scotland (1249-1286). Her mother died in 1283, and none of King Alexander's children survived him. When he died in 1286, Scottish nobles declared his granddaughter, Margaret, age four, queen. In 1290 her great-uncle, England's King Edward I, arranged for her marriage to his son, the future King Edward II. On the voyage to England, Margaret fell ill and died at the age of eight.

Suggested Reading:

(1)   Mackie, J. D. *A History of Scotland*. Harmondsworth, Middlesex: Penguin Books, Ltd., 1984. pp. 35, 45, 61-63, 135.
(2)   Runciman, Steven. *A History of the Crusades*. Cambridge: Cambridge University Press, 1952, 1987. vol 3, *The Kingdom of Acre*. pp. 401-402.
(3)   Langer, William L., Ed. *World History*. Boston: Houghton Mifflin, 1980. pp. 214, 217, 218.

Margaret Tudor

Queen, regent of Scotland (1513-1514)

She was born in 1489, the elder daughter of King Henry VII, who ruled England from 1485 to 1509, and Elizabeth, daughter of King Edward IV, who ruled from 1461 to 1483. In 1503 she married James IV, king of Scotland from 1488 to 1513, and bore a son who became James V when his father died in 1513. Margaret ruled as regent for her son. In 1514 she married Archibald Douglas, earl of Angus, and, since he was a partisan of England, the Scottish Parliament removed her from the regency. In 1527 she divorced Douglas and married Henry Stewart, whom her son made Lord Methven when he came to the throne the following year. Margaret and her third husband were James' most trusted advisors for the first six years of his majority, but James became angry at his mother for sharing state secrets with her brother, King Henry VIII of England. She retired to Methven Castle where she died in 1541.

Suggested Reading:

(1)   Myers, A. R. *England in the Late Middle Ages*. Harmondsworth, Middlesex: Penguin Books, 1952. vol. 4, p. 205.

(2) Langer, William L., ed. *World History*. Boston: Houghton Mifflin, 1980. p. 396.

Margareta (or Margaret of Alsace or Margaret I)

Countess, ruler of Flanders (1191-1194)

She was the daughter of Gertrude, whose father Robert I ruled 1071 to 1093, and Thierry I (or Dirk I) of Lorraine. She was the sister of Thierry of Alsace, who ruled Flanders from 1128 to 1157/68, and the aunt of Count Philip, who ruled from 1157/68 to 1191. (Philip was co-regent with his father Thierry from 1157 to 1168.) In 1171 Margareta married Baldwin V, count of Hainault, who then became Baldwin VIII, count of Flanders. In 1172 they had a son, Baldwin IX, who would become count of Flanders and Hainault in 1244 and, in 1278, emperor of Constantinople. When her nephew Philip died in 1191, Margareta succeeded him, but she died in 1194. Her son succeeded her that year.

Suggested Reading:

(1) Morby, John E. *Dynasties of the World*. Oxford: Oxford University Press, 1989. pp. 90, 93.
(2) Egan, Edward W. et. al., eds. *Kings, Rulers, and Statesmen*. New York: Sterling Publishing Company, 1976. p. 52.

Margaretha

Guardian for Otto II the Lame, count of Gelderland and Zutphen (1229-1234)

She was the daughter of Duke Henry I of Brabant. In 1206 she married Gerhard III of Gelre (Gelderland), count of Gelderland and Zutphen. It was a marriage designed to unite two antagonistic dynasties. In c. 1220 they had a son, Otto II, called Otto the Lame (not to be confused with Otto the Lame of Lüneburg, r. 1434-1446). When Gerhard III died in 1229, Otto succeeded his father with Margaretha serving as guardian until he came of age in 1234.

Suggested Reading:

(1) *Britannica Micropaedia*. Chicago: The University of Chicago Press/ Encyclopedia Britannica, Inc. 1983. vol VII, p. 626.

Margrethe II (Margaret)

Queen of Denmark (1972-)

She was born in 1940, the daughter of Frederick IX, king of Denmark from 1947 to 1972, and Ingrid, who was the daughter of crown prince Gustaf VI Adolf (or Adolphus) of Sweden (r. 1950-1973). In 1953 King Frederick signed a new constitution which permitted female succession to the throne for the first time in over 500 years. In 1967 Margrethe married Henri de Laborde de Monpezat, a French diplomat, who was then referred to as Prince Consort Henrik. The couple has two sons: Frederick, born in 1968, and Joachim, born in 1969. She acceded to the throne when her father died in 1972, the first queen to rule Denmark since 1412. She became, at age 31, the youngest queen regnant in the world, in the world's oldest existing monarchy. She is popularly called "The Queen of Democracy." A talented artist, she is best known for her illustrations of *The Lord of the Rings*. With her husband, she wrote *All Men Are Mortal*.

Suggested Reading:

(1) *International Who's Who 1987-1988*. London: Europa Publications Ltd., 1987. p. 963.

(2) Moritz, Charles, ed. *Current Biography Yearbook 1972*. New Haven: The H.W. Wilson Co., 1972. pp. 306-308.

(3) Morby, John E. *Dynasties of the World*. Oxford: Oxford University Press, 1989. pp. 150, 152.

(4) Egan, Edward W. et. al., eds. *Kings, Rulers and Statesmen*. New York: Sterling Publishing Company, 1976. p. 114.

Marguerite

Countess, ruler of Blois (1218-1230)

She was the eldest daughter of Isabella, daughter of King Louis IX of France, and Thibault V (Theobald), king of Navarre, who also ruled Blois until his death in 1218. She acceded to the throne when her father died in 1218. She married three times. Her third husband, Gauthier d'Avesnes, ruled with her. She died in 1230 and was succeeded by Marie de Chatillon.

Suggested Reading:

(1) Egan, Edward W. et. al., eds. *Kings, Rulers, and Statesmen*. New York: Sterling Publishing Company, 1976. p. 152.

Marguerite

Countess, ruler of Nevers (1384-1404). See Marguerite, Countess, ruler of Belgium

Marguerite de Thouars

Joint ruler of Dreux (1365-1377)

She was the daughter of Simon of Dreux and the sister of Peronelle. She and Peronelle were parceners of Dreux when their father died in 1365. In 1377 or 1378 they sold it to King Charles VI of France, who conferred it on the house of Albret.

Suggested Reading:

(1) Egan, Edward W. et. al., eds. *Kings, Rulers, and Statesmen*. New York: Sterling Publishing Company, 1976. p. 157.

Maria

Queen of Sicily (1377-1402)

She was the daughter of Frederick IV, ruler of Sicily from 1355 to 1377, except that until 1372, Sicily was claimed by Naples. She acceded to the throne in name only when he died in 1377. In 1390 she was abducted from Catania Castle and taken to Barcelona to marry her cousin, Martin the Younger, prince of Aragon, son of King Pedro IV. In 1392 he was crowned Martin I, king of Sicily. Martin and his relatives then set about to bring Sicily under Argonese control. Maria had one son, who died in 1402; she died the same year, having served her purpose, as far as the Argonese were concerned. Martin ruled for seven more years and was succeeded by his father.

Suggested Reading:

(1) Smith, Denis Mack. *History of Sicily*. New York: Dorset Press, 1968. vol. 1. p. 87.
(2) Egan, Edward W. et. al., eds. *Kings, Rulers, and Statesmen*. New York: Sterling Publishing Company, 1976. p. 274.

Maria Adelaide

Grand duchess of of the Grand Duchy of Luxembourg (1912-1969)

She was born in 1894, the eldest daughter of Grand Duke William IV, who reigned from 1905 to 1912. She succeeded him at the age of 18 upon his death in 1912. Maria Adelaide was not a popular ruler because of her reactionary policies. In August of 1914 Luxembourg was invaded by the German fifth army under the command of Crown Prince Wilhelm and the country was occupied for the remainder of World War I. Early in 1919, when German occupation had ended, Maria Adelaide was forced by popular opinion to abdicate in favor of her younger sister, Charlotte, whose cooperative economic and political policies more accurately reflected the times. Maria Adelaide died in 1924 at the age of 30.

Suggested Reading:

(1) Morby, John E. *Dynasties of the World*. Oxford: Oxford University Press, 1989. p. 97.
(2) Egan, Edward W. et. al., eds. *Kings, Rulers, and Statesmen*. New York: Sterling Publishing Company, 1976. p. 298.

María Ana Victoria of Spain (or Mariana)

Queen, regent of Portugal (1774-1777)

She was born María Ana Victoria in 1718, the daughter of Isabella of Parma and King Philip V, who ruled Spain (1700-1724 and 1724-1746). She was the sister of Philip VI (r. 1746-1759) and Charles III (r. 1759-1788). In

1721/2, at the age of two or three, she was contracted in marriage to Louis XV, age eleven. She was delivered to Paris, but in 1725 Louis's minister the Duc de Bourbon's mistress, the Marquise de Prie, hoping to maintain influence at court, conspired to have the marriage annulled so that Louis could marry Marie Leszcy_ska, daughter of the deposed king of Poland. María Victoria was sent back to Spain in disgrace, causing strained relations between Spain and France. María Victoria then married Joseph I, who later became ruler of Portugal (1750-1777). Joseph showed no interest in affairs of state. His entire reign was dominated by Sebastiao Jose Carvalho e Mello, who became marquis of Pombal in 1770. A ruthless dictator, Pombal nevertheless reformed finances and the army, broke the power of the nobility and the Church, and encouraged industry and trade. María Victoria and Joseph had a daughter, María I, born in 1734. In 1774 Joseph was declared insane and María Victoria was appointed regent. She began gradually to erode the power of Pombal. In 1777 her husband died, having never regained his health, and the reign was passed to María I.

Suggested Reading:

(1) Langer William L., ed. *World History* Boston: Houghton Mifflin, 1980. pp. 491-492.
(2) Durant, Will and Ariel. *The Age of Voltaire.* New York: Simon & Schuster, 1965. pp. 32, 273.
(3) Chapman, Charles E. *A History of Spain.* New York: Free Press/ Macmillan, 1946. p. 392.

Maria Anna of Austria (María Ana)

Queen, regent of Spain (1665-1676)

She was born in 1634, the daughter of Ferdinand III, king of Hungary (1625-1657), king of Bohemia (1637-1657), Holy Roman emperor (1637-1657), and his first wife, Maria Anna of Spain. In a lavish and extravagant ceremony, Archduchess Maria Anna of Austria became the second wife of Philip IV, who was king of Spain from 1621 to 1665. She had two children: Margareta Teresa, born in 1651, who married Emperor Leopold I, and Charles V, born in 1661, who succeeded to the throne at the age of four upon his father's death (1665). Maria Anna served as regent for over ten years, but her leadership was hampered by her dependence upon her Jesuit advisors and her preference for foreigners. In addition, she was preoccupied in combatting French King Louis XIV's attack on Spanish possessions in The Netherlands. Court nobles led by John Joseph of Austria gained the upper hand in the government and eventually forced Maria Anna to resign. She died in 1696.

Suggested Reading:

(1) Chapman, Charles E. *A History of Spain*. New York: A Free Press/ Macmillan, 1946. pp. 269, 284.
(2) Langer, William L., ed. *World History*. Boston: Houghton Mifflin, 1980. pp. 417, 486.

Maria Carolina

Queen, defacto ruler of Naples and Sicily (1777-1798 and 1799-1806)

She was born in 1752, the daughter of Maria Theresa, empress of Austria from 1740 to 1780, and Holy Roman Emperor Francis I. She was the sister of Marie Antoinette. In 1768 she married King Ferdinand IV, king of Naples (1759-1808), and later, as Ferdinand I, king of the Two Sicilies (1816-1825). Ferdinand allowed Maria Carolina to assume much of the authority to rule which had hitherto been held by the regent Tanucci. Affairs of state were conducted chiefly by her. The birth of a male heir, Francis I, in 1777, gave her the authority, according to her marriage contract, to sit on the council of state. She soon brought about the complete downfall of Tanucci and allied herself, perhaps romantically as well as politically, with an English adventurer, Lord Acton, of obvious British persuasion. When her sister Marie Antoinette was executed, Maria Carolina engaged Naples in the Austro-British campaign against the French Revolution. In 1798 the French seized Naples and renamed it the Parthenopean Republic, Maria Carolina, Ferdinand and their children were forced to flee for their lives. A year later, after the overthrow of the new republic, the royal family returned to Naples and ordered the execution of the republic's partisans. In 1805 she requested the aid of Russian and British fleets in yet another conflict with France. Again in 1806, Naples was overrun by the French and the royal family fled to Sicily. She had long since acquired a hatred of Sicilians. She once wrote, "The priests are completely corrupted, the people savage, the nobility of questionable loyalty." Once she even suggested that the British buy Sicily from her for six million pounds. When the Sicilians adopted a new constitution, she could see what it took others years to see: that it was a baronial document that discriminated against the common people and that parliament was a farce designed to divert people's attention from what the nobles were doing. After she quarreled with the British ambassador, he persuaded Ferdinand to exile her from Sicily. She returned to Austria alone in 1811, where she died three years later. In addition to her son, she was survived by five daughters: Maria Teresa, who married Emperor Francis I of Austria; Louisa Amelia, who married Ferdinand III of Tuscany; Maria Amelia, who married Louis Philippe, king of France; Cristina, who married Felix of Sardinia; and Maria Antonia, who married Ferdinand VII, king of Spain.

Suggested Reading:

(1) Smith, Denis Mack. *History of Sicily*. New York: Dorset Press, 1968. vol. 2. pp. 325, 335-338, 341, 348.
(2) Langer, William L., ed. *World History*. Boston: Houghton Mifflin, 1980. pp. 496, 497, 702.

Maria Christina (or Christina)

Duchess, governor general of Austrian Netherlands (1780-1789)

Maria Christina was born in 1742, one of 16 children of Maria Theresa, empress of Hungary and Bohemia (1740-1780) and Holy Roman Emperor Francis I, who ruled from 1745 to 1765. She married Albert, duke of Saxe-Teschen. Maria Christina governed the Austrian Netherlands, which is present day Belgium, during the reign of her brother, Holy Roman Emperor Joseph II, whose edicts abolishing many religious bodies were so unpopular that Maria Christina was hesitant to implement them. In retaliation to the edicts, the estates of Hainault and Brabant refused to pay taxes in 1788, and in 1789 revolution erupted. The Austrians were forced to retreat to Luxembourg. Maria Christina died in 1798.

Suggested Reading:

(1) Egan, Edward W. et. al., eds. *Kings, Rulers, and Statesmen*. New York: Sterling Publishing Company, 1976. p. 52.

Maria Christina of Austria

Queen, regent of Spain (1885-1902)

She was born in 1858 in an area of Austria that is now in Czechoslovakia. In 1879 she became the second wife of King Alfonso XII, ruler of Spain from 1874 to 1885. They had three children: Maria de la Mercedes, Maria Teresa, and Alfonso XIII, who was born after his father died. When Alfonso XII died in 1885, Maria de la Mercedes, the elder daughter, technically became hereditary queen until her brother was born in 1886. The ex-queen, Isabella II, attempted to intervene, but her meddling only strengthened Maria Christina's position. Maria Christina served as regent for both children until Alfonso XIII was declared of age to govern in 1902. Even then, Alfonso at first allowed his mother to continue to rule. During her regency, she alternated power between the liberals, led by Praxedes Mateo Sagasta, and the conservatives, led by Antonio Canovas del Castillo. The Spanish-American War of 1898 left Spain weakened and the Spanish Empire decimated, with the loss of Cuba, Puerto Rico, Guam, and the Philippines. Maria Christina resigned her regency in 1902. She died in 1929 in Madrid.

Suggested Reading:

(1) Chapman, Charles E. *A History of Spain*. New York: The Free Press/ Macmillan, 1946. p. 506.
(2) Langer. William L., ed. *World History*. Boston: Houghton Mifflin, 1980. pp. 695, 696-697.

María Cristina I of Naples (or Cristina)

Queen, regent of Spain (1833-1840)

She was born in Naples in 1806 and became the fourth wife of King Ferdinand VII, who ruled Spain from 1814 to 1833. They had two daughters: Isabella II and Luisa Fernanda. In 1833, two months before her husband's death, Maria Christina influenced him to set aside the Salic Law, thus allowing their daughter, María Isabel (Isabella II), to succed him and depriving his brother, Don Carlos, of the throne. On the death of Ferdinand, María Christina became regent with absolute power. Realizing she needed the support of the liberals, she liberalized the constitution and sanctioned certain anti-clerical measures. In 1833 she made a secret morganatic marriage to Fernando Muñoz which, when discovered, made her highly unpopular. In 1834 Don Carlos, determined to win the throne for himself, instigated the First Carlist War, aimed at María Christina and the liberals. The Carlists were defeated in 1837 but the war was not officially concluded until 1839. Don Carlos left the country for France. Meantime, María Christina was pressured into appointing a Progressist minister and accepting a new compromise constitution (1837). In 1840 General Baldomero Esparto, Progressist leader, revolted, forcing Maria Christina to resign her regency and leave the country, making way for Esparto to assume the regency. She later made an attempt to return and participate in the government, but failed, and she retired in exile to France in 1854, where she died in 1878.

Suggested Reading:

(1) Chapman, Charles E. *A History of Spain*. New York: The New Press/Macmillan, 1946. pp. 497-500.
(2) Ridley, Jasper. *Napoleon III and Eugenie*. New York: Viking Press, 1980. pp. 142, 144, 152, 157.
(3) Langer, William L., ed. *World History*. Boston: Houghton Mifflin, 1980. pp. 694-696.

Maria II da Gloria

Queen of Portugal (1826-1828 and 1834-1853)

She was born in 1819 in Brazil, the daughter of King Pedro IV, ruler of Brazil from 1826 to 1831, and Leopoldina of Austria. Pedro inherited the Portuguese throne from his father, John VI, who ruled as a constitutional monarch. Pedro drew up a charter providing for a parliamentary government similar to Britain's for Portugal, but he refused to leave Brazil to implement it. After a few months he abdicated and ceded the throne to his seven-year-old daughter Maria da Gloria, with her uncle Miguel as regent. She was betrothed to her uncle but did not marry him. In 1828, Miguel led a *coup d'etat* and proclaimed himself king. Maria da Gloria fled to England and contacted her father, asking him to come to her aid. In 1831 Pedro abdicated the Brazilian throne and traveled to England to lead the fight for the restoration of Maria to the Portuguese throne. With the help of England and France, the Miguelists were defeated. Maria was restored in 1833 and assumed power in 1834. She was first married to

Auguste Beauharnais, who soon died. In 1836 she married Duke Ferdinand of Saxe-Coburg. They had five children: Pedro V, who ruled from 1853 to 1861; Fernando; Luis I, who ruled from 1861 to 1889; John, and Leopoldina. Maria da Gloria's reign was a troubled one, primarily because of her choice of chief ministers. She appointed the amibtious duque de Saldanha, who dominated politics during much of her reign and who brought Portugal to the brink of civil war at one point. She died in childbirth in 1853.

Suggested Reading:

(1) Langer. William L., ed. *World History*. Boston: Houghton Mifflin, 1980. pp. 491, 698, 699.
(2) Ridley, Jasper. *Napoleon III and Eugenie*. New York: Viking Press, 1980. p. 85.
(3) Morby, John E. *Dynasties of the World*. Oxford: Oxford University Press, 1989. p. 120.
(4) Egan, Edward W. et. al., eds. *Kings, Rulers, and Statesmen*. New York: Sterling Publishing Company, 1976. p. 379.

Maria de la Mercedes (or Mercedes)

Queen infanta of Spain (1885-1886)

She was born in 1880, the elder daughter of King Alfonso XII, who ruled Spain from 1875 to 1885, and Maria Christina of Austria. When her father died in 1885, there was no male heir, so Maria de la Mercedes, age five, succeeded him. However, several months later her mother gave birth to a boy, Alfonso XIII, who became the new king at birth. Maria de la Mercedes was married to Carlo, Conti de Caserta di Bourbon, but she had no children. She died in 1904.

Suggested Reading:

(1) Langer, William L., ed. *World History*. Boston: Houghton Mifflin, 1980. p. 695.

María Estela Martínez de Perón

See Perón, Isabel

Maria (or Mary or Marija) of Anjou

"King" of Hungary, Queen of Croatia (1382-1385 and 1386-1395)

She was born in 1370, the daughter of Elizabeth of Bosnia and Polish King Ljudevit, or Louis the Great, king of Hungary (1342-1382) and king of Poland (1370-1382), and the older sister of Jadwiga (Jadviga), who inherited the Polish throne. While Marija was still a child, she was betrothed to Sigismund of Luxemburg,

In 1378, at the age of eight, Maria was married to Sigsmund of Luxembourg, age ten, Prince of Bohemia and son of Holy Roman Emperor and King of Bohemia Charles IV. Sigismund was later to become king of Hungary from 1387, king of Germany from 1411, king of the Lombards from 1431, and Holy Roman emperor from 1433. The couple had no children. When her father died in 1382, the Hungarian nobility, which had previously agreed to accept Jadwiga as "king of Hungary", elected instead Maria, age twelve, who also inherited the throne Croatia, with her mother assuming the regency. But Croatian nobility objected to the rule of the two queens. A conspiracy headed by Ivan Palizna planned to detach Croatia and invite Stjepan Tvrdko, king of Bosnia, to rule. When Nikola Gorjanski, the queen's advisor, learned of the conspiracy, he brought both queens, backed by a strong army, from Hungary to Croatia. The plot failed, and Palizna fled to Bosnia, while the queens received a royal welcome. Before her return to Hungary, Maria presided over a session of the Parliament, the *Sabor*. Soon, however, her position was challenged again. A new plot to unseat the queen was organized by the Horvat brothers, Pavao, bishop of Zagreb, and Ivanis, *Ban* of Macva. They invited Maria's cousin, Prince Charles II of Durazzo and Naples, whose father Steven V had ruled Hungary (1270-1272), to assume the Croatian throne. Charles gladly traveled from Naples to accept the reins of government. After a year in Croatia, he moved on to Hungary, determined to unseat Marija there, as well, which he did (1385). However, Queen Elizabeth and her advisors devised their own plan to overthrow him, and Charles was assassinated. Marija returned to the throne for a second time in 1386.

Following Charles' assassination, the Horvat brothers joined forces with Palizna, who returned from Bosnia, and determined to take control of the Croatian government. Again Gorjanski and the two queens set out for Croatia with an army. This time, however, the army was defeated. Both queens were captured and taken Palizna's castle, Novigrad on the Sea. Charles' widow insisted that Elizabeth be executed.

When Marija's husband, Sigismund of Luxemburg, learned that she was being held prisoner, he left for Hungary to assume the crown for himself. In 1387 he was crowned king consort. The Hungarians received him warmly, and he assembled a strong army and requested the help from the Venetian navy so as to invade Croatia and free Maria. With the Venetians blockading Novigrad's sea approach, the army laid siege by land. Eventually Palizna surrendered Marija in exchange for his own safe return to Bosnia. The Horvats also took refuge in Bosnia, while Maria and Sigismund returned to Hungary to face mounting threats by the Turks for the rest of their reign. She died in 1395 at the age of 25.

Suggested Reading:

(1) Dvornik, Francis. *The Slavs in European History and Civilization.* New Brunswick, NJ: Rutgers University Press, 1962. pp. 60-62, 83, 436.
(2) Langer, William L., ed. *World History.* Boston: Houghton Mifflin, 1980 pp. 339, 342.

Maria of Austria

Dowager Queen of Hungary, governor of The Netherlands (1530-1555)

She was the daughter of Queen Juana of Spain and Philip of Hapsburg. She was the sister of Holy Roman Emperor Charles V, and of Ferdinand, king of Bohemia. She married Louis II, who was king of Hungary from 1516 to 1526. Following his death in 1526, and the death in 1930 of Margaret, duchess of Savoy and governor of The Netherlands, Dowager Queen Maria was appointed governor of The Netherlands by her brother, Emperor Charles. She ruled until her death in 1555.

Suggested Reading:

(1) Geye, Pieter. *The Revolt of the Netherlands.* London: Ernest Benn, 1958. p. 38.

María I of Braganza

Queen of Portugal (1777-1816)

She was born María Victoria in 1734, the daughter of King Joseph I Emanuel, ruler of Portugal from 1750 to 1777, and María Ana Victoria of Spain. Her father suffered from insanity from 1774, and her mother became regent. When he died in 1777, María succeeded him as María I. She married her uncle Pedro III and ruled jointly with him until his death in 1786, and from then on she ruled alone. She consented to the trial of the dictator Pombal, who had usurped her father's power and authority, but she pardoned him because of his old age and sent him into exile. Her reign was characterized by peace and prosperity. She and Pedro had one son, John VI. In 1792 Queen María suffered a mental breakdown, and her son took over the government. In 1799 John assumed the title of prince regent. In 1807 Napoleon invaded Portugal and the family was forced to flee to Brazil. María remained in Brazil even after Napoleon's defeat. She died there in 1816.

Suggested Reading:

(1)   Chapman Charles E. *A History of Spain*. New York: The New Press/ Macmillan, 1946. p. 392.
(2)   Langer, William L., ed. *World History*. Boston: Houghton Mifflin, 1980. pp. 191, 192)

Maria Theresa

Empress of Hapsburg Empire, queen of Bohemia and Hungary, archduchess of Austria, ruler of Luxembourg, etc. (1740-1780).

She was born in 1717, the older daughter of Charles VI, king of Bohemia and Hungary from 1711 to 1740, and Elizabeth Christina of Brunswick. When her father died in 1740, Maria Theresa succeeded him in the midst of the War of Austrian Succession. That same year she married Francis Stephen of the house of Lorraine, grand duke of Tuscany from 1737 to 1765, later Francis I, emperor of the Hapsburg Empire (1745-1765). Two of their children, Joseph II and Leopold II, were emperors, and one was Maria Antoinette. At her accession the monarchy was exhausted, the people discontented and the army weak. Only seven weeks after her father's death, Frederick III the Great of Prussia marched in and took over the Austrian province of Silesia, precipitating the Silesian Wars of 1740-1742 and 1744. She lost Silesia to Frederick and never forgave the loss. The Seven Years' War which ensued (1756-1763) was a world war, fought not only in Europe but also in North America and India, with Britain and Prussia fighting France, Austria and Russia. Maria Theresa managed to bear 16 children in 20 years while she first established her right to rule, then negotiated an imperial crown for her husband, and meanwhile introduced economic reforms, strengthened the central government and the army. She improved the economic climate of The Netherlands and enjoyed wide popularity there. She died at the age of 63 in 1780.

Suggested Reading:

(1) Crankshaw, Edward. *Maria Theresa*. New York: Viking Press, 1969, 1971.

(2) Roider, Karl A., Jr., ed. *Maria Theresa*. Englewood Cliffs, N.J.: Prentice Hall, 1973.

Marie

Countess, ruler of Boulogne (1159-1173)

She was the daughter of Countess Mahaut de Boulogne (who was Queen Matilda of England), ruler of Boulogne from 1125 to 1150, and King Stephen I, who ruled England from 1135 to 1154. She was the sister of Count Eustache IV, who succeeded their mother upon her death and ruled from 1150 to 1153, and of Guillaume II, who ruled after his brother died in 1153 to 1159. When Guillaume died in 1159, Marie succeeded him. She was married to Matthieu d'Alcase. They had a daughter, Ide, who succeeded her mother upon Marie's death in 1173.

Suggested Reading:

(1) Egan, Edward W. et. al., eds. *Kings, Rulers, and Statesmen*. New York: Sterling Publishing Company, 1976. p. 152.

Marie (or Mary of Brabant)

Countess, ruler of Brabant (1260)

She was the second wife of Holy Roman Emperor Otto IV, whom she married c. 1213. Otto was deposed in 1215 and died in 1218. Marie did not remarry and had no children. When Countess Mahaut de Dammartin died in 1260, the fief of Boulogne passed to Marie. Eventually it passed to Robert VI, Comte d'Auvergne.

Suggested Reading:

(1) Egan, Edward W. et. al., eds. *Kings, Rulers, and Statesmen*. New York: Sterling Publishing Company, 1976. p. 152.
(2) Langer, William L., ed. *World History*. Boston: Houghton Mifflin, 1980. p. 224.

Marie de Bourbon

Princess, ruler of Achaea (1364-1370)

She was the widow of Robert II (r. 1333-1364). His brother Philippe II disputed her right to rule and eventually won out (r. 1364-1373).

Suggested Reading:

(1) Carpenter, Clive. *The Guinness Book of Kings, Rulers, & Statesmen*. Enfield, Middlesex: Guinness Superlatives Ltd., 1978. p. 1.

Marie de Bourbon Montpensier

Duchess, ruler of Auvergne (1608-1627)

She was born in 1606, the daughter of Henri, duke of Montpensier, who ruled Auvergne from 1602 to 1608, and Henriette de Joyeuse. At age three, she succeeded her father upon his death. She married Jean Baptist Gaston, duke of Orleans. In 1627 they had a daughter, Anne-Marie-Louise, who inherited her mother's rule when Marie died the same year.

Suggested Reading:

(1) Egan, Edward W. et. al., eds. *Kings, Rulers, and Statesmen*. New York: Sterling Publishing Company, 1976. p. 151.

Marie de Chatillon

Countess, ruler of Blois (1230-1241)

She inherited Blois when Countess Marguerite of Navarre died in 1230. She was married to Hugues de Chatillon, count of Saint-Pol. They had a son, Jean de Chatillon, who became count of Blois and Chartres when his mother died in 1241.

Suggested Reading:

(1) Egan, Edward W. et. al., eds. *Kings, Rulers, and Statesmen*. New York: Sterling Publishing Company, 1976. p. 152.

Marie de Médicis

Regent of France (1610-1617), defacto ruler until 1631, governor of Normandy (1612-1619)

She was born in 1573 in Florence, Italy; the daughter of Francesco de Medici, grand duke of Tuscany, and Joanna of Austria. In 1600 she married King Henry IV, (r. France 1589-1610). In 1601 she gave birth to the future Louis XIII and subsequently had five more children. When Henry was assassinated in 1610, Marie was named regent for her son Louis XIII. She chose as her chief minister a Florentine friend, Concino Concini, whom she named marquis d'Ancre. In 1612 she became governor of Normandy as well, a post she held until 1619. She was the first woman governor of a major province. She later traded this post for the government of Anjou. Even after Louis came of age in 1614, she continued to rule France. In 1619 Concini was assassinated, and Marie was banished to Blois, but she escaped and, with the help of the future Cardinal-duke of Richelieu, she set up court at Angers. After the death of the king's favorite, the duke of Luynes, in 1621, Marie and Richelieu gained control of affairs. She obtained a cardinal's hat for Richelieu and saw to it that Louis appointed him chief minister. When Richelieu rejected alliance with Spain and opted to side with the Hugenots, Marie demanded that he be dismissed. Eventually, instead, Louis banished his mother again (1631). She went to the Spanish Netherlands, then to Cologne, where she died in 1642, penniless.

Suggested Reading:

(1) Durant, Will and Ariel. *The Age of Voltaire*. New York: Simon & Schuster, 1965. pp. 26, 313.
(2) Hare, Christopher. *The Most Illustrious Ladies of the Italian Renaissance*. Williamstown, MA: Corner House, 1972. p. 211.
(3) Harding, Robert R. *Anatomy of a Power Elite*. New Haven, CT: Yale University Press, 1978. pp. 127, 129, 175, 226.
(4) Trevor-Roper, Hugh. *The Golden Age of Europe*. New York: Bonanza/Crown, 1987. pp. 153, 158, 166, 172, 173.

Marie d'Savoy-Nemours

See Jeanne de Nemours.

Marie-Louise

Regent of France (1812), duchess of Parma (1815-1847)

She was born in Vienna in 1791, the eldest of 12 children of Holy Roman Emperor Francis II (r. 1792-1806) and ruler of Austria as Francis I (1804-1835), and his second wife, Maria Theresa of Naples-Sicily. When Napoleon, eager for a royal heir, decided to divorce his beloved Josephine, the Austrian foreign minister, Count (later Prince) Klemens von Metternich, suggested 19-year-old Marie-Louise as Napoleon's second wife. They married in 1810 and in 1811 their son, Napoleon II, was born. In 1812, during Napoleon's Russian campaign, Marie-Louise served as regent. The marriage marked a turning point for Napoleon. According to historian Owen Connelly, "Marie-Louise made him so happy that he lost his compulsion to work." Whether she was equally happy is questionable. Napoleon still corresponded with Josephine, and there were rumors that he was the father the children of Marie—Louise's sister-in-law, Archduchess Sophie. After his first abdication in 1814, her father whisked her and her son back to Austria. The Congress of Vienna gave Marie-Louise the Italian duchies of Parma, Piacenza, and Guastalla, with sovereign power to rule in her own right, reverting to the house of Bourbon at her death. She refused to accompany Napoleon to Elba, and after he threatened to abduct her, they became completely estranged. By the time he died in 1821, she had already given birth to two children by Adam Adalbert, Graf von Neipperg. They married shortly after Napoleon's death. She established a moderate rule in Parma and maintained the previously enacted French reforms. Neipperg died only two years after their marriage, and in 1824 she took a third husband, Charles-Rene, Comte de Bombelles. In 1832 her son Napoleon II died in Vienna of tuberculosis. Marie-Louise died in Parma in 1847.

Suggested Reading:

(1) Putnam, John J. "Napoleon." *National Geographic*. 161 February 1982: 165-170.
(2) Langer, William L., ed. *World History*. Boston: Houghton Mifflin, 1980. pp. 644, 650.
(3) Sédillot, René. *An Outline of French History*. New York: Alfred A. Knopf, 1967. pp. 290, 306.

Marija

See Maria of Anjou

Marozia Crescentii

Ruler of Rome (A.D. 928-932)

She was the daughter of Roman senator Theophylact Crescentii and his wife Theodora. The patrician Crescentii family was of the landed aristocracy which controlled Rome during the nadir of the Papacy. At the time of Marozia, the Papacy was a local and secular institution. Italy was without effective native rule. Marozia was the mistress of Pope Sergius III and mother of his son John, later Pope John XI. She married Alberic I of Spoleto, margrave of Camerino, who, with her father, restored Sergius III to the Papacy. Alberic and Marozia had a son, Alberic II. After Alberic I died in 928, Marozia overthrew and imprisoned Pope John X, raised her illegitimate son to the Papacy, and took control of Rome until her son Alberic II assumed power in 932. Following the death of her first husband, she married, successively, Marquess Guido, Guy of Tuscany, and, after he died, his half-brother, Hugh of Provence, king of Italy from 926 to 932. In 932 her son Alberic II rose up against her and drove out King Hugh.

Suggested Reading:

(1) Previté-Orton, C. W. *The Shorter Cambridge History of the Crusades.* Cambridge: Cambridge University Press, 1952, 1982. vol. 1, *The Later Roman Empire to the Twelfth Century.* pp. 359, 437.

(2) Langer, William L., ed. *World History.* Boston: Houghton Mifflin, 1980. p. 230.

Martha

Queen mother, de facto ruler of Russia (1613-1619)

She was the wife of Philaret Romanov, who had been placed in captivity in Poland, while she had been forced into a convent by Boris Godunov. She was the mother of Michael Romanov, elected tsar of Russia in 1613. Young Michael had no education preparing him to rule, so he left the direction of affairs of state to the ambitious Martha, who left the convent, and other relatives. In 1619 Philaret was freed to return to Moscow, where he was elevated to patriarch. He assumed the reins of government and ruled "brutally" in the name of his son, eliminating other relatives and even Martha.

Suggested Reading:

(1) Dvornik, Francis. *The Slavs in European History and Civilization.* New Brunswick, NJ: Rutgers U. Press, 1962. p. 490.

Mary

Duchess, ruler of Burgundy and Luxembourg (1477-1482)

She was born in 1457, the daughter of Charles the Bold (r. 1467-1477) and Margaret of York. In 1474, Louis XI (the Spider) formed the Union of Constance, a coalition of foes of Burgundy, and opened war on Charles the Bold. Charles was killed in battle in 1477. Louis attempted to unite Burgundy with the crown, but Flanders stood firmly by Mary. The Union of Constance was a formidable foe for a widow alone; she soon married the Archduke Maximilian of Austria (r. Hapsburg Empire 1493-1519). The couple had two children: Philip (the Handsome), who married Joanna of

Castile and was regent of Spain; and Margaret, who first married John of Spain and then Philip of Savoy. Mary died in 1482. Their son Philip became duke of Burgundy.

Suggested Reading:

(1) Langer, William L., ed. *World History*. Boston: Houghton Mifflin, 1980. pp. 303, 324, 327, 406, 427.

Mary I (or Bloody Mary or Mary the Catholic)

Queen of England (1553-1558)

She was born in 1516, the daughter of Henry VIII, king of England (r. 1509-1547), and Catherine of Aragon, whom he divorced (1533), claiming marriage to his brother's widow was incestuous and thus Mary was a bastard. His next wife, Anne Boelyn, forced Mary to serve as lady-in-waiting for her own daughter, Elizabeth. Mary was also coerced into admitting the illegality of her mother's marriage to her father. After Anne Boelyn was beheaded, Mary's lot became easier; she was made godmother to Henry's third wife Jane Seymour's son, Edward. One by one she watched Henry's wives come and go, secretly practicing her Catholicism, waiting for a marriage partner to materialize. Her bastard status limited her marital opportunities, even though, in 1544, she was named in succession to the throne after Edward. When Edward died in 1553, one threat to her succession, Lady Jany Grey, had to be deposed after a nine-day "reign," and then Mary became, at age 37, the first queen to rule all of England in her own right. She set about restoring the ties to the Catholic Church severed during her father's reign. To that end, she determined to marry Philip of Spain, son of Holy Roman Emperor Charles V. The people of Tudor England distrusted Spaniards, and his Catholicism was of grave concern to nobles who had profitted when Henry VIII confiscated Catholic lands. Sir Thomas Wyatt led a Protestant insurrection which Mary countered with an impassioned plea to her citizenry. Wyatt was executed, and Mary married Philip in 1554. Soon after, the Papal Legate absolved England from the sin of its 20-year break with Rome. The Church restored heresy laws (1555), and some 280 heretics were burned. "Bloody Mary" was blamed for the slaughter. Philip returned to Spain when his father died (1555) and came to England only once more during their marriage. That was in 1556, to persuade her to take arms against France to assist Spain's interests. In 1558 Calais, an English possession for more than two centuries, was taken by the duke of Guise. This loss was one from which she never recovered. Ten months later she was dead.

Suggested Reading:

(1) Hudson, M. E. and Mary Clark. *Crown of a Thousand Years*. New York: Crown Publishers, 1978. pp. 78, 82-89.
(2) Trevor-Roper, Hugh. *The Golden Age of Europe*. New York: Bonanza/ Crown, 1987. pp. 26, 40, 190.
(3) Langer, William L., ed. *World History*. Boston: Houghton Mifflin, 1980. pp. 395-396, 398-399, 417.

Mary II

Queen of England (1689-1694)

She was born in 1662, the daughter of James II, ruler of England from 1685 to 1688, and Anne Hyde. Although both parents were Catholic converts, Mary was reared as a Protestant. In 1677, at age 15, she was married to her cousin, William of Orange, stadholder of Holland, and went to Holland to live. Her initial disappointment on meeting William, who was 12 years older than she and four inches shorter, eventually disappeared. However, she never reconciled to William's long-standing love affair with her lady-in-waiting, Elizabeth Villiers. Despite Mary's obvious dislike of Elizabeth, William insisted that she be retained in the queen's retinue. In 1688 English bishops wrote to William, a champion of Protestant causes, inviting him to invade England. It was an invitation which William and Mary welcomed. William's invasion met with scant resistance, for the country wanted a Protestant ruler. King James fled to France, and after a half-hearted attempt to regain his throne, retired to France permanently. Mary quickly made it known that she had no intention of reigning alone: she was the prince's wife, she said, and never meant to be "other than in subjection to him." They were crowned joint sovereigns in 1689. However, during her six years as Queen of England, she reigned alone for much of the time, since William was abroad attending to matters of state in Holland, or was conducting his military campaigns against France or Ireland. Mary enjoyed great popularity and ruled with vigor, sensitivity and dynamism during William's absences, but when he was in England, she quickly retired. Her chaplain wrote that if her husband retained the throne of England, "it would be done by her skill and talents for governing." Her estrangement from her father and from her adopted homeland, Holland, troubled her, but more vexing were her constant quarrels with her sister Anne, whose friends, Sarah and John Churchill, actively disliked William. She, in turn, mistrusted them and thought that Anne was entirely too much in their thrall. Mary died prematurely of smallpox at the age of 32 (1694).

Suggested Reading:

(1) Hudson, M. E. and Mary Clark. *Crown of a Thousand Years*. New York: Crown Publishers, 1978. pp. 112-114.
(2) Langer, William L., ed. *World History*. Boston: Houghton Mifflin, 1980. pp. 463, 465-467, 553.

Mary of Guise (or Mary of Lorraine)

Queen, regent of Scotland (1554-1560)

She was born in 1515, the eldest daughter of Claude of Lorraine, founding duc de Guise who ruled from 1528 to 1550, and Antoinette de Bourbon-Vendome. In 1533 she married Louis d'Orleans, duc de Longueville. They had one son, Francois, born in 1534. In 1537 her husband died. The following year she married King James V, ruler of Scotland from 1513 to 1542. Their daughter, Mary Stuart, was born a few days before James died in 1542. English King Henry VIII tried in vain to gain control of the kingdom at that time, but he failed. In 1554 James, earl of Arran, was deposed from the regency for 12-year-old Mary in favor of Queen Mary. In the beginning of her regency, Mary, a Catholic, actually cultivated Protestants and ruled with such religious tolerance that the Protestants even supported her 1558 decision to marry her daughter fo the future king of France, Francis II. However, heavy-handed French influence soon induced her to change her tolerant attitude toward Protestants and to attempt to suppress the growth of Protestantism in Scotland. Her actions sparked a civil war in which the Protestants were aided by England and the Catholics, by France. Mary was driven from office but returned, only to be on the verge of defeat again. Her health failed, and from her deathbed she called a conference of nobles from both sides and pleaded for reason and for a compromise. She died in 1560 before she could see her request honored.

Suggested Reading:

(1)   Mackie, J.D. *A History of Scotland*. Harmondsworth, Middlesex: Penguin Books, 1984. pp. 133, 136-139, 149.

Mary of Lorraine

See Mary of Guise

Mary Stuart

Queen of Scots (1542-1567)

Born in 1542, she was the only child of King James V, ruler of Scotland from 1513 to 1542, and Mary of Guise. Mary was born the year her father died. To keep Henry VIII from gaining control of the fatherless child, Mary's mother sent her to France when she was five years old, where she was reared in the household of King Henry II and Catherine de Medicis. In 1558 at age 16, she was married to their eldest son, 14-year-old Francis II, later ruler of France from 1559 to 1560. That same year, Elizabeth Tudor, a Protestant, acceded to the throne of England and Mary, a Catholic, was next in the line of succession. Two years later her husband died, and she soon returned to Scotland. For the first years of her majority rule, she refrained from interfering in religious affairs, even choosing Protestant advisors. Then she made the fatal mistake of falling in love with her cousin, Lord Darnley, who was unpopular with all factions. Despite all protests, she married him in 1565. Through plots and counter-plots, including the murder of her secretary Rizzio before her eyes, Darnley tried in ensure the succession for his heirs. Mary bore a son, James VI, in 1566, but by now she was convinced that Darnley had meant to kill her. One account says that Mary developed an adulturous relationship with the earl of Bothwell before he murdered Darnley in 1567, and that Mary was aware of Bothwell's plot. Whatever her foreknowledge of events was, afterward Bothwell abducted her, ravished her and subsequently married her. But the marriage set Scottish nobles up in arms; they exiled Bothwell, imprisoned Mary on the island of Loch Leven, and forced her to abdicate in favor of her son. The following year she fled to England, but Elizabth held her in prison for 18 years. Then, in 1586, suspecting Mary of being involved in a plot to assassinate her, Elizabeth consented to have Mary put to death.

Suggested Reading:

(1) Mackie, J.D. *A History of Scotland*. Harmondsworth, Middlesex: Penguin Books, 1984. pp. 134, 136-139, 153-175, 202, 308.

(2) Orfield, Olivia. *Death Trap*. Elgin, IL: Performance Publishing Co., 1979.

Mathilde

Countess, ruler of Nevers (992-1028)

She was the daughter of Otto Guillaume, count of Burgundy and Nevers from 987 to 992. She married Seigneur of Maers, Moncearx and Auxerre. They had a son, Renaud, who succeeded his mother as Count Renaud I of Auxerre and Nevers, on her death in 1028.

Suggested Reading:

(1) Egan, Edward W. et. al., eds. *Kings, Rulers, and Statesmen*. New York: Sterling Publishing, 1976. p. 159.

Matilda

Abbess, regent of Germany (996)

She was the daughter of Otto the Great, Holy Roman Emperor from 962 to 972, and Adelaide of Burgundy. She was a sister of Otto II, Emperor from 973 to 983. From 954 to 968 she was Abbess of Quedlinburg. When her 15-year-old nephew, Otto III, went to Italy to receive his imperial crown in 996, he installed his very able aunt Matilda, described as "a woman of great wisdom and strength," as his regent.

Suggested Reading:

(1) Löwenstein, Prince Hubertus zu. *A Basic History of Germany*. Bonn: Inter Nationes, 1964. p. 30.

Matilda (or Empress Maud)

Uncrowned queen of England (1141), regent of England (1154)

She was born in 1102, the only daughter of King Henry I, ruler of England from 1100 to 1135, and Edith (Also called Matilda) of Scotland. She was the grandaughter of William the Conqueror. Fierce, proud, and cynical, she developed an early, consuming interest in politics. In 1114 at the age of 12, she was married to Holy Roman Emperor Henry V, who lost her estates in his second campaign for expansion. The couple had no children. In 1120 her brother William, heir to the English throne, died, and in 1125 her husband died. Her father then recalled her to England, naming her his heir and arranging her marriage to 14-year-old Godfrey Plantagenet, count of Anjou. She was 29 years old. In 1133 the couple had a son, Henry II, destined to rule England from 1154 to 1189. She had two more sons, Geoffrey and William. When King Henry I died in 1135, her cousin Stephen of Blois, son of Henry's sister Adela, in a sudden *coup d'état*, usurped the throne. It took Matilda four years to gather her supporters, but in 1139, she invaded England to claim her throne from the usurper. It was two years before her forces could capture Stephen and send him in chains to Bristol Castle. She was proclaimed *Domina Anglorum*, "Lady of the English," and Queen in April, although she was not crowned at the time. But by November, her demands for money and her quarrels with the church had soured many of her supporters, who had second thoughts about crowning her. Hostility toward her mounted to such an extent that at one time she was forced to masquerade as a corpse to escape Stephen's supporters. Eventually Stephen was set free, and Maud was again obliged to elude her would-be captors, this time by wearing white so as to blend with the snow around Oxford Castle. Finally, after many battles and much intrigue, Matilda could see that she was beaten, and in 1148 she retired to Normandy. Her son Henry II acceded to the throne in 1154, and she ably performed her duties as regent for him during the first few years of his reign. She died in 1167, having composed the words to appear on her tombstone: "Here lies Henry's daughter, wife and mother; great by birth, greater by marriage, greatest by motherhood."

Suggested Reading:

(1) Stenton, Doris Mary. *English Society in the Early Middle Ages.* Harmondsworth, Middlesex: Penguin Books, Ltd., 1965. pp. 35-36, 225.

(2) Hudson, M. E. and Mary Clark. *Crown of a Thousand Years.* New York: Crown Publishers, 1978. pp. 26-27.

Matilda of Flanders

Duchess, regent of Normandy (c. 1066-?)

She was the daughter of Count Baldwin (Beaudoin) V of Flanders and the wife of William I (later, the Conqueror), Duke of Normandy. William based his claim for the throne of England on the fact that Matilda was a descendant of Alfred the Great. Her father was a descendant of Baldwin II, who married Alfred's daughter Aelfthryth. While William was conquering England (1066), Matilda ruled Normandy. The couple had four children: Robert Curthose, later duke of Normandy; William II Rufus (the Red), ruler of England (1087-1100); Adela, wife of Stephen II of Blois, ruler of England (1135-1154); and Henry I, ruler of England (1100-1135). Matilda died in 1083.

Suggested Reading:

(1) Previté-Orton, C. W. *The Shorter Cambridge Medieval History.* Cambridge: Cambridge University Press, 1982. vol. 1, *The Later Roman Empire.* pp. 382, 608.
(2) Heer, Friedrich. *The Medieval World.* tr. Janet Sondheimer. New York: Mentor/NAL, 1962. p. 318.
(3) Duff, Charles. *England and the English.* New York: G.P. Putnam's Sons, 1954. p. 83.

Matilda of Tuscany

Duchess, co-ruler of Central Italy (1071-1076), sole ruler (1076-1089)

She was born in 1046, the daughter of Boniface of Canossa, Marquis of Tuscany, and his wife Beatrice. Her father's assassination in 1052 and the deaths of her older brother and sister left her the sole heir of an enormous fortune, including the holdings amassed by her grandfather, Otto Adalbert, founder of the House of Attoni. In 1054 Beatrice married Godfrey the Bearded of Upper Lorraine, Emperor Henry III's most dangerous foe in Germany. In 1055 Henry arrested Beatrice and Matilda, age nine, sending them to Germany, while Godfrey fled. Later Henry and Godfrey became reconciled and released Beatrice and Matilda. Godfrey died in 1069, and Matilda married his son, Godfrey the Hunchback, and settled in Lorraine. In 1071 she lost her only child, so she returned to Italy, where she reigned with her mother until Beatrice's death in 1076. Then she became sole ruler of a large, wealthy and powerful domain. She remained all her life a powerful ally of the Papacy. In was at her castle of Canossa that Emperor Henry IV stood barefoot in the snow for three days in order to receive absolution from the Pope. There were few aspects of Italian or Papal life about which her wishes did not have to be considered. In 1089 Pope Urban II arranged a marriage between Matilda and Welf V, Duke of Bavaria and Carinthia. She was 43 and he only 17. Henry IV, intent on enlarging his holdings, invaded northern Italy, but Matilda, with her vast resources, was able to hold out against him in the hills. After he had seized the crown of Italy, Matilda and Pope Urban convinced his son Conrad to revolt against Henry (1093). Her death in 1115 created a furor, for in 1086 and 1102 she had donated her allodial lands to the Papacy, while her will named Henry V as the recipient. The resolution of the dilemma this caused was reached only after years of strife.

Suggested Reading:

(1) Duff, Nora. *Matilda of Tuscany*. London: Cambridge Press, 1909.

(2) Previté-Orton, C. W. *The Shorter Cambridge Medieval History*. Cambridge: Cambridge University Press, 1982. vol. 1, *The Later Roman Empire*. pp. 457, 485, 491, 494, 496, 497.

(3) Painter, Sidney. *The Rise of the Feudal Monarchies*. Westport: Greenwood Press, 1982. pp. 103-104.

(4) Langer, William L., ed. *World History*. Boston: Houghton Mifflin, 1980. pp. 221-223, 232-236, 314.

Matilda (or Mathilde)

Princess, ruler of Achaea (1313-1318)

She was the daughter of Isabelle, ruler of Achaea from 1301 to 1307, when she was deposed by Philippe II (r. 1307-1313). When Philippe died, she assumed the throne. Following her death in 1318, Robert, king of Naples, succeeded her.

Suggested Reading:

(1) Carpenter, Clive. *The Guinness Book of Kings, Rulers, & Statesmen*. Enfield, Middlesex: Guinness Superlatives Ltd., 1978. p. 1.

Maud

Empress. See Matilda.

Merkel, Angela

Cancellor of Germany (2005-), President of the European Council (2007)

She was born Angela Dorothea Kasner on July 17, 1954 in Hamburg, Germany, the oldest child of Horst Kasner, a Lutheran minister, and his wife Herlind Jentzsch, a language teacher. Her younger siblings were Marcus and Irene Kasner. In 1954 her father received a pastorship at the church in in Brandenburg, and the family moved to Templin. Thus Merkel grew up in the countryside 80 km (50 miles) north of Berlin in the Socialist German Democratic Republic [East Germany]. Her mother was a member of the Socialist Democratic Party and her grandparents lived in East Prussia. At that time it was most unusual for citizens to travel freely from East Germany to West Germany, and it was unusual for an East German family to own two automobiles. Therefore, it is fair to conclude that Merkel's father probably had a "sympathetic" relationship with the communist regime, since otherwise such freedom and perquisites for a Christian pastor and his family would have been impossible in East Germany.

Like most students, Angela Kasner was a member of the Free German Youth (FDJ), the official, socialist-led youth organization and moved up in its ranks. However, she was confirmed as a Christian rather than take part in the Jugendweihe, a secular coming-of-age ceremony popular in East Germany at the time.

She was educated in Templin and at the University of Leipzig, where she studied physics from 1973 to 1978. In 1977 she married physicist Ulrich Merkel, from whom she was divorced in 1982. The marriage produced no children. From 1978 to 1990 she was at the Central Institute for Phyusical Chemistry of the Academy of Sciences in Berlin-Aldershof, both as a student and as a research scientist. In pursuit of her doctoral degree (*Dr. rer. nat.*), she became fluent in Russian, earning a state prize. Her doctoral thesis was on quantum chemistry.

After the fall in 1989 of the Berlin Wall separating East and West Germany, Merkel joined the *Demokratischer Aufbruch* whose intent was to promote democracy in the new unified Germany. Following the first and only democratic election held in the East German state, she became the deputy spokesperson of the new pre-unification caretaker government under Lothar de Maizière. Then, at the first post-reunification general election in December 1990, she was elected to the Bundestag from electoral districts Rügen and Nordvorpommern and the city of Stralsund, which have remained her electoral district. Her party merged with the west German CDU and she became Minister for Women and Youth in Helmut Kohl's third cabinet. In 1994, she was made Minister for the Environment and Reactor Safety, which gave her greater political visibility and a platform on which to build her political career. As one of Kohl's protégées and his youngest cabinet minister, she was referred to by Kohl as "*das Mädchen*" ("the girl").

In 1998 she married Berlin chemistry professor Joachim Sauer, who had two adult sons by a previous marriage.

In the general elections of that year, the Kohl government was defeated and Merkel was made Secretary-General of the CDU, and in the following year she engineered CDU victories in six of seven regional elections, giving her party a creditable presence in the Bundesrat (states legislative body). When a donor financing scandal implicated Kohl, Merkel criticized her former mentor and his chosen successor Wolfgang Schäuble. In April 2000 the party threw out both men and elected Merkel as its first female chairperson. This was a bold step for the conservative, Catholic, male-dominated CDU, whose largest constituencies were in southern and western Germany, while Merkel was a Protestant from Protestant northern Germany. She remained chairwoman of the CDU and its sister party Bavarian Christian Social Union (CSU) from 2002 to 2005 and leader of the conservative opposition in the lower house of the Parliament, the Bundestag.

In 2005 she cobbled together a Grand Coalition of the CDU, CSU and Social Democratic Party of Germany (SPD) and after the November election and became Chancellor of the reunited Germany, the first woman to lead the nation since it became a modern nation in 1871. Her election was doubly significant since she came from East Germany, although born in the west. Her main campaign promise was to reduce unemployment. Once elected, her other primary concerns were health care reform and energy development.

In 2007 Merkel became a member of the Council of Women World Leaders. *Forbes Magazine* in 2006 and 2007 named her the most powerful woman in the world. In 2007 when she chaired the G8 summit, she was only the second woman to do so, the other being Margaret Thatcher. She,

Thatcher and Kim Campbell were the only three women ever to serve on the G8 at that time.

Because Merkel worked for better German-American relations, even supporting the invasion of Iraq against strong public opposition, she was criticized as an "American lackey." However, she differed vocally on some of the policies of the Bush administration following the invasion.

In 2007, over the objections of China, she met with the Dalai Lama for "private and informal talks." This recognition of the leader of Tibet so angered China that it cancelled talks with German officials, including Justice Minister Brigitte Zypries. Earlier that same year, as President-in-office of the European Council, she had visited the Middle East and offered Europe help to re-start Israeli and Palestinian peace negotiations. On another trip to Israel the following year, she addressed the Knesset, speaking of Germany's "Holocaust shame."

Suggested Reading:

(1) "East German past of iron lady unveiled," by Luke Harding. *The Observer,* June 26, 2005.

(2) "Merkel visits Mideast as EU president," *International Herald Tribune,* April 1, 2007.

(3) "Germany's First Fella, Angela Merkel Is Germany's Chancellor; But Her Husband Stays Out Of The Spotlight." CBS News.

(4) "Germany in political gridlock after neck-and-neck election." by Luke Harding. *The Guardian,* September 23, 2005.

Europe Section N

Nicole (or Nicola)

Duchess, ruler of Lorraine (1624-1625)

Nicole was the daughter of Henry II, duke of Lorraine, who ruled from 1608 to 1624. She became duchess of Lorraine upon her father's death in 1624. That same year she married her cousin Charles (later Charles IV, r. 1625-1634), son of her father's brother Francis II of Vaudémont. Francis, in a neat bit of finagling, arranged the marriage in order to wrest the duchy out of her control. The following year Francis abolished female succession so that he himself could be proclaimed duke. He then abdicated in favor of his son Charles IV (sometimes called Charles III). Nicole died in 1657.

Suggested Reading:

(1) *Britannica Micropaedia*. Chicago: Encyclopedia Britannica Press, 1983. vol. 2, p. 758.
(2) Morby, John E. *Dynasties of the World*. Oxford: Oxford University Press, 1989. p. 158.
(3) Egan, Edward W. et. al., eds. *Kings, Rulers, and Statesmen*. New York: Sterling Publishing Company, 1976. p. 128.

Europe Section O

Olga

Queen, regent of Greece (1920)

She was the wife of King Alexander I, ruler of Greece from 1917 to 1920. On October 25, 1920, King Alexander died from blood poisoning, having been bitten by a pet monkey. Queen Olga became regent until December, when former King Constantine I, Alexander's father who had previously abdicated, resumed the throne.

Suggested Reading:

(1)   Langer, William L., ed. *World History*. Boston: Houghton Mifflin, 1980. p. 1024.

Olympias (or Olumpias, Myrtale, Polyxena, or Stratonice)

Queen regent of Macedonia (317 B.C.)

She was born c. 375 B.C., the daughter of King Neoptolemus of Epirus. A follower of Orpheus and Dionysus, she met King Philip II of Macedon at the Sanctuary of the Gods on the island of Samothrace and in 357 B.C. became his principal wife. At that time she had apparently been called Myrtale and was perhaps renamed Olympias beginning the following year after Philip's victory in the Olympic Games. That same year, their son, Alexander III (the Great) was born in Pella, in Macedonia.

Two decades later, in 337 B.C., when Philip married Cleopatry Eurydice, Olympias and Alexander fled to Epirus. Alexander later moved on to Illyria and eventually reconciled with his father. After Philip was assassinated in 336, possibly by his wife or his 20-year-old son, Olympias returned to

Macedonia and, with her son now in power, forced Cleopatra Eurydice to commit suicide.

While Alexander was absent on military expeditions to Asia, Olympias quarrelled repeatedly over governing policy with the Macedonian viceroy, Antipater, but Alexander invariably supported Antipater against his mother. Eventually, she returned to Epirus (c. 331). Alexander died in 323, and Antipater died four years later, having appointed Polyperchon as his successor over the European part of the empire. This threatened Antipater's son Cassander's power.

Antipater had brought Alexander's Bactrian wife Roxane and their son Alexander IV (c. 323-c. 311 B.C.) to Macedonia; however, after Antipater's death, Roxane fled with the infant king to Epirus, to take refuge with Queen Olympias.

After Antipater's death, Polycheron invited Olympias to return to Macedonia to serve as regent for her grandson Alexander IV, but at first she refused. Finally, in 317, when Cassander put Philip II's mentally handicapped son Phillip III Arrhidaeus on the throne, Olympias returned with Polyperchon and invaded Macedonia in the name of her grandson. In this endeavor she was supported by Macedonian soldiers. She killed Philip III and many others and forced his wife Adea to commit suicide. But in 316 Cassander blockaded Olympias at Pynda. He imprisoned Roxane and Alexander IV and condemned Olympias to death, but his soldiers preferred to desert to her rather than carry out her execution.

Her death eventually came at the hands of relatives of her former victims, whom she had slain at the time of the invasion. Alexander IV was murdered in c. 310-309.

Suggested Reading:

(1) Peters, E. E. *The Harvest of Hellenism.* New York: Barnes & Noble Books, 1996. pp. 48, 53, 72, 76-77, 79.

(2) Worthington, Ian, ed. *Ventures into Greek History.* Oxford: Clarendon Press, 1994. pp. 357-380. Carney, E. D., "Olympias, Adea Eurydice, and the End of the Argead Dynasty".

(3) Bowder, Diana, *Who Was Who in the Greek World.* Oxford: Phaidon Press, 1982. pp. 324-325.

Europe Section P

Pauline

Princess and Duchess, ruler of Guastalla (1806)

Guastalla, located in northern Italy, was probably founded by the Lombards in the 7th century. In 1406 it was designated a county, and from 1539 it was ruled by the Gonzagas of Mantua. In 1621 it became a duchy, and in 1746 it passed to Austria and to the Spanish Bourbons.

Napoleon I, wanting to found a dynasty bearing his name, realized that someday one of the plots against his life might succeed. He knew that the individual is mortal, but family endures. He sought to protect his place in history by bestowing kingdoms upon his brothers and sisters. In 1806 he revived the tiny six-square-mile duchy of Guastalla as an "independent principality", appointing his second surviving sister, Pauline Bonaparte, as its ruler. This feckles lady, whose likeness Canova had carved in stone, was known for her beauty, vanity, lusts, and extravagance. Although she found it amusing to have been made a sovereign, she could not bother to leave the luxuries of Paris in order to rule. She took office on March 30, 1806 and abdicated on May 24 of the same year. She was the principality's only ruler.

Suggested Reading:

(1) Carpenter, Clive. *The Guinness Book of Kings, Rulers, & Statesmen.* Enfield, Middlesex: Guinness Superlatives Ltd., 1978. p. 145.

(2) Sédillot, René. *An Outline of French History.* tr. Gerard Hopkins. New York: Alfred A. Knopf, 1967. p. 306.

Pedini-Angelini, Maria Lea

Co-Captain Regent of San Marino (1981)

San Marino, located on the Adriatic side of Central Italy, and surrounded on all sides by Italy, is the world's oldest independent republic. It has a unique system of government, which calls for two Captains-Regent, elected by the Great and General Council, a parliament of 60 members elected for five-year terms. These Captains-Regent serve as heads of state, to preside over the executive branch, called the Congress of State, which is composed of ten members chosen by the Council. The Captains-Regent serve only a six-month term and may not be re-elected until after a three-year period has passed.

From 1945-1957, the country was ruled by a coalition of communists and socialists. In 1957 the Christian Democratic Party, aided by communist dissidents, took control. In 1978 a coalition led by communists again came to power, and it was during this period that Maria Lea Pedini-Angelini served as Co-Captain Regent.

Suggested Reading:

(1) *Britannica Macropaedia*. 1983. vol. 16. pp. 223-224.
(2) *Funk & Wagnalls New Encyclopedia*. 1986. vol. 23. p. 123.

Petronilla

Queen of Aragon (1137-1164)

She was born c. 1136, the daughter of King Ramiro II, ruler of Aragon from 1134 to 1137. Ramiro was a monk, the brother of King Alfonso I, ruler from 1102 to 1134, who named Ramiro to succeed him on his death. The pope freed Ramiro from his vows so that Ramiro could emerge from retirement only long enough to marry and produce an heir. He betrothed her to Ramón Berenguer IV, count of Barcelona, then soon abdicated and returned to his monastary, leaving Queen Petronilla under the guardianship of Ramón, who was only six at the time. Thirteen years later, in 1150, she married Berenguer, now king of Catalonia. Petronilla was never allowed to exercise authority during Berenguer's life. She had a son, Ramón Berenguer, who changed his name to the more Aragonese-sounding Alfonso II. By inheritance, Alfonso acceded to the throne of Catalonia in 1162 when his father died. Queen Petronilla abdicated the throne of Aragon in 1164, in favor of Alfonso. He was the first to rule in his own right over Aragon and Catalonia, which came to be known as the kingdom of Aragon.

Suggested Reading:

(1)   Chapman, Charles E. *A History of Spain*. New York: The Free Press/ Macmillan, 1946. pp. 78-79.
(2)   Langer, William L., ed. *World History*. Boston: Houghton Mifflin, 1980. pp. 250, 252.

Placidia, Galla (or Aelia)

Augusta, regent of the Western Roman Empire (A.D. 425-433)

She was born in A.D. 390, the daughter of Emperor Theodosius I, ruler from 379 to 395, and his second wife Galla, daughter of Valentinian I. She was the half-sister of Flavius Honorius, who ruled from 393 to 423. In 410 the Goths, under the command of Alaric, sacked Rome and took Galla Placidia prisoner. In 414 she married Alaric's successor, Athaulf in Narbonne. Athaulf was assassinated the following year. In 416 she was restored to the Romans, and the next year she unwillingly submitted to a political union, marriage to her half-brother's generalissimo, Constantius. They had a son, Valentinian, born in 419, and at least one daughter, Honoria. In 421 Constantius was declared Augustus and co-emperor, but he died Flavius Honorius died in 423 and, after a brief usurpation by Johannes during which Galla Placidia fled with her son to Constantinople, was succeeded in 425 by Galla Placidia's son, Valentinian, age six. Galla, as regent, actively supported by Bonifatius (Boniface), who bore the title Master of the Soldiers of the eastern army. At first her influence was dominant in affairs of state, but when she tried to replace her own Master of Soldiers with Boniface, he enlisted the help of the Huns, and by 423 his authority was unchallenged. Galla Placidia then turned her attention to adorning the city of Ravenna with a number of churches. She died in Rome in 450.

Suggested Reading:

(1)   Bowder, Diana, ed. *Who Was Who in the Roman World*. Ithaca, NY: Cornell University Press, 1980. pp. 4-5, 46, 146, 413-414, 556-557.
(2)   Previté-Orton, C. W. *The Shorter Cambridge Medieval History*. Cambridge: Cambridge University Press, 1952, 1982. vol. 1, *The Later Roman Empire to the Twelfth Century*. pp. 78, 86-88.

(3)   Langer, William L., ed. *World History*. Boston: Houghton Mifflin, 1980. pp. 134, 158-159.

Plavsic, Biljana

President of the Bosnian Serb Republic (1996-1997)

She was born in 1930 into a wealthy merchant family from Visoko. Her father, a biologist, was director of natural sciences at Sarajevo's museum. She also became a biologist, studying botany and plant viruses in Zagreb and in New York in the early 1970's as a Fulbright scholar. She was married briefly to a prominent Sarajevo lawyer, then divorced and became dean of natural sciences at Sarajevo University. When she failed to get the post as biology chair at the Academy for Arts and Sciences in 1990, she became active in the newly formed Serbian Democratic Party and rose rapidly to a position of prominence. She became an ardent supporter of Radovan Karadzic and the Serb cause: ethnic partition and a pure Serb state. When Karadzic was elected president the self-proclaimed Republika Srpska, she became vice president. She was elected president when Karadzic, charged with masterminding "ethnic cleansing" genocide against the Muslims, was deposed under the terms of the Dayton peace accords. He was forced into hiding in Pale, where he planned to continue to direct the republic from behind the scenes, setting up his own police force, government, and state media. Following her inauguration, she unexpectedly turned against the ideological irredentist Karadzic, renouncing his involvement in Serbian war crimes. The country, financially crippled by blockage of aid for noncompliance with the Dayton peace agreement of November 1995, was torn between loyalty to Karadzic and Plavsic, who had the cautious support of NATO and the United States. Still fiercely nationalistic, she favored a return to the monarchy. "With a parliamentary monarchy, each four years you can change the prime minister, but there is always stability in the state," she said in a September 1997 interview. "Now there is one stable roof over the Serb people, our church. Why not have the other roof, a monarchy?" But foreign assistance was not enough to overcome the hard-liners in parliament. In August of 1997, NATO-led forces of British and Czech peacekeepers took over a police station in Banja Luka when it was learned that a large quantity of arms were stored there in preparation for a coup attempt against Plavsic's government. Later in the month a similar police station seizure in Brcko was carried out in the presence of an angry mob sympathetic to former president Karadzic.

Subsequently, Plavsic, a pragmatic nationalist, was ousted from the ruling Serbian Democratic Party, calling into question her political survival as well as the fate of the Bosnian Serb Republic.

Suggested Reading:

(1) "Cracking Down on Bosnia's War Criminals" *World Press Review*. September 1997: 5.

(2) Rubin, Elizabeth. "The Enemy of Our Enemy" by Elizabeth Rubin. *The New York Times Magazine*. 14 September 1997: 58-61.

(3) "U.S. Warns Bosnian Serbs to Honor Accords". *The New York Times*. 31 August 1997: 6.

(4) Erlanger, Steven. "NATO Faces a Crossroads in Bosnia". *The New York Times*. 31 August 1997: 6.

(5) Hedges, Chris. Bosnian Vote Could Backfire on West". *The New York Times*. 23 November 1997: 4.

(6) Rüb, Matthias. "Threats to Bosnia's Peace". *World Press Review*. October 1997:4.

(7) "Difficult Choices". *World Press Review*. November 1997: 19.

(8) Hedges, Chris. "Officials See Risk in New NATO Push for Bosnia Peace". *The New York Times*. 24 August 1997: 1, 4.

Plectrudis von Ecternach

Queen, regent, acting Major Domina of Austrasia and Neustria (714-716)

Born before 665, she was the daughter of Count Palatine Hugobert von Ecternach (d. ca. 697) and his wife, Irmina, who became Abbess of Oeren and was later named a Saint. Plectrudis inherited "the Lands between the Rhine, Moselle and Meuse" after her mother entered a convent. She married Pepin II of Herstol (Heristal), mayor (Major Domus) of Austrasia and Neustria from 687 to 714. The couple had at least one son, Grimoald, who died in 714, the same year his father died. All of Pepin's sons had predeceased him except one illegitimate son, Charles the Bold (Martel). Following the Frankish custom, Pepin's will divided the kingdoms among his boy grandsons as mayors under the regency of Queen Plectrudis. She did not rule long before civil war broke out among various rival factions. Between 716 and 719 Pepin's illegitimate son Charles overcame the Neustrians in three battles and took control of the kingdoms. She died ca. 725.

Suggested Reading:

(1) Previté-Orton, C. W. *The Shorter Cambridge Medieval History.* Cambridge: Cambridge University Press, 1952, 1982. p. 159.

Europe Section R

Ranocchini, Glorianna

Co-Captain-Regent of San Marino (1984, 1989-1990)

San Marino, a land-locked country completely surrounded by Italy, is the oldest independent country in the world. The republic is led by heads of state called Co-Captains-Regent, who are elected for six-month terms and re-electable only after three years. The Co-Captains-Regent preside over the ten-member Congress of State, the executive branch of the government. These members and the Captains-Regent are all elected from among the parliamentary body, called the Great and General Council, members of which are elected for terms of five years.

Glorianna Ranocchini, who had been elected to a seat on the Great and General Council, first came to power in 1984, while a coalition led by Communists controlled the Council. In 1986 a new Christian Democrat-Communist coalition was formed. Glorianna Rancchini, returned to the Council in the general elections of 1988, was again named to the post of Captain-Regent in 1989, serving until April 1990.

Suggested Reading:

(1) *Britannica Macropaedia* vol. 16, "San Marino". 1990. pp. 223-224.
(2) *Funk & Wagnalls New Encyclopedia*. vol. 23, "San Marino", 1986. p. 123.

Robinson, Mary

President of Ireland (1990-1997)

Born Mary Bourke in Ballina, County Mayo, in 1944, she was educated in a convent school in Dublin. Her parents, Aubrey Bourke and Tessa

O'Donnell, were doctors who subscribed to the *Irish Times*, considered a Protestant newspaper, which was banned at her school. She campaigned successfully for the ban to be lifted. She studied law, did post-graduate work at Harvard law School, and at 25 became Trinity College's youngest law professor. Although her family was staunchly Catholic, she married a Protestant solicitor, Nicholas Robinson, and they had three children. As a civil liberties lawyer, she entered politics for and became a senator at age 25. As a former member of the Irish Labor Party, she campaigned for the underdogs in Irish society. She also campaigned for the decriminalization of homosexuality, for equal rights for women, and against the prohibition of information on abortion. On her run for the presidency, she asked for and received a mandate to extend the hand of friendship to Northern Ireland's two communities. She was sworn in as the first woman president of Ireland on December 3, 1990. Of voters who elected her to what was then a largely symbolic but representative position, she said, "Instead of rocking the table, they rocked the system."

Prior to Robinson's tenure in office, successive presidents did little but sign documents and appeared at state occasions. But Robinson changed the image of the Irish presidency into one of vitality and action and became one of the most admired leaders in the world.

In May of 1995, President Robinson described the 150th anniversary of the great potato famine of 1845-47 as a time fo break the silence about this national disgrace and to decipher the puzzles and mysteries surrouding it. Was the famine a national disaster, was the landlord system at fault, or was the British laissez-faire colonial system in effect an act of genocide? Whatever the causes, the famine changed the country's character forever. It marked the end of the Celtic church, the Irish language, and the landlord class. It brought on the massive exodus to America, so that today, there are more Irish in the United States than in Ireland. It has been considered so shameful that even Irish literature has shunned it. However, Robinson hoped the commemoration would be cathartic, such that the Irish people would then look back to the golden age of the 7th and 8th centuries with renewed pride in Ireland's accomplishments.

She became a key figure in helping consolidate the peace process between the two Irelands. She was the first Irish president to open dialogue with the British Royal Family, paying a visit to Buckingham Palace for tea with the queen, and hosting a visit of the queen's children in Ireland.

She did not confine her interest to civil rights at home. She took several fact-finding trips to parts of Africa suffering from famine and the ravages of war. In 1996 her name was being mentioned as a possible successor to Boutros-Ghali as UN Secretary-General. Her popularity among many diverse factions had grown during her first term, which was a seven-year one. The recipient of numerous honorary degrees and international humanitarian awards, she was said to be admired by Queen Elizabeth. She instilled great loyalty among her staff at Phoenix Park. Loyalist women from Belfast sang her praises, as did Lord Jenkins, co-founder of Britain's Social Democratic Party, who praised her for her "wisdom and humanity."

Acknowledged as a "fervent internationalist," Robinson was quoted in the London *Observer* (April 21, 1996) as believing that order, national or international would be attained one step at a time. "We need to build lots of bridges," she said.

At the end of her term, she announced "with great reluctance" her decision not to run for re-election, although her success was assured, as no candidate opposed her. Upon leaving her post, she joined the United Nation as head of Human Rights.

Suggested Reading:

(1) "Here's to You, Mrs. Robinson". *World Press Review.* July 1996: 49.
(2) Connolly, Anne. "Ghosts of the Famine". *South China Morning Post*, Hong Kong, 11 November 1995. Reprinted in *World Press Review* February 1996: 39-40.
(3) Makem, Peter. "President Robinson Departs". in "Letter from Ireland". *Irish Edition.* www.us-irish.com. 24 November 1997.
(4) "Outpouring of Warmth for Retiring Irish President". www.us-irish. com. 24 November 1997.

Europe Section S

Sancha, Queen

Titular ruler of León (1037-1038)

Sancha was the daughter of Anfonso V (r. 999-1028) and Urraca I, and the sister of Vermudo III (r. 1028-1037), who died without leaving an heir. Sancha's mother was the sister of Sancho el Mayor, king of Navarre (r. 1000-1035), who, during his lifetime, managed to bring all of Christian Spain under his influence.

Following the death of Alfonso V in 1028, Garciía Sanchez, count of Castile, negotiated a marriage with the young Sancha that would have bolstered his position in relation to both León and Navarre. But before the marriage could be celebrated, he was assassinated in the city of León (1029). Because King Sancho of Navarre was married to García Sanchez's sister, he immediately claimed Castile in his wife's name and installed his son Ferdinand I (Fernando) as count. He then arranged a marriage between his son and his niece, Sancha. In 1034 the Navarrese king seized control of the city of León, forcing Vermudo to flee to Galicia. But King Sancho died the next year and Vermudo immediately repossessed León. Thus Sancha was once again in line to inherit the throne upon Vermudo's death in 1037.

Her husband Fernando then ruled from 1038 until his death in 1065. The couple had two sons who ruled: García, the youngest, who ruled Galicia (1065-1071), until his brother Sancho took it from him; Sancho II the Strong, who ruled Castile (1065-1072) and was killed while wresting León from his other brother; and Alfonso VI, who ruled León (1065-1109), having reclaimed it after his brother Sancho's assassination. Alfonso's daughter Urraca, managed to do what her grandmother could not: she ruled León in her own right (1109-1126).

Suggested Reading:

(1)   Reilly, Bernard F., *The Kingdom of León-Castilla under Queen Urraca*. Princeton: Princeton University Press, 1982. pp. 6-9.

Schavan, Annette

German Minister in Merkel's Cabinet (2005-)

She was born on June 10, 1955 in Jüchen. She is a member of the Christian Democratic Union, a conservative political party in Germany. From 1995 to 2005 she was Minister of Culture, Youth, and Sports for the German state of Baden-Würtemberg. She created a controversy when she refused to allow a Muslim teacher to wear a head scarf in school, while allowing Catholic nuns to wear their habits. In 2006 she received the Else Mayer Award for her work for feminists. In 2005 she was named by Chancellor Angela Merkel to her Grand Coalition Cabinet. She became Federal Minister of Education and Research.

Suggested Reading:

(1)   Official Site of Annette Schavan.

Schmidt, Ursula (Ulla)

German Minister for under Schroeder (2001) Angela Merkel's Cabinet (2001-)

She was norn on June 13, 1949 in Aachen, Germany. In 1976 she was a candidate of the Communist League of West Germany for the Bundestag (Federal Assembly) in Aachen. In 1983, she changed to the Social Demovratic Party and is active in the "Seeheimer Kreis," the far right wing of the party. The Communist League dissolved two years later.

In 2001 she was named Federal Minister for Health under Gerhard Schröder, replacing Andrea Fischer. A year later, she became Federal Minister for Health and Social Security. When Angela Merkel formed her Grand Coalition of Cabinet members, Schmidt again became Federal Minister for Health, but social security returned to the purvey of the Minister of Labour. In 2009 she created a minor furor when she criticized statements made by Pope Benedict XVI about the futility of condoms in the prevention of AIDS

Suggested Reading:

(1) Official Site of Ulla Schmidt.
(2) "Pope's comments on condoms draw criticism from France and Germany." *Canadian Press,* 2009.

Seaxburh

Queen of the kingdom of Wessex (672-674)

She lived (ca 636-around 700). She was the daughter of Pybba and the sister of Penda of Mercia. She married Cenwalh (Cenwealh), who ruled from 642-672. When Cenwalh repudiated his wife, her brother Penda drove him from his throne. After Cenwalh died, Seaxburh ruled for two years.

She was followed by Aescwine (Centwine), a descendant of former King Cynric, or Cynegils (r. 534-560).

Suggested Reading:

(1) Aycock, Leslie. *Arthur's Britain.* Harmondsworth, Middlesex: Penguin Books, 1971. p. 343.
(2) Morby, John E. *Dynasties of the World.* Oxford: Oxford University Press, 1989. p. 66.

Seaxburh, Dowager Queen

Regent of Kent (664-666)

Also known as Saint Seaxburh or Sexburga of Ely, she was the oldest daughter of King Anna of East Anglia and his second wife, Saewara. She married King Erconbert (Eorcenberht) of Kent (640-664), and after he died of the "yellow plague", she reigned on behalf off her son, Egbert I. After he came of age, she became abbess of Minister-in-Sheppey and later of Ely, where her sister, St. Etheldreda of Ely had been Abbess. Another sister and both of her daughters; Ermengilda and Ercongota were saints as were her grandchildren: St. Werburga of Chester, St. Wulfade and St. Rufinus. She lived ca. 636-around 700. Egbert died in 673.

Suchocka, Hanna

Prime Minister of Poland (1992-1993)

Hanna Suchocka was born on April 3, 1946 in the western Polish village of Pleszew, about 60 miles from the city of Poznan. Her family, considered leading citizens of the community, owned a pharmacy and lived in a large apartment above it. Although church attendance was not condoned in Communist-dominated Poland, her family attended the Roman Catholic Church across the street from their home weekly. When she enrolled in the University of Adam Mickiewicz in Poznan, she wanted to study literature, languages or fine arts, but her parents wanted her to study pharmacy. As a compormise, she studied constitutional law, graduating in 1968. She was offered a one-year appointment as a junior faculty member contingent upon her joining the Communist Pary. She refused, because she wanted to have the freedom to attend church.

To save her legal career, she joined the Democratic Party, which was tolerated by the Communists but was neither Marxist nor atheist. After entering politics as a member of the Democratic Party, she was elected to the Communist Parliament in 1980, where she quickly gained a reputation as a compromiser.

In December of 1981, martial law was imposed and thousands of Solidarity leaders were sent to prison. Suchocka left the Democratic Party soon afterward, and when her term was up in 1984, she retired from Parliament. However, when the new post-communist government was installed, she returned to politics and was again elected to Parliament in 1989. She was in London in 1992 when a party member phoned to inform her that she was wanted to serve as prime minister. At first she refused, but within weeks it became apparent that she was the only politician trusted by both moderates and the new fundamentalist Catholic parties. When she took office in July, 1992 amid a severe economic recession, her primary task was to be steering the once-communist country into a system of free market economy. She began to institute austere measures to bring the country toward prosperity. Under her coalition government, the fourth government in as many years, Poland began to experience the first political stability since the demise of communism in 1989. She persuaded Sejm (Parliament) to accept a "mini-constitution" and to adopt an austere budget that would enable the country to obtain foreign aid. After much negotiation and compromise, she was able to procure passage of a mass privatization plan for state-owned industry. Her personal popularity was strong among all segments of Polish society, but her coalition government was less well liked. In the election in the fall of 1993 her coalition had dissolved, and her party, the Democratic Union, was defeated.

Suggested Reading:

(1) "Poland's Prime Minister Looks Ahead to Reform" by Francine S. Kiefer. *The Christian Science Monitor.* May 7, 1993, p. 8.
(2) "Her Year of Living Dangerously," by Stephen Engelberg. *The New York Times Magazine,* September 12, 1993, pp. 41,52,55.

Susanne (or Suzanne) de Bourbon

Duchess, ruler of Bourbonnais (1503-1521)

She was born in 1491, the daughter of Pierre II, sire of Beaujeu and duke of Bourbon from 1488 to 1505, and Anne of France. Her only brother, Charles, died young. When her father died (c. 1503), Susanne inherited the duchy of Bourbonnais. In 1505 she married Charles III, count of Montpensier, and had three sons, who all died young. She and Charles, who was the great-grandson of John I, duke of Bourbon (r. 1410-1434), administered the duchy until her death in 1521. Charles continued to rule, but a charge of treason against him led to the confiscation of Bourbonnais by the French crown upon his death in 1527.

Suggested Reading:

(1) Morby, John E. *Dynasties of the World.* Oxford: Oxford University Press, 1989. p. 82.
(2) Egan, Edward W. et. al., eds. *Kings, Rulers, and Statesmen.* New York: Sterling Publishing Company, 1976. p. 153.

Europe Section T

Telles, Leonora

See Leonora Telles

Teresa of Castile (or Teresa of Portugal)

Countess, regent of Portugal (1112-1128)

She was the illegitimate daughter of King Alfonso VI, ruler of Castile from 1072 to 1109, and Jimena Muñoz. She was the half-sister of Urraca, (r. León-Castile 1109-1126). Teresa married Henry of Burgundy, or of Lorraine, to whom, in possibly as early as 1093/5, Alfonso VI granted land called the county of Portugal. In 1109 they had a son, Alfonso Henriques (Enríquez), who at age three succeeded as count of Portugal upon Henry's death (1112). Soon after Teresa assumed the post as regent, she became embroiled in a struggle with Galicia and Castile. After the death of Queen Urraca in 1126, there followed ten years of wars between Portugal and Castile, as first Teresa and later her son attempted to gain independence from Castile. Portuguese defenses were easily overcome, and Teresa, being the daughter, half-sister and aunt of Castilian kings, agreed to accept Castilian domination of Portugal. Her son, at age 19, took command of the army, defeated the Castilians and drove his mother into exile (1128). In 1139 Portugal at last became a kingdom and Alfonso was proclaimed king. He continued to rule until 1185.

Suggested Reading:

(1) Chapman, Charles E. *A History of Spain*. New York: AFree Press/ Macmillan, 1946. pp. 74-75.
(2) Reilly, Bernard F. *The Kingdom of León-Castilla Under Queen Urraca*. Princeton, NJ: Princeton University Press, 1982. pp. 28, 129.

(3) Langer.William L., ed. *World History*. Boston: Houghton Mifflin, 1980. pp. 253-254.

Teuta

Queen of Illyria (c. 231 B.C.-227 B.C.)

Historians have dubbed Queen Teuta the Catherine the Great of Illyria. In Roman times, during and after the First Punic War, Illyria occupied a strip east of the Adriatic Sea making up the northwestern part of the Balkan Peninsula, which had been inhabited by an Indo-European people called the Illyrians since about the 10th century B.C. At the height of its dominance in the region, Illyria extended from the Danube River to the Gulf of Ambracia on the Adriatic, to the Sar Mountains. The Illyrian tribes, influenced by their equally barbarous Thracian neighbors, were adept at mounted warfare using the iron weapons from Inner Asia. Illyria consisted of many small backward kingdoms, the best known being located in present-day Albania with its capital at Scodra (Shkodër). In its prime, it was ruled by King Agron, whose wife was the celebrated Queen Teuta. Agron, with Demetrius II of Macedonia, defeated the Aetolians in c. 231 B.C. But Agron died, leaving a young son, for whom his widow Teuta became regent.

Queen Teuta took an aggressive stance against her neighbors. With part of her navy, she attacked Sicily and the Greek colonies on the coast, while at the same time her pirates harassed Roman commerce. Her activities so disrupted the Republic's rising commercial development that the Roman Senate declared war on her in 229. Rome send a huge army and fleet of 200 vessels under the command of Sentumalus and Alvinus to suppress her piracy. After two years of protracted warfare, Queen Teuta sued for peace (227 B.C.). Thereafter she was forced to pay tributes to Rome. The Hellenes, whom Teuta's pirates had also harassed, were so grateful that they admitted the Romans to the Isthmian Games and the Eleusinian Mysteries.

The rude tribes of Illyria were far from destroyed, however; in the difficult mountains and valleys of the interior, Teuta's successor Scerdilaidas had gathered his forces and was aided by Philip V of Macedonia. In 219 the Romans sent a second naval expedition that, after a protracted war, conquered the whole Balkan Peninsula. The last Illyrian king, Genthius, surrendered in 168 B.C. (or 165 B.C.).

Suggested Reading:

(1) Langer, William L. *An Encyclopedia of World History*. Boston: Houghton Mifflin Company, 1980. p. 99.
(2) Kinder, Hermann and Werner Hilgemann. *The Anchor Atlas of World History*, Vol. I. Trans. Ernest A. Menze. Garden City: Anchor/Doubleday, 1974. p. 81.
(3) www:albanian.com)

Thatcher, Margaret (Hilda)

Prime minister of Great Britain (1979-1990)

She was born Hilda Roberts in 1925, the daughter of Alfred Roberts, one-time mayor of Grantham, Lincolnshire. She attended Somerville College, Oxford, where she received a B.S. degree in chemistry and M.A. in law, specializing in taxation. She worked as a research chemist from 1947 to 1951. In 1951 she married Denis Thatcher; the couple had one son and twin daughters. She was called to the bar in 1953 and elected to Parliament six years later. After holding a number of political offices, in 1970 she became Leader of the Opposition, and four years later succeeded Edward Heath as Leader of the Tories. In May 1979 the conservatives won the election and Mrs. Thatcher, who belongs to the right wing of the conservative party, became the first woman in history to serve as Britain's prime minister. She has since become Britain's longest continuously serving prime minister in 160 years, and the longest serving leader in Western Europe. When Margaret Thatcher came into office, former deputy prime minister Lord William Whittlaw said, "England had reached an economic and social equivalent of Dunkirk." A breakdown in public services, labor unrest and industrial decline plagued the country. By and large, Ms. Thatcher's ultra-conservative economic moves reached far into the future. Once asked what she had changed in Britain, she answered, "Everything." Preaching free market, private enterprise, the value of hard work, self-discipline and thrift, she made respectable in Britain the spirit of capitalism which elsewhere in the world had become synonymous with greed and exploitation. However, for all her positive economic impact, a Gallup survey taken on the eve of her tenth year in office concluded that after Edward Heath, she was the least popular of English leaders. The survey found public perception that under Thatcher's rule there was more poverty, selfishness, greed, and crime in Britain. Her attempt at censorship of criticism of her administration was widely condemned, both at home and abroad. Too, the alleged business activities of her son Mark tainted the waning years of her administration. As early as 1984 she sent him to America when reports surfaced that he had made a career of questionable, perhaps illegal dealings. He was reported to have made his first fortune of some $18 million by parlaying his mother's position into becoming middleman in a controversial $30 billion deal to sell British arms to Saudi Arabia. Although Margaret Thatcher would later maintain that the arms deal was proper, private reports held that she was "heartbroken."

On November 22, 1990, urged by Conservative advisors, Margaret Thatcher resigned, throwing her support to John Major, who was elected her successor. However, the press's uncovering of her son's activities during and immediately after her term continued to throw a shadow across her record. The younger Thatcher had risen to director of Emergency Networks, which allegedly deducted $3 million in taxes from its employees' paychecks but failed to pass the money on to the government. Also pending were lawsuits alleging that the company pocketed medical insurance premiums as well. He next became involved with Ameristar Fuels Corporation which filed for bankruptcy and was sold in 1995, with four senior financial managers of the company being charged with serious malpractice. In 1996 the younger Thatcher faced trial for tax evasion.

Suggested Reading:

(1) Junor, Penny. *Margaret Thatcher: Wife, Mother, Politician*. London: Sidgwick & London, 1983.
(2) Baum, Julian, "Sizing up a Decade of British Radicalism." *The Christian Science Monitor*. 4 May 1989: 1-2.
(3) "The Sleaze Factor" *World Press Review*. December 1994: 27.
(4) "Sinking Son" *World Press Review*. June 1995: 43.

Theodolinda (or Theodelinda)

Queen, ruler of Lombards briefly (A.D. 590), regent of Lombards (A.D. 616-622)

The daughter of Duke Garibold of Bavaria, in ca. 590 she married King Authari, Lombard king from A.D. 584 to 590. When Authari died shortly after their marriage, the nobles of Lombard allowed Theodolinda to choose a new husband who would then also be king. She selected a Thuringian, Agilulf, duke of Turin. In 602 the couple had a son, Adaloald, who acceded to the throne when his father died in 616, and for whom Theodolinda was regent during his minority. A devout Catholic, she used her influence to help Catholicism triumph over Arianism in northern Italy. Theodolinda and Agilulf also had a daughter, Gundeberga, who married the Arian Rothari (Rother of legend), duke of Brescia, who ruled the Arians from 636 to 652 and who allowed the Catholic heirarchy to be reestablished in his kingdom. In 622 Theodolinda's son came of age, but shortly afterwards, in 624, he went berserk, went on a killing rampage, and murdered twelve Lombard nobles. He was deposed and later poisoned (c. 626). At that time, Theodolinda, who had devoted her life to religion and good works, retired in sorrow and died two years later.

Suggested Reading:

(1) Previté-Orton, C. W. *The Shorter Cambridge Medieval History.* Cambridge: Cambridge University press, 1982. vol. 1. *The Later Roman Empire.* p. 220.
(2) Gibbon, Edward. *The Decline and Fall of the Roman Empire.* Chicago: Encuclopedia Britannica Press, 1952. vol. 1, p. 607. vol. 2, pp. 107, 630.
(3) Langer, William L., ed. *World History.* Boston: Houghton Mifflin, 1980. p. 165.

Theophano

Regent of Germany (A.D. 984-991)

Although historians have called her one of the greatest women in world history, they do not agree on her history. She was either the daughter of the Eastern Roman Emperor Romanus II, ruler from 959 to 963, and his wife Theophano, or the niece or grandniece of Emperor John Tzimisces, ruler from 969 to 976, who had a licentious affair with Romanus' wife, Theophano. In ca. 972 she married Otto II, who ruled the German Empire from 973 to 983. In 980 they had a son, Otto III, who succeeded his father at age three upon Otto II's death of a fever. Immediately revolts flared up among the Slavs on one side and the Danes and Franks on another, all intent upon wresting power from the throne. It was the genius of Theophano that saved the empire. In her castle at Quedlinburg she maintained a brilliant court attended by scholars of great note. She presided over a magnificent diet at Nijmwegen, attended by numerous princes. Her forceful and intelligent presence quelled the dissent, which did not surface again until after her death in 991. She was succeeded in the regency by her mother-in-law, Adelaide.

Suggested Reading:

(1) Ostrogorsky. George. *History of the Byzantine State*. New Brunswick, NJ: Rutgers University Press, 1969, pp. 296, 314.
(2) Gibbon, Edward. *The Decline and Fall of the Roman Empire*. Chicago: Encylopedia Britannica Press, 1951. vol. 2, p. 320.
(3) Löwenstein, Prince Hubertus Zu. *A Basic History of Germany* Bonn: Inter Nationes, 1964. pp. 21-24.
(4) Langer, William L., ed. *World History*. Boston: Houghton Mifflin, 1980. pp. 176, 195, 230-231.

Dowager Duchess Theuderata di Friuli of Benevento (Italy)

Regent of Benevento, Italy (677-ca. 682)

When her husband, Romuald I died, she was first regent for their oldst son, Grimoald and then for the second, Gisulf I from 680 He died in 705.

Tymoshenko, Yulia

Prime Minster of Ukraine (2005, 2007-)

Yulia Tymoshenko was born on November 27th, 1960 in Dnepropetrovsk, Ukraine (then SSR), the daughter of Ludmila Nikolaevna Telegina and Vladimir Abramovich Grigean (her father left the family when Yulia was three years old).After leaving the school in 1979, she joined the economic faculty of Dnepropetrovsk State University to study cybernetic engineering. That same year, while studying there, she married Oleksandr Tymoshenko, the son of a mid-level Communist Party bureaucrat. Their daughter Eugenia was born in 1980.

Yulia began rising through a number of positions under the Komosomol, the official Soviet Communist youth organization. In 1984, she graduated from Dnepropetrovsk State University with a degree in economics and went on to earn a candidate degree—equilavent of a PhD—in economics. Since then, she has written about 50 papers.

In 1991 she became managing director of Ukrainian Oil Corporation, which laid the foundation for a new company, United Energy Systems of Ukraine. (UESU)

She moved into politics in 1996, winning a seat in the Ukranian Parliament (Verkhovna Rada) with a record 92.3% of the vote. She was re-elected in 1998 and became Chair of the Budget Committee. From 1999 to 2001, she was Deputy Prime Minister for Fuel and Energy in Viktor Yushchenko's cabinet. In January 2001 she was fired by President Leonid Kuchma during a conflict with industrialists. In 2002 she was re-elected as a member of Parliament. She was dubbed as one of the most beautiful women to ever enter politics by *The Globe and Mail* in 2001. In January 2005 she was appointed Acting Prime Minister of Ukraine under President Viktor Yushcenko. Two weeks later she was ratified by Verkhovna Rada (Parliament) by an overwhelming majority. But her government was dismissed by President Yushcenko during a live television address to the nation. She eventually formed a coalition with Our Ukraine—People's Self-Defense Bloc, also associated with the Orange Revolution. In December of 2007 she was once again elected Prime Minister.

Suggested Reading:

(1) Westcott, Kathryn. "The queen of Ukraine's image machine." BBC News, May 10, 2007

(2) MacDonald, Elizabeth; Chana R. Schoenberger. "The 100 most Powerful Women." *Forbes.* July 28, 2005,

(3) Feifer, Gregory. "Ukraine's Tymoshenko Likely Prime Minister." NPR, October 2, 2007.

(4) Biography of Yulia Tymoshenko: Personal Web Site of Yulia Tymoshenko.

(5) Olearchyk, Roman; Stefan Wagstyl. "A tough and populist maverisk." *Financial Times,* October 2, 2007.

Europe Section U

Ulrica Eleanora

Queen of Sweden (1718-1720)

She was born in 1688, the daughter of King Charles XI, ruler of Sweden from 1660 to 1697, and Ulrica Eleanora of Denmark. Her brother, Charles XII, succeeded their father on the throne. She was betrothed to Frederick of Hesse-Cassel, a Calvinist, but refused to marry him until her brother assured her the marriage would not jeopardize her accession to the throne in that Catholic country. The couple married in 1715 but remained childless. In 1718, while on a military expedition to Norway, Charles XII was shot and killed, and Ulrica Eleanora acceded to the throne. Charles Frederick, son of her late older sister Hedvig Sofia, challenged her right to rule. However, the riksdag accepted her reign on the condition that a new constitution be drawn up. This new document provided for a joint rule by the monarchy and the council when the riksdag was not in session. When the riksdag was sitting, principal decisions would be made by a secret committee made up of nobles, clergy and burghers. Peasants were to have a voice in matters concerning taxes. This new constitution ushered in Sweden's so-called Age of Freedom. Ulrica Eleanora, being completely devoted to her husband, bowed to his ambitions in 1720 by abdicating in his favor. She died in 1741.

(1) Derry, T. K. *A History of Scandinavia*. Minneapolis: University of Minnesota Press, 1979. pp. 159, 163, 166, 178.
(2) Langer, William L., ed. *World History*. Boston: Houghton Mifflin, 1980. pp. 441, 508.

Urraca, Doña

Queen, ruler of León and Castile united (1109-1126)

Doña Urraca was born c. 1081, the daughter of Constance and Alfonso VI, King of Leon from 1065 and King of Castile from 1072. She first married Raymond of Burgundy, a French knight who had come to participate in the Wars of Reconquista. She and Raymond had two sons before he died sometime prior to 1109. Her father spent most of his time fighting the Muslims. In his last battle with the Almoravids in 1108, his only son and Urraca's brother, Sancho, was killed. Alfonso immediately began making arrangements for his widowed daughter, who would now inherit the throne, to marry someone on whom he could count to continue to fight the Muslims. When her father died the next year, Urraca, still a widow, inherited both thrones, Leon and Castile. She bowed to her father's wishes and married King Alfonso I (the Battler) of Aragon, whom she detested. Evidence shows that she ruled her own kingdom had no intention of giving up her authority to him. Their constant scrapping kept the government in a turmoil and even curtailed the progress of the Cross in Spain during the First Crusade. Eventually she sent him back to Aragon via annulment. Neither her lover, the Count of Lara, nor her confidant, Archbishop Bernardo of Toledo, held sway over her decisions. Before her death, to assure that the throne did not fall into the hands of the greedy Argonese, she had her son, Alfonso VII, crowned with her.

Suggested Reading:

(1) Reilly, Kevin. B. *The Kingdom of León-Castilla under Queen Urraca 1109-1126*. Princeton: Princeton University Press, 1982.
(2) Runciman, Steven. *A History of the Crusades*. Cambridge: Cambridge University Press, 1952. vol.2, *The Kingdom of Jerusalem*. pp. 249-250.
(3) Langer, William L., ed. *World History*. Boston: Houghton Mifflin 1980. p. 250.

Europe Section V

Dr. Vaira Vīķe-Freiberga

President of Latvia (1999-)

Vaira Vike, the first woman president of Latvia, was born on December 1, 1937 in Riga, Latvia. Her parents were World War II refugees who left Soviet-controlled Eastern European in 1945 and lived in West Germany, Morocco, then Canada while Vaira was growing up. She studied at the University of Toronto and received a PhD in psychology from McGill University in 1965. For thirty-three years, from 1965 to 1998, she worked as a professor of psychology at Université de Montréal. During this time, she served as Vice-Chair of the Science Council of Canada and as president of several social science professional organizations. She was also active in the Latvian community in Canada. A large part of her research had focused on Latvian folk literature.

In 1998, Vaira Vīķe-Freiberga returned to Latvia to head the Latvian Institute, which is devoted to promoting Latvian awareness abroad. The following year, after the Latvian Parliament was unable to elect a President on the first round, she was drafted and became the country's first female President. Her approval rating was very high, ranging between 70% to 85%. She was easily reelected in 2003.

During her tenure, Latvia remained active in NATO and joined the European Union in 2004. She supported U.S. policy in Iraq. On numerous occasions, including an address to the joint session of US Congress, she called for Russia to admit to the Soviet occupation of the three Baltic nations.

In April 2005, United Nations Secretary-General Kifo Annan named Vīķe-Freiberga as a member of his team of global political leaders helping to promote his comprehensive reform agenda.

In September 2006 she was awarded an honorary doctorate by the University of Ottawa, and on September 16 of that year, the three Baltic States jointly announced Vīķe-Freiberga's candidacy for the post of United

Nations Secretary-General. When she addressed the General Assembly, she pledged that she would face "the challenges posed by the UN reform and promoting human rights, freedom and democracy, including gender equality". However, Russia, a permanent member of the UN Security Council, indicated it would not support any Eastern European candidate.

Vīķe-Freiberga was believed to enjoy the support of the White House. It was said that Riga was chosen to host the NATO Summit in 2006 partly thanks to her relationships with President Bush and Condoleeza Rice. These relationships may, on the other hand, have worked against her election as UN Secretary-General.

Vaira Vīķe-Freiberga is married to Imants Freibergs, a professor of computer sciences at Université du Québec à Montréal, and current president of the Latvian Information and Communications Technology Association. The couple met at a gathering of expatriate Latvians and were married at a low-key ceremony in Toronto. They have two children, Kārlis and Indra, but no grandchildren.

Suggested Reading:

(1)   Official Website of the President of Latvia

Victoria

Queen, ruler of the British Empire (1837-1901)

She was born Alexandrina Victoria, in 1819, the daughter of Edward, Duke of Kent, and Princess Victore of Saxe-Coborg. Her father died eight months later and she was reared by her mother, who would have been her regent but for the fact that King William IV of Hanover, Victoria's uncle and ruler since 1830, died shortly after her eighteenth birthday. Although Victoria inherited the crown of England, the crown of Hanover was barred to her by Salic law and went instead to her uncle Ernest, duke of Cumberland. For the first two and one half years of her reign she remained unmarried, vacillating about becoming betrothed to her cousin, Prince Albert of Saxe-Coburg-Gotha. She eventually married him, and thus began one of the happiest royal marriages on record. The couple had nine children who married into all the royal houses of Europe: Victoria married German Emperor Frederick III; English King Edward VII married Alexandra of Denmark; Alice married Louis of Hesse-Darmstadt; Alfred married Marie of Russia; Helena married Christian of Schleswig-Holstein; Louis married the Duke of Argyll; Arthur married Louise of Prussia; Leopold married Helena of Woldech; and Beatrice married Prince Henry of Battenburg. Not the most supportive of mothers, she often openly criticized her oldest son Edward in terms which would have crushed a lesser boy or man. Albert died of typhoid in 1861, and Victoria mourned for him for the next 40 years. Her long association with Benjamin Disraeli, the Conservative prime minister, and her grating relationship with his rival, William Ewart Gladstone, the Liberal leader, dominated her political concerns for many years. In a brilliant bit of public relations strategy in 1876, Disraeli secured for her the title of "Empress of India," and she became the symbol of the national mood and enthusiasm for expansion and empire building. By the very length of her tenure during a time of unprecedented growth, she outlived her detractors and gained the devotion of the nation. She celebrated both a Golden Jubilee in 1887 and a Diamond Jubilee in 1897. By the time of her death in 1901, she had restored, as Britain's longest-reigning monarch, both dignity and respect to the crown and affection for its wearer. She was succeeded by her eldest son, Edward VII.

Suggested Reading:

(1) Longford, Elizabeth. *Queen Victoria: Born to Succeed.* New York: Harper & Row, 1914.

(2) Fulford, Roger. *Hanover to Windsor.* Glasgow: Fontana/Collins, 1981. pp. 38-113.

(3) Ridley, Jasper. *Napoleon III and Eugenie.* New York: Viking press, 1980. pp. 579-588, 603-617, 622-623.

(4) Hudson, M. E. and Mary Clark. *Crown of a Thousand Years.* New York: Crown Publishing, 1978. pp. 132-135.

Vigdis

See Finnebogadottir, Vigdis

Vittoria

Duchess, ruler of Urbino (1623)

Urbino was a dukedom in central Italy, famous for its majolica, a tin-glazed earthenware. Vittoria was the heir of Duke Federigo Ubaldo (1621-1623), of the family of Della Rovere. She married Ferdinando II de'Medici, who in 1627 became grand duke of Tuscany, and who was a brilliant inventor of scientific instruments and a patron of the sciences. Vittoria acceded to the throne of Urbino upon the untimely death of Duke Ubaldo in 1623. At her death in 1631, Urbino was incorporated by reversion into the Papal States by Pope Urban VIII. In 1680 Urbino became part of the kingdom of Italy.

Suggested Reading:

(1) Egan, Edward W. et. al., eds. *Kings, Rulers, and Statesmen*. New York: Sterling Publishing, 1976. p. 277.

(1) Langer, William L., ed. *World History*. Boston: Houghton Mifflin, 1980. p. 425.

Europe Section W

Wallström, Margot Elisabeth

Swedish politician, European Commissioner for Institutional Relations and Communication Streategy (2004-), Vice President of Barroso Commission (2008)

She was born on September 28, 1954 in Skellefteå, Sweden, where she graduated fromhigh school in 1973. She did not receive a higher education. As with many women who maintain a home, her career started and stopped several times. She married and had two children. She entered politics at an early age. From 1974 to 1977 she was Ombudsman for the Swedish Social Democratic Youth League. From 1977 to 1979 she worked as a junior accountant at Alfa Savings Bank in Karlstad. In 1979 she stood for Parliament on the Swedish Social Democratic ticket. She won and remained a member of Parliament until 1985. In 1986 she became senior accountant for Alfa Savings Bank in Karlstad and served until 1987. In 1988 she returned to service in the Swedish government as Minister for Civil Affairs, which included Consumer Affairs, Women and Youth, serving until 1991. In 1993 she became a member of the Executive Committee of the Swedish Social Democratic Party, where she remains. Also, from 1993 to 1994 she was CEO of TV Värmland, the Regional Televisional Network of Värmland, a province on Sweden's west-central coast. In 1994 she became Minister for Culture, serving until 1996, when she became Minister for Social Affairs, serving until 1998. From 1998 to 1999 she was Executive Vice-President of Worldview Global Media in Colombo, Sri Lanka. From 1999 to 2004 she served as a Member of the European Commission for the Environment. It was because of her experience on this Commission that she was chosen in 2007 to write the Foreword for the Swedish translation of Al Gore's *An Inconvenient Truth*. From 2004 forward, she has served as First Vice President of the European Commission for Institutional Relations and Communication Strategy. In December 2006, Wallström was voted the most popular woman in Sweden, beating royals and athletes in a survey carried out by ICA-kuriren and Sifo. As of November 16, 2007, she became Chair of the Council of Women World Leaders Ministerial Initiative, replacing former U.S. Secretary of State Madeleine K. Albright.

Suggested Reading:

(!)   Wallstrom's cv: *www.ec.europa.eu.*
(2)   Sweden Loves Reinfeldt and Wallström." *The Local,* December 29, 2006.

Wieczorek-Zeul, Heidemarie

German Cabinet Minister (1998-)

She was born November 21, 1942 in Frankfort am Main. She joined the Social Democratic party in 1965 and is in the left wing of the party. She is often referred to as "Red Heidi." From 1974 to 1977 she chaired the youth organization of the Young Socialists. When Gerhard Schröder became Chancellor in 1998, she served as Minister for Economic Cooperation and Development. After his defeat to Angela Merkel in 2005, Weiczorek-Zeul retained her office as a member of Merkel's Grand Coalition Cabinet. In July 2006, Charlotte Knobloch, head of the Central Council of Jews in Germany, demanded her resignation after she had called Israeli use of cluster bombs "totally unacceptable under international law." In 2009 she took on Pope Benedict XVI after he voiced the opinion that the use of condoms did nothing to prevent the contraction of AIDS.

Suggested Reading:

(1)   *http://www.bmz.de/en/ministryleadershipzeul/lebenslaufBMin.pdf.*
(2)   "German Social Democrats Leader Quits Over Lie." *The New York Times.* April 5, 1993.

Wilhelmina

Queen, ruler of The Netherlands (1890-1949)

Wilhemina was born in 1880, the daughter of King William ruler of the Netherlands from 1849 to 1890, and his second wife Emma of

Waldeck-Pyrmont. When her father died (1890), she became, at the age of ten, queen of The Netherlands under the regency of Queen Emma. She was inaugurated (not crowned, because the crown belongs to the Dutch people) in 1898. The liberal ministry passed much social legislation during the first two years of her majority, including bills calling for improved housing, compulsory education for children, and accident insurance. In 1901 she married Duke Henry of Mecklenburg-Schwerin. The couple had a daughter, Juliana, born in 1909. Wilhelmina kept her country neutral during World War I, and after the German defeat, Kaiser Wilhelm sought and received refuge in The Netherlands. In 1920, the Dutch refused an Allied demand for his surrender. He lived in retirement, first at Amerongen, then at Doorn, where he died in 1941. Ironically, the Dutch kindness to the ex-ruler of Germany did not prevent the Nazis under Adolph Hitler from overrunning The Netherlands in May 1940. May was to become a pivotal month for the queen for the rest of the decade. She escaped with her family and the government to London the day before The Netherlands formally surrendered, May 14, 1940. Throughout the war, Queen Wilhelmina sent messages from England of hope for her people over Radio Orange. She returned May 3, 1945, after the Nazi surrender to find that her country had suffered extensive damage. Imminent large-scale famine was averted only by aid from the Allies. In May 17, 1948, the countries of The Netherlands, Belgium, Luxembourg, France and Britain signed a 50-year mutual assistance pact in Brussels. Four months later, due to ill health, Wilhelmina abdicated in favor of her daughter, Juliana. She lived in retirement at her palace, Het Loo, until her death in 1962 at the age of 82.

Suggested Reading:

(1) Langer, William L., ed. *World History*. Boston: Houghton Mifflin, 1980. pp. 674, 986, 1136, 1172, 1179.
(2) Shirer, William L. *The Rise and Fall of the Third Reich*. New York: Simon & Schuster, 1960. pp. 561, 640, 652, 721-723, 729.

Europe Section Y

Yelena Glinskaya (or Helen Glinski, Glinskij or Glinskaia)

Grand Princess, regent of Russia (1533-1538)

She was born ca. 1506 of a noble Tartar family, the niece of Prince Michael Glinski (Glinskij), a converted Orthodox Lithuanian magnate, who, during a dispute between contenders for the Polish-Lithuanian throne, Alexander I and Sigismund I, had switched sides, deserted, and moved to Russia. In c. 1529 Yelena became the second wife of Grand Prince Vasily III (Basil III), ruler of Russia from 1505 to 1533, whose marriage to his first wife Solomonia had been childless. Yelena bore Vasily two sons. Their firstborn son, born in 1530, became Ivan IV (later called the Terrible), ruler of Russia at the age of three when Vasily died. Grand Princess Yelena ruled in Ivan's name, disregarding the boyar duma and relying instead on her uncle, Prince Michael, until his death. Then she turned for counsel to her young lover, Ivan Ovchina-Telepnev-Oblensky, sparking unfounded rumors that Ivan was his son. Her late husband Basil III had engaged in territorial disputes with Poland-Lithuania without receiving asked-for assistance of the Hapsburgs. The Russians had made substantial gain in that ten-year conflict, acquiring the key city of Smolensk in 1514. In 1533 Yelena sent embassies both to Ferdinand I, king of both Hungary and Bohemia, and his brother, Holy Roman Emperor Charles V, hoping to bolster friendship with the Hapsburgs in case of another conflict with Poland-Lithuania. The dispute did flare again over the ownership of Smolensk: in 1534-1536 another war resulted in no gain for the Poles. Russia was able to keep possession of Smolensk. Meanwhile, the boyars families of Sujskij and Belskij fought among themselves for the privilege of then overpowering Yelena's regency and assuming it themselves. In 1538 Yelena died suddenly, possibly of poisoning, allegedly at the provocation of the boyars. Ivan IV imprisoned Yelena's advisor Oblensky and his sister, although he did not formally accuse them of implementing the murder plot.

Suggested Reading:

(1) Riasanovsky, Nicholas V. *A History of Russia*. Oxford: Oxford University Press, 1963, 1993. p. 143.
(2) Dvornik, Francis. *The Slavs in European History and Civilization*. New Brunswick, NJ: Rutgers University Press, 1962. pp. 273, 343, 378, 439, 442.
(3) Langer, William L., ed. *World History*. Boston: Houghton Mifflin, 1980. pp. 442, 444, 446.

Yolande de Bourgogne

Countess, ruler of Nevers (1266-1296)

She was the daughter of Countess Mahaut II de Bourbon (ruled Nevers 1257-1266) and Eudes de Bourgogne. She inherited the rule of Nevers when her mother died in 1266. She first married Jean Tristan de France, count of Valois, and after his death, she married Robert de Dampierre. She was succeeded in 1296 by Louis I of Flanders.

Suggested Reading:

(1) Egan, Edward W. et. al., eds. *Kings, Rulers, and Statesmen*. New York: Sterling Publishing Company, 1976. p. 160.

Europe Section Z

Zypries, Brigitte

German Minister of Justice (2002-)

Brigitte Zypries was born November 16, 1953 in Kassel, Germany. She studied law in Gießen from 1972 to 1977. She worked at Gießen University until 1985, when she became Assistant Head of Division at the State Chancellery of Hesse until 1988. She is a member of the Social Democratic party of Germany. After two years as a member of the academic staff at the Federal Constitutional Court, she was named Head of Division of the State Chancellery of Lower Saxony. In 1995 she became Head of the Department of the State Chancellery of Lower Saxony, a position she maintained through 1997. From 1998 to 2002, she served as State Secretary and was active in the Ministry for Women, Labour and Social Affairs of Lower Saxony. In the fall of 2002, she became Federal Minister of Justice in the Cabinet of Angela Merkel.

Suggested Reading:

(1) "Brigitte Zyprie's blog"
(2) "Madeleine paedophile gang theory 'is likely'." *The Scotsman*, March 6, 2007.

PART II

Women Leaders in the Western Hemisphere

Western Hemisphere Introduction

Central America accounts for the earliest documented women rulers in the Western Hemisphere. In the Nineteenth Century an American explorer and his wife, Augustus and Alice Le Plongeon, claimed to have deciphered Mayan hieroglyphs and unearthed the history of a Queen Moo, but only one other student of Mayan culture supported their claims, and they are generally thought to be spurious. (1)

Legitimate queens of the Maya have been discovered, however: Lady Zac Zuc and Lady Kanal-Ikal, both called "King of Palenque", and Lady Wac-Chanil-Ahau, Naranjo, all of whose activities are well-documented in glyphs. (2) What makes these historical records particularly interesting is the number of parallels of Maya culture with those much older ones in North Africa and the Middle East.

Dr. Hugh B. Fox, Professor Emeritus in the Department of American Thought and Languages at Michigan State University and author of six books on pre-Columbian cultures, describes an astounding find he made in the Musée de L'Homme in Paris that started him on a journey of discovery: a Mochica Indian pot from Peru bearing iconic symbols that were identical to some he had seen at the Louvre the day before on a Greek Sicilian pot. This led to a study of the connections between so-called New World art and language and that of the Old World, his conclusion being that the ancient Americas was the center of Old World myth. He found an 1871 book in French by Brazilian scholar Vincent Fidel Lopez linking Quechua, language of the Inca, with Sanskrit, and a 1953 book by A.H. and R. Verrill which ties Quechua to Sumerian, the ancient language of Gilgamesh.

Fox's research unearths a Phoenician presence in the New World from at least some time around 150 B.C. The Mochicas, he believes, are transplanted Hellenized Carthaginians. The Mochica "Indians" as a Phoenician colony becomes much less dramatic when we realize that there were Black Africans in the New World among the Olmecs and that the Maya god of merchants, Ek Chuah, is a Black African.

The Phoenicians were also in Mexico. According to Fox's contention, the Yope on the Mexican west coast were really Phoenicians. The Aztec spring god, Kipe Totec, is ultimately derived from the Phoenician god Adonis. The Aztec language is full of Greek and Latin loan-words. One of Fox's books shows a Mediterranean/Middle Eastern link to the New World dating back to at least 3,000 B.C. There are also links with the Far East, meaning that our world is much more ethnically mixed than we have believed. (3)

Is it any wonder, then, that Maya would have built pyramids much as did the Egyptians, and that, like "Pharaoh" Hapshetsut, among others, two of the Maya "Kings" were women? Another Maya woman ruled who did not take the title of "King," and there may yet be others discovered as more of the glyphs are deciphered.

These Maya rulers did not come to the throne as consorts or regents, but inherited the crown, much like their European counterparts. After the appearance of European colonizers in the New World, few women have inherited power, and even fewer have been elected to leadership positions at any level.

There have been exceptions. Unlike the situation in the Northern Hemisphere, several women have successfully traveled the road to the presidential palaces of South America on their own merit.

Prior to the 1998 presidential elections in Venezuela, the mayor of the Caracas municipality of Chacao led in opinion polls testing voter reactions to potential candidates. That the mayor happened also to be a former Miss Universe was the ingredient that made this story particularly newsworthy. Irene Sáez Conde, Miss Universe of 1981, had served with distinction for five years as mayor of one of the country's wealthiest districts. An independent who formed her own political party, she was being courted by both the country's major parties as the most serious contender if she chose to run—despite that she was female, tall, blond, and beautiful. Or perhaps, because of it. Who can forget that the dashingly handsome Peruvian novelist Mario Vargas Llosa stole the hearts of Peruvian women voters who hadn't a clue as to his political positions?

There have been women presidents the Western Hemisphere: Bachelet in Chile, Tejada in Bolivia, [Isabel] Perón and Fernandez de Kirchner in Argentina, Jagan in Guyana, Chamorro in Nicaragua, Pascal-Trouillot in Haiti. In the former kingdom of Brazil, it was a woman (Isabel) who freed 700,000 slaves. Women have served as prime ministers of Dominica (Charles), Haiti (Werleigh), Guyana (Jagan, the same one who later served as president), Canada (Campbell), and the Netherlands Antilles (de

Jongh-Elhage). Three governors-general have been female (Sauvé of Canada, Barrow of Barbados and Gordon of Belize).

In the northern portion of the Western Hemisphere, the first woman to become a United States presidential candidate was Victoria Claflin Woodhull, who ran in 1872 on the Equal Rights Party and was soundly defeated. (4) Her more prominent opponents were Horace Greeley and the incumbent, Ulysses S. Grant. Other than Kim Campbell of Canada, the best the United States has been able to manage are one Speaker of the House (Pelosi) and three Secretaries of State (Albright, Rice, and Clinton), but more than a few governors. Even prior to Arizona's statehood in 1912, women played a role in governing Arizona. Women were part of its constitutional convention and were allowed to vote years before women got the right to vote nationally. During more electoral contests in the state, there has been no mention of gender. Instead, the candidates touted their considerable experience and proven leadership as elected officials.

Native American groups have occasionally had women leaders. In the 1980s two large tribes, the Seminoles and Cherokees, were headed by women (Betty Mae Jumper and Wilma Mankiller), and history records at least four others.

At the close of the Twentieth Century, many tribes had begun electing presidents, chairpersons, and governors instead of chiefs, and at the time of this writing, an enormous number are women: Southern Paiutes: Evelyn James, president; Oneida: Deborah Doxtator, chairperson; Etowah band, Green Mountain Ani Yunwiwa: Ven Dhyani Ywahoo, Chief; Aleut: Rena J. Kudrin, president; Alturas: Norma Jean Garcia, chairperson; Aroonstook band of Micmac tribe: Mary Philbrook, tribal leader; Benton Paiute: Rose Marie Bahe, chairperson; Big Pine Reservation: Velma Jones, chairperson; Blue Lake Rancheria: Sylvia Daniels, chairperson; Buena Vista Rancheria: Lucille Lucero, chairperson; Cahuilla Band of Mission Tribe: Lois Candelaria, chairperson; Carson Colony: Sherri Johnson, chairperson; Chehlis: Mena Medina, Chairperson; Chuathbaluk: Darlene Peterson, Chief; Cortina Rancheria: Mary Norton, chairperson; Cow Creek Band of Umpqua Tribe: Sue Shaffer, chairperson; Coyote Valley reservation: Doris Renick, chairperson; Crow: Clara Nomee, chairperson; Dillingham Village: Sally H. Smith, president; Eastern Band of Cherokee: Joyce Conseen Dugan, Principal Chief; Evansville Village: Rhonda Musser, Chief; Eyak: Agnes Nichols, president; Fort McDermitt Tribal Council: Helen Snapp, chairperson; Fort Mojave Tribal Council: Nora Garcia, chairperson; Fort Sill Apache: Mildred Cleghorn, chairperson; Houlton Band of Maliseet Tribe:

Clair Sabattis, chairperson; Iqurmuit: Mary Belkoff, president; Jackson Rancheria: margaret Dalton, chairperson; Kaibab Paiute: Margaret Dalton, chairperson; Kaibab Paiute: Gloria Bulletts-Benson, chairperson; Kaw: Wanda Stone, chairperson; Kenaitze: Clare Swan, tribal chair; King Cove Agdaogux: Della Trimple, president; La Jolla band of Mission tribe: Doris J. Magante, chairperson; La Posta band of Mission tribe: Gwendolyn Parada, chairperson; Lone Pine Reservation: Sandra Jefferson Yonge, chairperson; Lovelock tribal council: Deanna Austin, chairperson; Lower Elwha: Carla J. Elofson, chairperson; Lytton Rancheria: Suzanne Steele-Tiger, chairperson; Manley Hot Springs tribe: Dixie Dayo, president; Manzanita: Frances Shaw, chairperson; Mentasta Lake tribe: Kathrun Johns, president; Mornogo band of Mission tribe: Adelaide Presley, chairperson; Muckleshoot: Virginia Cross, chairperson; Napamute: Agnes E. Charles, president; Belkofski: Maggie Kenezuroff, president; Cantwell: Ruby John, president; Chistochina: Evelyn Beeter, president; native Village of Council of Nome: Barbara Gray, president; Crooked Creek: Marie Inman, president; Gakona: Linda Tyone, president; Piamuit: Janes Napoleon, president; Solomon: Rose Ann Timbers, president; St. Michael Native Village: Susanna Horn, president; White Mountain Native Village: Dorothy Barr, president; Yakutat: Nettie Vale, president; Oneida: Deborah J. Dozator, chairman; Pauma band of Mission tribe; Florence Lofton, chairperson; Pinoleville: Leona Williams, chairperson; Pitka's Point: Ruth Riley, president; Ponca tribe of Nebraska: Deb Wright, chairperson; Port Graham Native Village: Eleanor McMullen, president; Pueblo of Sandia: Inez Baca, Governor; Qualingin tribe of Unalaska: Harriet Berikoff, president; Quinault Indian nation: Pearl Capoeman-Baller, chairperson; Redding Rancheria: Barbara Murphy, chairperson; Redwood Valley Rancheria: Rita Hoel, chairperson; Rohnerville Rancheria: Aileen Bowie, chairperson; Sac and Fox of the Missouri Tribal council: Sandra Keo, chairperson; San Pasqual: Diana Martinez, chairperson; Saxman: Shristine Collison, president; Shingle Springs Rancheria: Elsie Shilin, chairperson; Shismaref: Stella Weyiouanna, president: Shoonaq' tribe of Kodiak: Margaret Roberts, president; Siletz: Dolores Pigsley, chairperson; Sisseton-Wahpeton Sioux: Lorraine Rousseau, chairperson; Stockbridge Munsee tribal council: Leah Miller-Heath, president; Torres-Martinez band of Mission tribe: Helen Jose, chairperson; Trinidad Rancheria: Carol Ervin, chairperson; Twenty-nine Palms band of Mission Indians: June Mike, chairperson; Upper Sioux: Lorraine Gouge, chairperson; Ute: Judy Knight-Frank, chairperson; Village of Eagle: Ruth Ridley, First Chief; Kalskag: Annie Lou Williams, president; Ouzinkie: Angelina Campfield, president; Sleetmute:

Jane Zaukan, president; Walker River Paiute: Anita Collins, chairperson; Wampanoag: Beverly Wright, chairperson. (5)

The charge of these chiefs, presidents, and chairpersons is usually primarily the economic betterment of the tribe. Evelyn James' task, for example, was obtaining from the neighboring Navajo tribe by peaceful means Paiute lands which the U.S. government assigned to the Navajo when it expanded the Navajo reservation in the 1930s (6), while Ven Dhyani Ywahoo is the spiritual leader of her tribe charged with the mission to pass on the traditions of her ancestors. (7)

Notes:

(1) Peter Tompkins. *Mysteries of the Mexican Pyramids.* (New York: Harper & Row, 1976), 165-175.

(2) Linda Schele and David Freidel. *A Forest of Kings, The Untold Story of the Ancient Maya.* (New York: Quill/ William Morrow, 1990), 221-225, 227-228, 266, 467, 468, 478.

(3) Hugh B. Fox. *Stairway to the Sun.* San Francisco: Permeable Press, 1996.

(4) "Presidential Trivia" by Harold Faber. *The New York Times Magazine,* October 24, 1984.

(5) Names of current leaders of tribes and Native American nations can be obtained from the World Wide Web.

(6) Matt Kelley, Associated Press. "Land Agreement Would Give Tribe Their Own Land." *Houston Chronicle.* 11 January 1998: 23A.

(7) Ven Dhyani Ywahoo maintains her own website. For more information, contact *sunray@sover.net.*

Western Hemisphere Section A

Abbott, Grace

Social Reformer, planner of U.S. Social Security System (1934-1935)

Grace was born in Grand Island, Nebraska on November 17, 1878. She graduated from Grand Island College in 1898 and taught in the local high school for eight years while doing graduate studies at the University of Nebraska (1902) and the University of Chicago (summer of 1904). In 1907 she moved to Chicago and soon became a resident in Jane Addam's Hull-House. By the time the University of Chicago awarded her doctoral degree in Political Science (1909), Grace had become director of the Immigrants' Protective League. She worked to secure legislation protecting immigrants at Ellis Island, testifying before Congress against immigration restrictions and writing a book, *The Immigrant and the Community* (1917). During 1910-1917 she was on the faculty of what later became known as the University of Chicago's Graduate School of Social Service Administration. In 1917 she joined the staff of the Federal Children's Bureau, where she was responsible enforcement of the Child Labor Act of 1916 until 1918 when it was declared unconstitutional.

During World War I she was an adviser to the War Labor Policies Board and succeeded in having clauses prohibiting child labor written into all government war contracts. After the War, she returned to Illinois (1919) as Director of the Illinois State Immigrants' Commission. In 1921 President Warren G. Harding named her Head of the Children's Bureau, where she was involved in providing federal funds to states for programs in maternal and infant health care. This aid program was ended by Congress in 1929. From 1922 to 1934 she was also an unofficial representative of the United States at the League of Nations Advisory Committee on Traffic in Women and Children.

In 1934 she resigned the Children's Bureau and accepted a professorship in the University of Chicago's School of Social Service Administration, where her sister Edith was Dean. In 1934-1935, as a member of President Franklin D. Roosevelt's Council on Economic Security, Abbott helped plan the Social Security system. She was editor of the *Social Service Review* from 1934-1939. In 1935 and 1937 she served as U.S. delegate to the International Labor Organization. In 1938 she published her two-volume work, *The Child and the State*.

She died on June 19, 1939. In 1941 a collection of her papers was published entitled *From Relief to Social Security*.

Suggested Reading:

(1) McHenry, Robert, ed. *Famous American Women*. Springfield, MA: G & C Merriam Company, 1980, p. 1.

Abzug, Bella

Social activist, Congressperson (1971-1976)

Born Bella Savitsky on July 24, 1920 in the Bronx, New York City, the daughter of poor Russian immigrants. She graduated from Hunter College in 1942 and Columbia University Law School in 1945. While at Columbia she was an editor of the *Columbia Law Review*. She also did graduate studies at the Jewish Theological Seminary. In June of 1945 she married Martin M. Abzug. The couple raised two daughters. In 1947 she was admitted to the New York bar. For the next 23 years her practice consisted primarily of civil rights cases. She also worked for various causes, including peace and disarmament. She was particularly active opposing U.S. involvement in Vietnam. She was famous for her quote, "A woman's place is in the House—the House of Representatives." In 1970 she ran for the 19th Congressional District seat against Leonard Farbstein, a seven-term incumbent, whom she defeated, going on to win in the general election and becoming a member of the 92nd Congress. On her first day in Congress, she broke with tradition on the first day by offering a resolution calling for the immediate withdrawal of U.S. troops from Indochina. In 1976 she gave up her seat to run for the Senate, but she was defeated by Daniel Patrick Moynihan. In September 1977 she ran for the Democratic nomination for mayor of New York and was defeated. In February of 1978 she lost a special election to fill the congressional seat vacated by Mayor Ed Koch. In 1978 President Jimmy Carter named her co-chairman of the National Advisory

Committee on Women, but in January 1979 he dismissed her because of her criticism of the Administration's economic policies. She continued to work for women's causes. In 1986 her great supporter, her husband Martin died. In 1990 she co-founded the Women's Environment and Development Organization and as its president, became active in the United Nations and U.N. conferences, working to empower women around the world. She gave her last speech before the United Nations in March on 1998, and, after a long battle with breast cancer and heart disease, she died soon after, on March 31, 1998.

Suggested Reading:

(1) McHenry, Robert, ed. *Famous American Women.* Springfield, MA: G. & C. Merriman Company, 1980. p. 2.

(2) *www.jewishwomensarchive.org.*

Ajaw, Lady

See K'atun Ajaw

Ahpo-Hel

Co-ruler of Palenque (626-672)

She was the primary of Hanab Pakal (603-683), King of the Mayan empire of Palenque, in present-day Mexico. Some researchers believe that he made her his co-ruler, although this would have been very unusual, unless he were ill or away for an extended period. For the first nine years of their marriage, she had no children, but eventually she bore two sons to carry on the dynasty.

Albright, Madeline

U.S. Secretary of State (1997-2001)

She was born Marie Jana Korbelová on May 15, 1937 in Prague, Czechoslovakia, to Josef and Anna (Speglova) Korbel. She was one of two children; she had a brother, John. Later in her life, she was to follow in the footsteps of her father, who was a Czech diplomat. The family, which was Jewish, converted from Judaism to Roman Catholicism to escape persecution, a fact that Madeline didn't know until years later. Madeline (the French version of a nickname given her by her grandmother) attended a Swiss boarding school, where she adopted her nickname, again to avoid discrimination. Much later she converted to the Episcopalian church.

When Bohemia and Moravia were annexed by Germany in 1939, the family fled to London. Madeleine Korbel Albright was born in Prague, Czechoslovakia in 1937. Her father was an official in the Czech government-in-exile who fled to London, where she remembers enduring the blitz. Her father served in several diplomatic posts after World War II and when the Communists took over Czechoslovakia in 1948 he sent his family to the United States, where he ended up running the School of International Studies at the University of Denver (where one of his prize students was Condolezza Rice). On the personal side of the ledger Albright talks about her marriage to "Newsday" scion Joe Albright, which ended in divorce, raising her three daughters, and learning late in her life that her Jewish grandparents had died in Nazi concentration camps. Earning her doctorate from Columbia, Albright worked her way from being Edmund Muskie's senior legislative assistant to work for National Security Advisor Zbigniew Brezinski in the Carter Administration. When the Democrats returned to the White House in 1992, Albright moved into the upper stratosphere of American diplomacy where she proved herself to be a Wilsonian moralist whose hero was Dean Acheson. That may have saved her life, as many of her Jewish relatives in Czechoslovakia were killed in the Holocaust, including three of her grandparents, a fact she didn't learn until 1996.

After World War II, the family moved to Belgrade, where Josef Korbel served as Czechoslovakia's ambassador to Yugoslavia. When the Communists took control of Czechoslavakia in 1948, the family fled again, this time, in 1950, to the United States, where Josef became the founding dean of the Graduate School of International Studies at the University of Denver. Korbel later taught future Secretary of State Condoleezza Rice. Years later, at Josef's funeral, Rice gave the family a piano in the memory of her former teacher.

Madeline attended Denver's Kent High School, graduating in 1955. She became a naturalized U.S. citizen in 1957. She attended Wellesley College in Massachusetts on a scholarship, earning a BA with honors in Political Science in 1959, and married Chicago journalist Joseph Medill Patterson Albright that same year. The couple had met while Madeline had a summer job at *The Denver Post*. They had three daughters: twins Anne and Alice, and Katie. They divorced in 1983.

When the twins were born six weeks prematurely and remained hospitalized for a long period of time, Albright took a course in Russian to pass the time. By the end of their hospital stay, she was fluent in the language. She is also fluent in English, French and Czech, with good speaking and reading abilities in Serbian, Polish and German. While raising her family, she attended the School of Advanced International Studies at Johns Hopkins University, received a certificate from the Russian Institute at Columbia University, and she earned a MA there in 1968 and PhD in Public Law and Government in 1976, also at Columbia.

She was the chief legislative assistant to Senator Edmund Muskie from 1976 to 1978, serving as the Washington coordinator of the Maine for Muskie campaign, and worked both as a staff member of the National Security Council and of the White House from 1978 to 1981. She was a fellow at the Woodrow Wilson International Center for Scholars at Smithsonian Institution from 1981 to 1982. At the same time she also served as a Senior Fellow in Soviet and Eastern European Affairs and a Research professor in international affairs and director of women in foreign service at the School of Foreign Service at Georgetown University from 1982 to 1993, president of the Center for National Policy from 1985 to 1993, foreign policy coordinator for the [Walter] Mondale for President campaign in 1984. She gained recognition as a foreign policy adviser to vice-presidential candidate Geraldine Ferraro that year and to presidential candidate Michael Dukakis in 1988. She was vice chairman for the National Democratic Institute for Internal Affairs in Washington from 1984 to 1993. Shortly after President Bill Clinton was inaugurated, Albright was appointed ambassador to the U.N., her first diplomatic post, presenting her credentials on February 9, 1993. During her tenure at the U.N., she had a prickly relationship with U.N. Secretary-General Boutros Boutros-Ghali. She did not advocate taking action against the genocide in Rwanda. Later, in a PBS documentary, "Ghosts of Rwanda," she would comment, "It was a very very very difficult time, the situation was so unclear . . . . in retrospect it all looks very clear"

She remained the permanent representative of the U.S. United Nations in New York from 1993 to 1997, when she became Secretary of the U.S. Department of State under President Bill Clinton from 1997 to 2001. She was the nation's 64th Secretary of State and the first woman.

In 2000, Secretary Albright became one of the highest level Western diplomats ever to meet with Kim Jong-il, the communist leader of North Korea, during an official state visit to that country. In the aftermath of that country's 2006 announcement of testing of a nuclear bomb, members of the

Bush administration, which adamantly refused to consider dialogue with North Korea, criticized the Clinton administration for having encouraged diplomatic conversation with the dictator. But Albright jumped immediately to Clinton's defense and stoutly defended the Clinton policy, stating that "During that period North Korea didn't do any nuclear testing."

Following Albright's term as U.S. Secretary of State, many speculated that she might pursue a career in Czech politics, since Czech President Václav Havel talked openly about the possibility of Albright succeeding him when he retired in 2002. Albright was reportedly flattered by suggestions that she should run for office, but denied ever seriously considering it.

Albright and at least five other former members of the Clinton administration served on the Council on Foreign Relations board of directors. She is currently the Mortara Distinguished Professor of Diplomacy at the Georgetown University Walsh School of Foreign Service in Washington, DC.

In 2003, she accepted a position on the Board of Directors of the New York Stock Exchange. In 2005, she declined to run for re-election to the Board in the aftermath of the Grasso compensation scandal, in which the Chairman of the NYSE Board of Directors Dick Grasso had been granted $187.5-million dollars in compensation, with little oversight by the board on which Albright sat. During the tenure of interim chairman John S. Reed, she served as chairwoman of the NYSE board's nominating and governance committee. Shortly after the appointment of the board's permanent chairman in 2005, Albright submitted her resignation.

On January 5, 2006, she participated in a meeting at the White House of former Secretaries of Defense and State to discuss US foreign policy with Bush administration officials. On May 5, 2006 she was again invited to the White House to meet with former Secretaries and Bush administration officials to discuss Iraq. There was little evidence that the White House heeded any advice by these former Secretaries. In an interview to *Newsweek International* published July 24, 2006, Albright gave her opinion in United States' current foreign policy: "I hope I'm wrong, but I'm afraid that Iraq is going to turn out to be the greatest disaster in American foreign policy—worse than Vietnam."

Albright currently serves as chairperson of National Democratic Institute for International Affairs, as president of the Truman Scholarship Foundation, and as co-chair of the Commission on Legal Empowerment of the Poor.

In September 2006, with Václav Havel, she received the MiE Award for furthering the cause of international understanding.

After her retirement, Albright published her memoir, *Madam Secretary* (2003) and *The Mighty and the Almighty: Reflections on America, God, and World Affairs* (2006). In *Madam Secretary*, Albright wrote of how her mother told her that Condoleezza Rice was her father's favorite student.

Suggested Reading:

(1) *Who's Who of American Women 2006-2007*. New Providence, RI: Marquis Who's Who/ Reed Elsevier, Inc. 2005. p. 20.

Anderson, Helen Eugenie Moore

U.S. Diplomat, first woman ambassador (1949-1973)

Born Eugenie Moore on May 26, 1090, the daughter of a Methodist minister who held various parsonages, she attended Stephens College in Columbia, Missouri, Simpson College in Indianola, Iowa, and Carlton College in Northfield, Minnesota but earned no degree. In September 1930 she married John P. Anderson, an artist, of Red Wing, Minnesota. The couple had two children: Hans and Elizabeth Johanna.

Eugenie studied piano at Julliard during a two-year stay in New York before she and her husband returned to Red Wing. There she developed a lasting interest in foreign affairs and became a leader in Minnesota League of Women Voters. In 1944 she became Democratic Party chairman, helping to effect the Democratic-Farmer-Labor coalition. In 1946 she was made vice-chairman of the central committee. In 1948 she was a delegate to the Democratic national convention where she was named to the party's national committee. Her effective campaigning on behalf of President Harry Truman and Vice President Hubert Humphrey led to her appointment in 1949 as U.S. ambassador to Denmark. She was the first woman to hold that rank, her predecessors having held no rank higher than minister. She held the post until July 1953. Afterwards she remained active in politics and international affairs, becoming chairman of the Minnesota Commission for Fair Employment Practices in 1955-1960, member of the Democratic National Committee's advisory committee on foreign policy in 1957-1961, member of the American Delegation to the Atlantic Conference in London in 1959, and vice-chairman of the Citizens Committee for International Development from 1961-1962, In May 1962 President John F. Kennedy appointed her as U.S. Envoy to Bulgaria, where she served until December

1964. From August 1965 to September 1968, she was the US representative on the UN Trusteeship to the UN General Assembly; and from September 1967 she was senior advisor to the US delegation to the UN. From 1968 she held the title of special assistant to the Secretary of State, and from 1973 she was a member of the Commission on Minnesota's Future.

She died March 31, 1997.

Suggested Reading:

(1) *Encyclopedia Britannica.*
(2) McHenry, Robert, ed. *Famous American Women.* Springfield, MA: G. & C. Merriam Company, 1980. p. 8.

Apumatec

Queen of North American Indian tribe (1607)

Apumatec was encountered in Virginia by Capt. Newport's expedition on its first exploration inland from Jamestown, which did not proceed beyond the present site of Richmond. She was described by Gabriel Archer: "She had much copper about her neck; a crownet of copper upon her head. She had long black haire, which hanged loose downe her back to her myddle; which only part was covered with a deare's skyn, and ells all naked. She had her woemen attending on her, adorned much like herselfe (save they wanted copper) . . . Our captain presented her with guyfts liberally; whereupon shee cheered somewhat her countenance . . ."

Suggested Reading:

(1) Jones, Howard Mumford. *The Literature of Virginia in the Seventeenth Century.* Charlottesville: University of Virginia Press, 1968. pp. 19-20.

Section B

Bachelet, Michelle

President of Chile (2006-)

Michelle Bachelet was born in 1951, the daughter of an air force general, Alberto Bachelet, and an archeologist mother, Ángela Jeria. General Bachelet, who remained loyal to President Salvador Allende, was imprisoned by his comrades in 1973 after the coup that brought Augusto Pinochet to power. He died in prison of a heart attack. In the aftermath of the coup, Michelle and her mother were jailed, tortured, and exiled to Australia, then later to Germany for several years. Her only brother, Alberto, died in 2001.

Prior to the coup, while still in her teens, Michelle joined Chile's Young Socialists. When she and her mother returned to Chile after their long exile, Michelle, who had gone to Australia to study pediatrics, went to work with child victims of human rights abuses. She was multilingual, which helped her to rise rapidly in the ranks of the Young Socialists, speaking out for the return of democracy.

Along the way, she met and married architect Jorges Dávalos and bore two children before the couple divorced. In 1984 she had one more child out of wedlock by her boyfriend, Dr. Aníbal Henríquez.

In 1988 a plebiscite ousted the Pinochet regime, and Bachelet was in line to move into positions of responsibility in the government. By the mid 1900s she was an adviser in the ministry of health and was studying military strategy at Chile's national academy for political and military strategy—a course normally reserved for military commanders. Upon her graduation, she was awarded a presidential grant of honor and sent to Washington for a course at the Inter-American Defense College, where she again came in first in her class.

In 2000 she was made minister of health by President Ricardo Lagos. Within three months she ended the long queues for appointments at health centers. She said, "The state is at the service of people, not the opposite."

In January 2002 Lagos took the bold step of naming her defense minister. Her performance in that arena led to her candidacy for president in 2005. Her bid was particularly audacious, given that Chile is a Catholic country which legalized divorce only a few years ago. Bachelet, an avowed agnostic and a single mother, promised that if she won, exactly half of her cabinet appointees would be women. Her political detractors lambasted her for being overweight but a lightweight politically, her mother retorted, "Have they ever looked at her CV?"

At one point she returned to the prison where she had been held and forgave her torturers.

Suggested Reading:

(1) "Top Woman in a Macho World" by Diane Dixon. *Guardian Weekly,* June 16-22, 1006.
(2) Interview on "The View" ABC-TV, September 29, 2006.

Barnard, Kate

Political reformer, first woman ever elected to a statewide office in any state (1907-1914)

Born on May 23, 1875 in Geneva, Nebraska, Kate, whose mother died, was reared by relatives in Kansas until 1889, when she rejoined her widowed father in the newly opened Oklahoma Territory. She graduated from high school in Oklahoma City and afterward worked as a teacher and stenographer, becoming a clerk for the Democratic minority in the territorial legislature. In 1904 she was appointed to the Oklahoma Commission at the Louisiana Purchase Exposition in St. Louis. She became interested in providing aid for the underprivileged and was appointed matron of the Provident Association of Oklahoma City in December 1905. From that post she directed relief to hundreds of poor families, providing clothing and schooling to their children. She was instrumental in forming the Federal Labor Union in Oklahoma City and securing its affiliation with the American Federation of Labor. She played a major role in the 1906 "Shawnee Convention," a joint meeting of farmers and labor representatives to hammer out a platform to present to the state constitutional convention. Her primary interests were the planks on compulsory education and child labor abolition. The Democratic majority adopted her planks and established the office of state commissioner of charities and corrections. Barnard relinquished her post with the Provident Association to run for commissioner, and in the election of 1907 she was elected. She was the first woman ever elected to a statewide office in any state. She was reelected in 1910 and for seven years helped get progressive labor legislation passed. Her unannounced trip to Lansing, Kansas, to inspect the Kansas state prison where some 600 Oklahoma convicts were "contracted" out, exposed atrocious conditions and ended Oklahoma's contract with Kansas. She launched a similar campaign in Arizona in 1911-1912. In 1911 she began an investigation into widespread fraud in the state-court administered system of guardianship for Indian minors. Her efforts recovered nearly a million dollars for 1361 Indian children defrauded of oil, gas, timber and land rights. Her delving into graft ultimately caused the legislature to cut her staff and budget, and in 1914 she declined to seek reelection. She retired to Oklahoma City where she lived until her death on February 23, 1930.

Suggested Reading:

(1)   McHenry, Robert, ed. *Famous American Women*. Springfield, MA: G. & C. Merriam Company, 1980. pp. 20-21.

Barrow, Nita

Governor-General of Barbados (1990-1995)

Barbados is the easternmost island of the West Indies. In 1966 it became an independent state in the Commonwealth of Nations. The British monarch, the nominal head of state, is represented by a Governor-general, who presides over a privy council appointed by the Governor-general on advice from the Prime Minister. Control of the government rests in the hands of the Prime Minister and other ministers answerable to Parliament.

Nita Barrow was born in 1916. She was married to Errol Barrow, who was active in the Democratic Labor Party. In 1986 Errol Barrow became Prime Minister, but he died a year later. Nita Barrow continued to take an active part in politics, and in 1990 she was appointed Governor-general by Queen Elizabeth II. She held the post until 1995.

Suggested Reading:

(1)   Barbados Bureau on Information and Tourism.

(2)   *Funk & Wagnalls New Encyclopedia*, vol. 3. 1996. p. 273.

Batz' Ek', Lady

Queen Mother of Caracol (618-634)

She was born in 566 and arrived at Oxwitza at the age of 18. She married Knot Ajaw, King of Caracol, a Mayan kingdom in present-day Mexico. Knot Ajaw had ruled for 31 years at the time of the marriage. The couple had a son, K'an II who ruled after his father died in 618 until 658. For the first fifteen years of K'an II's reign, Lady Batz' Ek' as Queen Mother had a great deal of political power until her death in 634.

Betancourt Pulecio, Íngrid

Colombian Congresswoman and Senator, Presidential Candidate (1994-2002)

Íngrid Betancourt Pulecio was born in Bogotá. Her mother, Yolanda Pulecio, was a well-known beauty queen, a former Miss Colombia, and political activist who later represented the poor southern neighborhoods of Bogotá in Congress. Her father, Gabriel Betancourt, was minister for the General Gustavo Rojas Pinilla dictatorship (1953-1957) and later a diplomat, posted to the embassy in Paris, where Íngrid grew up. Their house was frequently visited by leading Colombian personalities and intellectuals. She attended the *Institut d'Etudes Politiques de Paris*, an elite school of higher education. After graduating, she married fellow student Fabrice Delloye, and they had two children, Melanie and Lorenzo. Her husband was in the French diplomatic service, and they lived in various countries, including. New Zealand. Briefly during the 1980s she lived in Quito, Ecuador, working as an aerobics instructor.

After the 1989 murder of Colombian presidential candidate Luis Carlos Galán, who was running on an anti-drug-trafficking platform, Íngrid returned to Colombia to help her country. Beginning in 1990, she worked at the Ministry of Finance, from which she resigned to enter politics in 1994. Her first campaign distributed condoms, with the motto that she would be like a condom against corruption. The south of Bogotá supported her, thanks partially to the name recognition from her mother, who helped her campaign.

She was elected to the Chamber of Representatives in 1994 and launched a political party, the Green Oxygen Party. During her term, she criticized the administration of President Ernesto Samper, who was accused of corruption after accepting money for his electoral campaign from the Cali drug cartel. Sometime during this period, she divorced her French husband and later married a Colombian.

In 1998 she ran for Senator and won by the largest number of votes of any candidate in that year's Senate election. The presidential candidate Andrés Pastrana Arango persuaded her to endorse him, and she campaigned on his behalf. Ultimately he was proclaimed the victor, but Ingrid claimed he reneged on the promises he made to her when she agreed to do support him.

After the 1998 election, Ingrid wrote a memoir. Initially, it could not be published in Colombia, because of the polemics against former President Samper and others, so it came out first in France. It was later published in English in 2002 as *Until Death Do Us Part*. During her Senatorial term, death threats from unknown parties induced her to send her children to New Zealand for safety.

In 2002 Betancourt ran for President and decided to go to the demilitarized zone in the town of San Vicente del Caguán to meet with the FARC (Revolutionary Armed Forces of Colombia), which despite three years of negotiations, continued its practice of hi-jacking, kidnapping, extortion, military attacks, and distribution of weapons. Several Colombian political figures continued to attempt to visit the demilitarized zone even as the "peace talks" with FARC fell apart. Most candidates for political office who intended to do so backed off when authorities warned them of the danger. However, Íngrid Betancourt insisted to be taken to the former DMZ by a military aircraft. President Pastrana and other officials turned down this petition arguing that they could not guarantee her safety during the turmoil that would follow the retaking of the DMZ. Additionally, aiding a Presidential candidate meant that the government was rendering its resources to Betancourt's private political interests.

When denied transport aboard a military helicopter that was heading to the zone, she decided to head into the DMZ via ground transport, together with her campaign manager, Clara Rojas, who was later named running-mate for the 2002 election, and a handful of political aides.

On February 23, 2002, she was stopped at the last military checkpoint before going into the former DMZ. Military officers insisted that Betancourt and her party not continue in their effort to reach San Vicente del Caguán, the village used for the peace talks. San Vicente's mayor was the only Green Oxygen Party elected official in the entire country by then. Intense fighting was taking place inside the DMZ and the security situation was rapidly deteriorating. Betancourt dismissed their warnings and continued her journey, and was kidnapped by FARC, who held her for six years. Her name still appeared on the ballot for the presidential elections; her husband promised to continue her campaign. In the end, she achieved less than 1% of the votes. The Presidential election was eventually won by Álvaro Uribe Vélez.

Her relatives and those of most of FARC's political hostages strongly rejected any potential rescue operations, due to the tragic death of Antiquia Governor Guillermo Gaviria Correa, his peace advisor and several soldiers, kidnapped by the FARC during a peace march in 2003. They were shot at close range by the FARC when the government launched an army rescue mission into the jungle.

A day after Betancourt's kidnapping several non-government organizations led by Armand Burguet were organized in Europe and around the world to lobby for her liberation. The committee initially consisted of some 280 activists in 39 countries. In February 2006, France urged the FARC to seize the chance offered by a European-proposed prisoner swap, accepted by Bogotá, and free dozens it had held for up to seven years. Foreign Minister Philippe Douste-Blazy said it was "up to the Revolutionary Armed Forces of Colombia to show they were serious about releasing former Colombian presidential candidate Ingrid Betancourt and other detainees".

In an interview with French newspaper *L'Humanité* in June 2006, Raul Reyes, a leader of the FARC, said that Betancourt "is doing well, within the environment she finds herself in. It's not easy when one is deprived of freedom."

Many prisoners were reported ill. In May 2007, a kidnapped member of the Colombian National Police, Jhon Frank Pinchao, managed to escape. He claimed that Betancourt was being held in the same prison camp he had been in and that she had attempted to escape several times, but had been recaptured and "severely punished". He also reported seeing Clara Rojas, who had given birth to a son, Emmanuel, while in captivity.

On July 26, 2007, Melanie Delloye, Íngrid Betancourt's daughter, reported two French diplomats had been unable to confirm that Íngrid Betancourt was still alive. On November 11, 2007, Venezuelan President Hugo Chávez told French newspaper *Le Figaro* that he hoped to be able to show French President Sarkozy proof that Betancourt was alive before their meeting on November 20. On November 18 Chávez announced to the French press that he had been told by a FARC leader that she was still alive.

On November 30, 2007 the Colombian government released information that they had captured three members of the urban cells of the FARC in Bogotá who had videos and letters from people held hostage by the FARC, including Betancourt. A letter intended for Ingrid's mother, Yolanda, found at the same time, was published in several newspapers.

In 2008, Venezuelan President Hugo Chávez and the International Red Cross organized humanitarian operations to receive several civilian hostages whose release had been announced by FARC. The first, Operation Emmanuel, led to the successful release of Clara Rojas and Consuelo González. On February 27, 2008, the second operation was carried out, freeing four former members of the Colombian Congress. One released hostage described Ingrid Betancourt. as "exhausted physically and in her morale . . . Ingrid is mistreated very badly, they have vented their anger on her, they have her chained up in inhumane conditions." Another said that she has Hepatitis B and is "near the end." President Sarkozy said he was prepared to go personally to accept her release if necessary.

On March 27, 2008, the Colombian government offered to free hundreds of guerrilla fighters in exchange for Betancourt's release. On March 31, 2008, Colombian news station Caracol quoted several sources saying Betancourt had stopped taking her medication and stopped eating, and was in desperate need of a blood transfusion.

On April 2, 2008, Betancourt's son, Lorenzo Delloye, addressed the FARC and President, Álvaro Uribe, to facilitate the freeing of Ingrid to keep her from dying. On April 7, 2008, 5,000 marchers, led by Argentine President Cristina Fernandez and French First Lady Carla Bruni-Sarkozy, demonstrated near the Paris Opera to show support for Betancourt.

Six years after her capture, she was rescued by Colombian forces with US help. Two days after her rescue, she arrived in Paris to thank the nation that had championed her cause. "I owe everything to France," she said, after a warm greeting by President Nicolas Sarkozy and his wife Carla. "France is my home. You are my family."

In comments to Europe 1 Radio, she said, "I was in chains all the time, twenty-four hours a day, for three years. I tried to wear those chains with dignity, even if I felt that it was unbearable."

Asked if she had been tortured, she said, "Yes, yes," and said her captors had fallen into "diabolical behavior," adding, "It was so monstrous I think they themselves were disgusted." She called her rescue "a miracle of the

Virgin Mary" and said, "You need tremendous spirituality to stop yourself falling into the abyss."

Pope Benedict XVI invited her to meet with him the following week.

Speaking at the Élysée Palace with Mr. Sarkozy later, Ms. Betancourt said she walked perhaps 200 miles a year. "I walked with a hat pulled down over my ears because all sorts of things fall on your head, ants that bite you, insects, lice, ticks, with gloves because everything in the jungle bites, each time you try to grab on to something so that you don't fall, you've put your hand on a tarantula, you've put your hand on a thorn, a leaf that bites, it's an absolutely hostile world, with dangerous animals. But the most dangerous of all was man, those who were behind me with their big guns."

On the flight to France, news agencies reported, Ms. Betancourt said: "I owe my life to France. If France hadn't fought for me, I wouldn't be here making this extraordinary journey."

It was a signal honor for the French president to meet the plane, which he had sent to Colombia with her children to reunite the family and bring them all back to France.

At one point, Ms. Betancourt grabbed Mr. Sarkozy's hand and said, "I owe so much to this extraordinary man who did so much for me," and she praised France for aiding her family, providing moral support and for pressing the Colombian government to find a nonviolent way to rescue her. "France opposed a military operation that would put the lives of the hostages at risk, particularly my life," she said. "So in a sense you saved my life."

She asked Mr. Sarkozy for his continuing help in freeing the other 700 or so hostages held by the Revolutionary Armed Forces of Colombia (FARC). She was freed along with three American contractors and 11 Colombians. He answered, "Let it be clear, we will continue."

While the French saw Ms. Betancourt as a symbol of their own sense of political activism—an ecologist, an educated person with a social conscience, independent and brave—many in Colombia saw her as a dilettante, an exile who returned to teach the natives how to live and who courted publicity.

Mr. Sarkozy's own role became a topic of heated internal politics. The rescue operation, carried out by Colombian forces with American guidance, was done with no French involvement whatsoever and no forewarning to Paris. That prompted the Socialist he defeated for the presidency, Ségolène Royal, to belittle the diplomatic role the president had played. "Nicolas Sarkozy had absolutely nothing to do with this liberation," she said in an interview during a visit to Canada. She called his diplomatic efforts "useless."

Mr. Sarkozy's allies leaped to counterattack. Prime Minister François Fillon said Ms. Royal was behaving like "a little girl in the playground" while Frédéric Lefebvre, a spokesman for Mr. Sarkozy's political party, said that Mr. Sarkozy had displayed "total commitment these past 12 months in the search for all possible ways" to ensure Ms. Betancourt's release.

French officials also dismissed Swiss reports that bribes had been paid to the FARC and that the rescue was a staged affair.

In 2009 a new opinion emerged, told by three fellow inmates in a book, *Out of Captivity, Surviving 1967 Days in the Colombian Jungle*. Here, the aristocratic politician greeted as a heroine in 2008 is depicted as selfish and haughty by the American military contractors who were held in the same prison.

Keith Stansell, 44-year-old ex-Marine and co-author of the book, said in an interview, "I don't want to attack her, but truth is very savage. We were infected enough with her behavior in the jungle. Now I just want to get immunized."

The book, co-authored by Thomas Howes and Marc Gonsalves, tells of their forced jungle marches, contracting numerous tropical diseases, and being chained to one another to discourage escape. It portrays Betancourt as putting herself at the top of a hostage hierarchy, hoarding used clothing and writing materials, determining bathing schedules, hiding information from a transistor radio that she concealed, even having a tantrum about the color of mattress she was given, which was baby blue. Describing the hidden radio, Gonsalves, 36, reported Stansell's telling Betancourt that unless she shared the radio information with her fellow captives, he was going to have to turn her in. Even on the day of their rescue, Stansell said, "I can get over just about anything, but I don't know about Ingrid. Forgive? Yes. Move on? Yes. Respect? No."

Relations between Betancourt and Clara Rojas, who was also writing a book about their years in captivity, continued to be strained following their release. Another former hostage, Luis Eladio Pérez, a former Colombian lawmaker who formed a close relationship with Betancourt during their years in the jungle, told in a book in 2008 of dissension and tension among the hostages because of her position as a daughter of a patrician diplomat and former beauty queen, "Ingrid is a person who generates a great deal of envy. Not even the kidnapping had taken away that karma, above all because 90 per cent of the news stories . . . about the kidnapping were about her, as if the rest of us did not exist."

Suggested Reading:

(1) Betancourt, Íngrid. *Until Death Do Us Part: My Struggle to Reclaim Colombia*. New York: Harper Collins, 2002.
(2) "5,000 March in Paris for Betancourt." AP News, April 7, 2008.
(3) "Betancourt, in France, Details Her Captivity" by Steve Erlanger and Alan Cowell. *The New York Times*. July 5, 2008.

Section C

Campbell, Kim

Prime Minister of Canada (1993)

She was born in 1947, was educated as a lawyer, and became a professor before entering politics. In 1988 she was elected to Parliament and moved swiftly through the ranks of Canada's ruling Progressive Conservative Party. She was soon appointed Minister of Indian Affairs and later Minister of Justice. In January of 1993 she was appointed Minister of Defense. In June of 1993 she was elected Canada's first woman prime minister, after telling her supporters, " . . . whether I win or lose, our party is ready for a leader from either founding gender . . . . Our choice as a party is clear: We can respond to the winds of change or we can be swept away." She took over a country bitter over government cutbacks of social programs and a 11.4 percent unemployment rate.

One of her first tasks was to tackle the federal and provincial deficits by calling a special meeting with provincial premiers aimed at reaching a spending agreement before a scheduled summit with other world leaders. In July, 1993 Campbell represented Canada at the three day G-7 summit in Tokyo. G-7 stands for the Group of Seven of the world's leading industrial nations: Japan, Canada, Britain, Italy, France, Germany, and the United States. The group discussed terrorism, ethnic wars such as the one in Bosnia, and nuclear threats, but could reach little consensus on how to deal with the violence in Bosnia. They did agree to supply aid to Russian Boris Yeltsin's government. The summit allowed Campbell to stand out as the only woman among those world leaders.

Back home, Campbell worked to solidify the conservative base in Canada's western provinces before she faced elections. By law she had to call for elections no later than the end of November. Although an August 1993 Gallup poll showed Campbell's approval rating at 51 percent, the highest level for a prime minister in 30 years, her popularity was not enough to pull her Progressive Conservatives ahead of the Liberal Party, led by Jean Chrétien.

Suggested Reading:

(1) "Canada's Tories Name a Woman as New Premier." *The New York Times*. 14 June 1993: A1, A4.
(2) Clayton, Mark. "Canada's Campbell Turns to the Race Ahead". *The Christian Science Monitor*. 15 June 1993: 6.
(3) Jones, Clayton. "Security Issues Crowd Agenda at Tokyo Summit". *The Christian Science Monitor*. 9 July 1993: 1, 4.
(4) Clayton, Mark. "Kim Campbell Sets Out to Show She's No 'Kim Mulroney'". *The Christian Science Monitor*. 25 August 1993: 3.
(5) Farnsworth, Clyde H. "How Women Moved Up in Canada. *The New York Times*. 20 June 1993: E5.

Camelia-Romer, Suzanne

Prime Minister of Netherlands Antilles (1993, 1998-1999)

Chamorro, Violeta Barrios de

President of Nicaragua (1990-1996)

Born Violeta Barrios in Rivas, Nicaragua in 1929, she was the daughter of a wealthy cattle baron and his wife. She received her education in women's colleges in Texas and Virginia. At the age of 20 she married Pedro Juaquín Chamorro Cardenal, who became editor of the family newspaper *La Prensa*, in 1952. The couple had four children, Pedro Juaquín, Claudia, Carlos Fernando, and Cristina. Chamorro Cardenal's crusades against Anastasio Somoza's regime resulted in his imprisonment in 1956. After he was exiled to a remote village, he escaped to Puerto Rica, where Violeta and the children joined him and where the family lived for several years.

In 1978, while Violeta was in Miami, Chamorro Cardenal was assassinated. Violeta took over directorship of *La Prensa* that year and entered politics the following year, becoming one of five members of a revolutionary junta that brought Daniel Ortega Saavedra into power. Two of her children, Claudia and Carlos Fernando, took an active part in the revolution. But after nine months, Violeta Chamorro left the government, claiming that what had promised to be a pluralistic democratic government had instead become a Marxist Communist government. Part of her husband's family broke away from *La Prensa* to form a pro-government newspaper, *El Nuevo Diario*, and Violeta Chamorro directed *La Prensa*, which became the focus of opposition to the Sandinista government. Two of her children, Pedro Juaquín and Cristina, followed her, while the other two remained in the Sandinista camp.

In 1990 a 14-party coalition chose Violeta Chamorro to be its candidate in a democratic election for president of Nicaragua. On February 15, 1990, she became the first woman to be elected president of a nation in the western hemisphere.

After one year in office, her only solid accomplishment was bringing peace and a semblance of democracy to a country long ravaged by civil war and dictatorship. However, the economy, left in ruins by the Sandinistas, had continued to disintegrate.

By the summer of 1993, Chamorro had come under such intense political pressure both in Nicaragua and abroad that political observers wondered whether she would be able to finish the remaining three years of her term. Her government faced almost insurmountable problems as a result of a depressed economy, the accelerating guerrilla activity, and hostile political opposition from both extremes. Critics accused her of detachment, leaving government details to her controversial son-in-law and chief of staff, Antonio Lacayo. In public she continued to display the sense of humor, dignity, trademarks of Nicaragua's first family which has been compared to the Kennedy family in the United States.

In February 1995 Chamorro and the National Assembly began arguing over constitutional reforms. In June, she and the legislators had finally agreed on a number of reforms she had requested, and the Assembly approved her choices for Supreme Court judgeships.

In the months prior to the election in 1996, Chamorro and her supporters had formed a new party, the National Project, one of whose goals was to overthrow the Nepotism Law, prohibiting her son-in-law, Lacayo, from running for president in 1996. Former Sandinista Vice President Sergio Ramírez, new leader of a breakaway party called the Renewed Sandinista Movement, agreed to back the removal of the law and allow Lacayo to run "in the interests of social peace."

Violeta Chamorro retired on January 10, 1997.

Suggested Reading:

(1) Krauss, Clifford. "Bush's Uneasy Welcome for Violeta Chamorro". *The New York Times*, 4 April 1991: 3E.

(2) Constable, Pamela. "Nicaragua's Change Slow under Chamorro". *The Houston Chronicle*, 28 April 1991: 23A.

(3) Trotta, Dan. "Chamorro's Days Numbered in Nicaragua?". *The Houston Chronicle*. 1 August 1993: 28A.

(4) "Maneuvers at the Top" *World Press Review* August 1995, p. 26.

(5) *Who's Who in the World 1997*. New Providence, RI: Marquis Who's Who/ Reed Elsevier, Inc. 1996. p. 238.

Charles, Mary Eugenia

Prime minister of Dominica (1980-1995)

The granddaughter of former slaves, the daughter of John Baptiste and Josephine Delauney Charles, Mary Eugenia was born on May 15, 1919 in Pointe Michel, Dominica. Dominica, an island in the Caribbean, was a British possession at that time. Her father, who lived to be 107 years old, was founder of the Penney Bank. She received a B.A. degree from the University of Canada and studied law at the London School of Economics and Political Science. In 1949 she returned to Dominica, the first woman attorney-at-law on the island. She became interested in politics in 1968, while fighting a sedition law which stifled dissent. She was appointed to the legislature in 1970 and to the house of assembly in 1975. There she became leader of the opposition. It was partly through the efforts of the Dominica Freedom Party, which she co-founded, that Dominica gained independence from Great Britain in 1978. In the election of 1980 her party gained the majority and she became Prime Minister. Charles instituted immediate measures of economic reform. She set about to corral the tax evaders and to put an end to governmental corruption. In 1985 she won a second five-year term and was also made minister of foreign affairs, finance, economic affairs, and defense. Her primary concern was improving the quality of life for her people. "We should give the people not luxury but a little comfort—a job, the means to build a house, assistance for agricultural pursuits," she said in an interview. "We will never be rich, but I think we can be a self-reliant nation with a little thrift and a little development." To that end Charles has sought to encourage tourism to some extent, but she has been adamant about preserving the island's ecology and national identity. Dominica has no casinos, no night clubs, no duty free shops, and Charles had no intention of encouraging them. "We want to bring in the kind of tourists who like what we already have here. We especially are encouraging naturalists . . . . We don't want hordes of tourists who expect to go to night clubs every night," she told an interviewer. She was described as a no-nonsense leader, a pragmatist. A strict constitutionalist, her colleagues considered her a brilliant lawyer and a savvy politician "with considerable charm." Of women's rights on her island, Charles said, "In Dominica, we really live women's lib. We don't have to expound it." It was Eugenia Charles who petitioned President Ronald Reagan's help against Cuban infiltration of Grenada, which led to the U.S. invasion of Grenada in 1983.

Charles, who was called "the Iron Woman of the Caribbean", served two terms as prime minister, retiring in 1995. In 1991 Britain's Queen Elizabeth named her a Dame of the British Commonwealth. She lived with her father until he died in 1983 at the age of 107, saying she never met anyone she wanted to marry. In 2005 she fell and suffered a broken hip and was transported to Martinique to undergo a surgical repair. She died of complications in Martinique at the age of 86. She was survived by two brothers.

Suggested Reading:

(1) Moritz, Charles, ed. *Current Biography Yearbook, 1986.* New York: The H.W. Wilson Co., 1986. pp. 88-91.

(2) *International Who's Who 1987-1988.* New Providence, RI: Reed Elsevier, 1997. p 256.

(3) Okey, Roberta, "Trekking Nature's Terrarium" *Americas* Sept./Oct. 1987: 8-13.

(4) Walter, Greg, "Interview." *People.* November 1983: 20, 46.

(5) Sanders, Charles L., "Interview" *Ebony.* January 1981: 16.

(6) *Who's Who in the World 1997.* New Providence, RI: Marquis Who's Who/ Reed Elsevier, Inc. 1996. p. 243.

(7) "Eugenia Charles Dies" *Jamaica-Gleaner.com,* September 8, 2005.

Clinton, Hillary Rodham

U.S. Secretary of State (2009-)

Hillary Diane Rodham was born October 26, 1947 in Chicago, Illinois. She attended Wellesley College, where she was the first student to deliver the commencement address in 1969. She earned a law degree in 1973 from Yale University Law School, where she met her future husband, William Jefferson Clinton. She was a Congressional legal counsel until 1974, when she moved to Arkansas and, in 1975, married Bill Clinton. The couple had one daughter, Chelsea. Hillary continued practice of law, co-founding in 1977 the Arkansas Advocates for Children and Families, and in 1978 becoming the first female chair of the Legal Services Corporation. In 1979 she became the first female partner in Rose Law Firm. During that period she was listed twice on the list of One Hundred Most Influential Lawyers in America.

While she was carving out her law career, her husband had entered the political arena, becoming Governor of the State of Arkansas in 1979. She served as First Lady of Arkansas from 1979 to 1981. Clinton was defeated for re-election but ran again in 1983 and was successful in regaining the governorship. Hillary Clinton again served as First Lady from 1983 to 1992. She took an active part in her husband's administration, heading a task force to improve the Arkansas school system.

In 1993 Bill Clinton became President of the United States, and Hillary served as First Lady for two terms. Early in his first term, her Clinton health care initiative was shot down by the U.S. Congress. Late in his second term, she staunchly defended him against accusations of sexual misconduct, to which he later admitted. Public skepticism as to the soundness of their marriage continued to follow her even after they left Washington.

The Clintons moved to New York, where she was elected to the U.S. Senate in 2001. She was the first female to serve in the Senate from New York. Her election was the first time a First Lady had run for public office. In the early months of President Bush's administration, she voted for the Iraq War Decision, but she later criticized its conduct of the war and opposed most of its domestic policies. In 2006 she was re-elected by a wide margin. She ran for President in 2008 and received more delegates than any other female in U.S. history, but she ultimately lost to Barak Obama. President Obama then named her to become Secretary of State. She was the first former First Lady ever to serve in a President's cabinet.

Suggested Reading:

(1) Milton, Joyce. *The First Partner: Hillary Rodham Clinton*. William Morris, 1999.
(2) Estrich, Susan. *The Case for Hillary Clinton*. HarperCollins, 2005. pp. 66-68.

Section G

Ginsburg, Ruth Bader

Associate Justice on the U.S. Supreme Court (1993-)

Ruth Joan Bader was born March 15, 1933 in Brooklyn, N.Y., the second daughter of Nathan and Celia Amster Bader. She attended James Madison High School. Her mother died of cancer the day before her graduation. She received a BA degree from Cornell University in 1954 and married fellow student Martin D. Ginsburg, later a professor of law at Georgetown University Law Center. When she enrolled at Harvard Law School that same year, she was one of only nine women in a class of more than 500. Their first child, Jane, was born in 1955. Shortly thereafter her husband was diagnosed with cancer and during his treatment period, Ruth attended classes and took notes for them both, typed his papers, cared for both baby and husband, and managed to make the Harvard Law Review. Later, when Martin accepted a job in New York, she transferred to Columbia Law School and became the first woman to be on both the Harvard and Columbia Law Reviews. She received her LLB from Columbia, tying for first in her class. In 1965 their son James was born.

In private practice, Ginsburg spent much of her energies as an advocate for equal citizenship for men and women as a constitutional principle. She was a volunteer lawyer for the American Civil Liberties Union and was on the faculty of both Columbia Law School and Rutgers School of Law in Newark (1963-1872). For 13 years she served as a federal judge on the United States Court of Appeals for the District of Columbia Circuit. At the request of Vice President Al Gore, she administered his oath of office. Then in 1993 President Bill Clinton appointed her to the Supreme Court. She was the second female Justice—Sandra Day O'Connor being the first—and the court's first Jewish woman. She generally voted with the more liberal wing of the court.

In 1999 she underwent surgery for colorectal cancer and underwent chemotherapy for eight months while continuing her court duties. She did not miss a single day on the bench throughout her treatment. In 2009 she was again hospitalized for surgery pertaining to pancreatic cancer, being released eight days after surgery and returning to work nine days after that. Two days later she was present when President Barak Obama addressed a joint session of Congress.

Suggested Reading:

(1) Bayer, Linda. *Ruth Bader Ginsburg*. Philadelphia: Chelsea House Publishers, 2000.
(2) Clinton, Bill. *My Life*. New York: Vintage, 2005.

Gonzáles, Consuelo

Colombian Congresswoman (1990s)

Consuelo Gonzales de Perdomo, a former Congresswoman, was the mother of two daughters, Patricia and Fernanda, and one grandchild Maria Juliana. In 2002 she, along with other political activists, was taken prisoner by the Colombian leftist guerrilla group, Revolutionary Armed Forces of Colombia (FARC), who demanded return of a number of guerrilla prisoners in exchange for her freedom. After more than six years in captivity, her release, along with that of Colombian vice presidential candidate Clara Rojas, was facilitated by the Belgian Minister of Foreign Affairs, Karel De Gucht.

Her daughters and grandchild welcomed her in Caracas, Venezuela, following her release on July 10, 2008 in the Colombian forest of Guaviare.

Gordon, Minita

Governor-general of Belize (1981-1993)

Formerly the crown colony British Honduras, Belize is located on the east coast of Central America. In 1973 the name was changed from British Honduras to Belize, and in 1981 the colony gained independence and became a member of the British Commonwealth of nations with Queen

Elizabeth II as head of state. In Belize and several other Commonwealth nations, the monarch is represented by a Governor-general.

The Governor-general, appointed by the British monarch, presides over national and international defense, foreign affairs, and the civil service, but wields no real power for governing.

Minita Gordon was born in 1930. After receiving an excellent education, she served in several positions including member of the National Assembly. When Belize received her independence in 1981, Minita Gordon was appointed its first Governor-general by Queen Elizabeth II. Because Guatemala refused to recognize Belize's independence, 1500 British troops, under Gordon's command, remained on Belize soil to maintain peace. Gordon served for twelve years, retiring in 1993.

Suggested Reading:

(1)   Funk & Wagnall's New Encyclopedia Vol. 3, 1986, *Belize*. p. 412.

Section H

Hull, Jane

Governor of Arizona (1997-2003)

She was born Jane Dee Bowerstock August 8, 1935 in Kansas City, Missouri. She received a degree in Education from the University of Kansas. She taught in an elementary school in Kansas City.

A Republican, Hull later claimed that she moved to Arizona in 1962 after she was inspired by a Barry Goldwater speech. She worked in the Goldwater Presidential Campaign of 1964. She married Dr. Terry Hull, who was a public health physician at Navaho Nation. The couple had four children. She taught at Navaho Nation schools in Chinle, Arizona and returned to school at Arizona State University for a graduate degree.

She entered politics in the 1970s, serving in the Arizona House of Representatives from 1979 to 1998, seven terms. She was Speaker of the House from 1989 to 1992 and Speaker Pro Tem from 1992 to 1993, the first female Speaker in Arizona history.

In 1994 she was elected Arizona Secretary of State, which has no lieutenant governor. When Governor Fife Symington was forced to resign in 1997 after a conviction for fraud, Hull, as next in line, was sworn in as governor.

The following year, she was elected to the office in her own right, the first woman to be elected to the position. For the first time in U.S. history, all five top elected executive positions in one state were held by women: besides Hull, there were Betsey Bayless, secretary of state; Janet Napolitano, attorney general; Carol Springer, treasurer; and Lisa Graham Keegan, superintendent of public instruction. By Arizona law with limits a governor's term to eight years, she was barred from seeking a second full term, and she was succeeded by Napolitano.

Hull's relations with Senator John S. McCain were strained, and in the 2000 presidential elections she supported George W. Bush. In 2004 she was a public delegate to the United Nations General Assembly.

Suggested Reading:

(1) "Women Assuming Governorship, 4 Next-highest Posts in Arizona" by David Schwartz. *Houston Chronicle*, January 3, 1999.

Section I

Isabel Peron

See Peron, Isabel

Isabel

Princess, regent of Brazilian Empire (1871-1872 and 1876-1888)

Isabel was born in 1846, the daughter of Dom Pedro de Alantara, Pedro II, second and last emperor of the Brazilian Empire, who ruled from 1840 to 1889. King Pedro was a wise and able ruler, and his daughter was educated to become one as well. She married a Frenchman, Gaston d'Orleans, Comte d'Eu. In 1971, 1876 and 1888, King Pedro, anxious to improve Brazil's relations with Europe, personally made extended visits to European heads of state. He also visited the U.S. president in 1876. During those protracted absences, Isabel acted as regent. Although Pedro and Isabel as his regent did much to enhance education, remove corruption, abolish slavery and enhance revenues, their popularity waned. In 1888 Isabel decreed complete emancipation without compensation to owners, and about 700,000 slaves were freed. The slave owners withdrew their support of the king. Support for a republic grew, as did dissatisfaction with Isabella and her French husband. The army, which Pedro had barred from dabbling in politics, hatched a conspiracy and revolted in 1889. Pedro abdicated and he and Isabel and their family sought exile in Europe. Isabel died in Europe in 1921.

Suggested Reading:

(1) Langer, William L., ed. *World History*. Boston: Houghton Mifflin, 1980. p. 855.
(2) Egan, Edward W. et. al., eds. *Kings, Rulers, and Statesmen*. New York: Sterling Publishing Company, 1976. p. 61.

Ix Yo K'in, Lady

Queen of Tikal (511-527)

Tikal was a Mayan City-State located in northwestern present-day Guatemala. Ix Yo K'in was born in 505, the daughter of King Chak Tok Ich'aak II, who died in 511. Her name means Baby Jaguar. Ix Yo K'in became Queen when she was six years old, the nineteenth successor to the throne. She was also known as Lady Kalomte' because she was assigned a coregent, Kalomte' B'alam, a famous warrior. She ruled for sixteen years and was succeeded by King K'inich Muwaan Jol.

Section J

Jagan, Janet

Prime minister (1997), President of Guyana (1997-)

She was born Janet Rosenberg in 1921, the daughter of Jewish immigrants living in Chicago. She trained as a nurse at Northwestern, and met a young man training at Northwestern University Dental School, Cheddi Jagan (b. 1918 in Port Mourant, Jamaica of East Indian parents). In 1943 they married and moved to Guyana, at that time a British colony called British Guiana on the northeastern shore of South America. The couple had two children and in time became citizens of Guyana. Fifty per cent of Guyana's population is of East Indian extraction, and thirty-one per cent is of black African extraction.

In the late 1940's she helped her husband found the People's Progressive Party, a predominantly East Indian (male) organization. While Cheddi Jagan became a member of the legislative council (1947-1953), Janet Jagan co-founded, in 1946, the Women's Political and Economic Development Organization and, in 1953, she founded its successor, the Women's Progressive Organization. In that year, unlimited suffrage was granted to the citizens of Guyana by the British government. In 1955, after an ethnic split in the WPO's leadership, Indian members of the Women's Progressive Organization were encouraged to join the hitherto mostly male People's Progressive Party.

As her husband rose in positions of leadership, Janet Jagan served as a member of the legislative assembly. In 1961 Guyana achieved full self-government under the British umbrella, and the People's Progressive Party gained the majority in the legislative assembly. Cheddi Jagan became the first premier of Guyana, and Janet Jagan became health minister. But the austere economic measures which President Jagan introduced the following year resulted in riots that pitted African and Indian factions against each other. British troops returned more than once to restore order.

In 1963 elections were held again, and, when no one could secure a majority, Forbes Burnham of the People's National Congress was chosen to form a coalition government. On May 26, 1966 Guyana was declared an independent nation, and it became a member of the United Nations the same year. On February 23, 1970 Guyana became a republic, and Arthur Chung (b. 1918) of the People's National Congress became president.

In the elections of 1992, Cheddi Jagan's People's Progressive Party again gained a majority in the National Assembly, and Jagan became president of Guyana, an office he held until his death in March, 1997, of a heart attack. Jagan's deputy, Samuel A. Hinds, succeeded him pending elections the following December, and his widow, Janet Jagan, became prime minister, the first woman to hold that high post.

On September 1, 1997, she accepted her party's nomination to run for the presidency. On December 15, 1997, she won by an overall majority, and on December 19, she was sworn in as president of the Republic of Guyana, becoming the first woman to hold the highest office in the land. Samuel A. Hinds was elected prime minister, and Bharrat Jagdeo became vice president. As was expected, the opposition People's National Congress, which had been in power from 1970 to 1992, challenged the results.

The newly elected President Jagan expressed the desire that her son Joey Jagan, who had been living in the Caribbean, return to Guyana and succeed at the helm of the People's Progressive Party. Thus she would be grooming him for future leadership of the republic. However, critics described the younger Jagan as a "loose cannon" who might destroy the fragile economic development of the country.

Suggested Reading:

(1) Ishmael, Safraz W., "People's Progressive Party Civic Homepage". www. pppcivic.org. December, 1997. Prepared by Ishmael from University of Maryland School of Physics.
(2) Seenarine, Moses, "Keeping the Natives at Bay: Janet Jagan in Guyana." Saxakali Publications, Oct. 29, 1997.

de Jongh-Elhage, Emily

Prime Minister of the Netherlands Antilles (2006-)

The Netherlands Antilles, previously known as the Netherlands West Indies or Dutch Antilles/West Indies, is part of the Lesser Antilles and consists of two groups of islands in the Caribbean Sea: Curacao and Bonaire, off the coast of Venezuela; and Sint Eustatiujs, Saba and Sint Maarten, lying southeast of the Virgin Islands. The islands form an autonomous part of the Kingdom of the Netherlands. Their economy depends mostly upon tourism and petroleum.

Emily Saïdy Elhage was born on December 7, 1946 to parents of Lebanese heritage. She graduated from the Curacao Teachers' College in 1965, married de Jongh, and worked as a teacher until 1982. In 1987 she went into real estate and became a prominent agent during the next eight years. In 1995 she entered politics as a member of the Party for the Restructured Antilles (PAR). The party nominated her as a Member of the Island Council (Parliament) for the Curacao PAR. She held the post of President of the Preparatory Committee of the Island Council for three years. In December of 1998 she became Commissioner of Public Works and Public Housing for Curacao, a post she held until June of 1999.

In October 2005 she was unanimously elected the leader of the Party for the Restructured Antilles and as such has been instrumental in bringing about the new status of the Islands. The Netherlands Antilles is scheduled to be dissolved as a unified political entity on December 15, 2008, at which time the five constituent islands will attain new constitutional statuses within the Kingdom of the Netherlands. PAR won the elections for Parliament in January of 2006 and she was sworn in as Prime Minister on March 26, 2006, succeeding Etienne Ys, who had previously stepped down as party leader. De Jongh-Elhage simultaneously held the post as Minister of General Affairs and Foreign Relations.

Suggested Reading:

(1) *Womenandglobalsecurity.org*. International Women Leaders Global Security Summit. The Annenberg Foundation Trust, Sunnylands.

Jumper, Betty Mae

Chief of Seminole Nation (1960s)

She was born ca. 1927 in Florida and graduated from a reservation high school in Cherokee, North Carolina. She studied nursing in Oklahoma and went into field work with the U.S. Public Health Service. She then returned to Florida to the State Seminole Reservation, the Big Cypress Reservation, and has been active in the affairs of the tribe ever since. In the Seminole nation the clans are perpetuated through the women. She was elected chief in the 1960s. An interviewer in 1969 described her as bright, jolly, and vivacious. As chief, her main concern was to raise the living standards of her tribe through education. She once cited the government-funded Head Start program as the most important boost for Seminole children's education. She said, "Many of the kids went into the first grade without knowing English. So they couldn't learn much, and they never did catch up. With Head Start they start out even." The program was dismantled by President Reagan. Of her people, Jumper said, "We don't want to be white people; we want to be Seminoles. We want the modern things, and we want to live nicely, but we want to do it among friends." Jumper mentioned the greatest trial of Indian youth who go away to college or military service is loneliness.

Suggested Reading:

(1) Capron, Lewis, "Florida's Emerging Seminoles." *The National Geographic*. November 1969: 716-734.

Section K

Kalomte, Lady

See Ix Yo K'in

Kanal-Ikal of B'aakal, Lady

Maya "King" of Palenque (A.D. 583-604)

Palenque was a Mayan kingdom located in the present-day Yucatan area of Mexico. Yohl Ik'nal did not come to the throne as a consort or regent, but ascended to the throne following the death of her father, Kan B'alam I or Chan Bahlum (b. A.D. 524, r. 572-583). She was also called Lady Kanal Ikal, Ix Yohi Ik'nal, Lady Olnal, Kan-Ik, Lady Ik, or K'anal-Ik'al. She was one of a very few Mayan women to bear full royal titles and to rule in her own right for an extended period—in her case, more than two decades. She had at least two sons. One was Ai Ne' ohl, or Ac-Kan, who succeeded her on the throne on January 4, 605 after her death on November 7, 604. Another son, Pacal I, had a daughter, Lady Kanal-Ikal's granddaughter, named Zac-Kuk, who later also inherited the throne. The fact that Lady Kanal-Ikal appears prominently in her great-grandson Pacal the Great's records, makes it likely that she commissioned the inscriptions and temple constructions during her reign.

Suggested Reading:

(1) Schele, Linda and David Freidel, *A Forest of Kings The Untold Story of the Ancient Maya*. New York: Quill/William Morrow, 1990. pp. 219-221, 223, 224, 467.

K'atun Ajaw, Lady

Politically influential Queen of Pietras Negras (687)

Lady Ajaw was born as Princess of Amana in Mexico and married King K'inich Yo'nal Akh II. Although she had no vested power, records indicate that during her husband's reign, she wielded considerable power.

Suggested Reading:

(1) Schele, Linda and David Freidel, *A Forest of Kings The Untold Story of the Ancient Maya*. New York: Quill/William Morrow, 1990.

Kirchner, Cristina Elizabeth Fernández de

President of Argentina (2007-)

She was born on February 19, 1953 in Tolosa, La Plata, the daughter of Eduardo Fernández and Ofelia Esther Wilhelm. She attended the National University of La Plata where she studied law, and where she met her future husband, Néstor. They were married in 1975 and had two children: Máximo and Florencia. She began her political career as a member of the Peronist Youth movement of the Justicialist Party, but for a while she and her husband abandoned politics and entered private law practice in Río Gallegos. A decade later she returned to politics and won a seat in the Santa Cruz legislature, which she held until 1995, when she was elected to the Senate representing Santa Cruz. She moved to the Chamber of Deputies in 1997 and returned to the Senate in 2001.

She was pivotal to the success of her husband's presidential bid in 2003, although he came into office with the smallest number of votes (21.9%) on record. During his term, Cristina, as First Lady, became a good-will ambassador much in the style of the beloved Eva Perón, with whom she was often compared.

In the 2005 elections Kirchner was the favored candidate for Senator from the province of Buenos Aires, representing the Front for Victory Party. Her chief rival was Hilda González de Duhalde, wife of former President Eduardo Duharde, whom she handily defeated.

Her husband decided not to run for a second term as president but announced that his wife would run instead. It was speculated that, since a standing president can be re-elected only once, the husband and wife team planned to alter power to keep the office in Peronist hands as long as possible. In the October 2007 general election, she ran for the presidency representing the leftist ruling Front for Victory Perónist party. She ran by one of the widest margins since the country reverted to democratic rule in 1983. She became Argentina's first elected female President and the second female ever to serve—the other being Isabel Martinez de Perón (1974-1976). Her four-year term began on December 10, 2007. The following year *Forbes* magazine ranked her thirteenth among the 100 most powerful women in the world.

Fernández finally won the election in the first round with 45.3% of the vote, followed by 22% for Elisa Carrió (candidate for the Civic Coalition) and 16% for former Economy Minister Roberto Lavagna. Eleven others split the remaining 15%.

Suggested Reading:

(1) "Argentine First Lady Seeks Presidency." AP. *The New York Times*.

Kirkpatrick, Jeane

United Nations Ambassador, shaper of foreign policy under Ronald Reagan (1981-1985)

She was born Jeane Duane Jordan on Nov. 19, 1926, in Duncan, Okla., the daughter of Welcher F. and Leona (Kile) Jordan. Her father was an oil wildcatter who moved from town to town searching for a gusher that he never hit.

She earned an AA degree from Stephens College in Missouri, then moved to New York, where she earned a BA degree from Barnard College in 1948, a MA degree from Columbia University in 1950 and a PhD from Columbia in 1968. Meantime, she went to Washington as a research analyst at the Intelligence and Research Bureau of the State Department, where she met her future husband, Evron M. Kirkpatrick. Fifteen years her senior, he was a veteran of the wartime Office of Strategic Services, and he soon became the head of the American Political Science Association. They married in 1955 and had three sons—Douglas Jordan, John Evron and Stuart Alan. Mr. Kirkpatrick died in 1995. The oldest son, Douglas, died in 2006.

In 1967, before completing her doctoral dissertation, she was appointed associate professor at Georgetown University. In 1968 she earned a doctorate in political science at Columbia University. Georgetown made her a full professor in 1973 and gave her the endowed Leavey Chair five years later.

She supported Jimmy Carter in 1976 and came close to being chosen for an ambassadorship in his administration. But she had become deeply disenchanted with her party. She joined the Committee on the Present Danger, a neoconservative organization which warned throughout the late 1970s of a disastrous downturn in every aspect of American strength, from nuclear warheads to national image. Arguing against President Carter's emphasis on civil rights, she first entered Ronald Reagan's inner circle on the strength of a 10,000-word article she published in the neoconservative magazine Commentary in November 1979. The article, "Dictatorships and Double Standards," drew a bright line between right-wing pro-American governments and left-wing anti-American ones.

It was said that Mr. Reagan read the article closely. Richard V. Allen, who later became the first of his six national security advisers, introduced him to Ms. Kirkpatrick. They met at a February 1980 dinner party given by George F. Will, the syndicated columnist.

She later recalled that she wondered aloud how she, a Democrat all her life, could join his team. Mr. Reagan confided, "I was a Democrat once, you know." He won her over. After his election a year later, Ms. Kirkpatrick became the United Nations ambassador and "Dictatorships and Double Standards" became an important part of the foreign policy of the United States.

Reagan was said to have a simple view of foreign policy: it was a battle between the US and the Evil Empire, with other nations backing one side or the other. When he came to office in 1981, 51 members of the Committee on the Present Danger won positions of significant power in his administration. Ms. Kirkpatrick was the first American woman to serve as United Nations ambassador. She was the only woman, and the only Democrat, on President Reagan's National Security Council. No woman had ever been so close to the center of presidential power without actually residing in the White House. On accepting the post, she vowed to serve only during Reagan's first term. She claimed to detest the job, comparing it to "death and taxes."

Her mission was to wage rhetorical warfare against Moscow and its allies. She sought to restore the international standing of the United States after its defeat in Vietnam and the captivity of Americans in Iran. At the United Nations, she defended Israel's 1982 invasion of Lebanon and the American invasion of Grenada in 1983. She argued for El Salvador's right-wing junta and against Nicaragua's left-wing ruling council, the Sandinistas.

In private, she supported American efforts to sustain the contras, the rebel group that tried to overthrow the Sandinistas with CIA help. She was a crucial participant in a March 1981 National Security Planning Group meeting that produced a $19 million covert action plan to make the contras a fighting force.

Her high-profile performance at the United Nations made her President Reagan's favorite envoy. He told her, "You're taking off that big sign that we used to wear that said, 'Kick Me,'" He admired her strong diplomatic stands and her undiplomatic language. In a letter to 40 third world ambassadors in October 1981, she accused them of spreading "base lies" and making "malicious attacks upon the good name of the United States."

President Reagan brought her into his innermost foreign policy circle, the National Security Planning Group. There she weighed the risks and rewards of clandestine warfare in Central America, covert operations against Libya, the disastrous deployment of American marines in Lebanon, the invasion of Grenada and support for rebel forces in Afghanistan.

Her most notorious performance came during the 1982 Falklands war when she made little effort to disguise her distaste for US support of Britain. Reliable evidence pointed to her regular contacts with members of the Galtieri junta in Argentina to pass on details of US intentions.

She was part of a national security team that was often at odds. Her relationship with Reagan's first Secretary of State, four-star General Alexander M. Haig Jr., "started off bad and got worse over time," Mr. Adelman said in an oral history of the Reagan years. She had something Mr. Haig found that he lacked: the president's ear.

Ms. Kirkpatrick was at the June 1984 National Security Planning Group meeting that began the secret initiative that later became known as the Iran-contra affair. Congress had cut off funds for the contras. Defense Secretary William J. Casey wanted to obtain money from foreign countries in defiance of the ban.

Ms. Kirkpatrick was in favor. "We should make the maximum effort to find the money," she said. Secretary of State George P. Shultz was opposed. "It is an impeachable offense," he said. President Reagan warned that if the story leaked, "we'll all be hanging by our thumbs in front of the White House."

Over the next two years, millions skimmed from secret arms sales to Iran went to the contras. The story did leak, as Mr. Reagan feared, and his administration was shaken by Congressional investigations and criminal charges. Robert C. McFarlane, who had won the national security position over Ms. Kirkpatrick, pleaded guilty to misinforming Congress.

Mr. McFarlane said he should have stood up against the secret initiative to support the contras. But "if I'd done that," he said, "Bill Casey, Jeane Kirkpatrick and Cap Weinberger would have said I was some kind of commie."

By then Ms. Kirkpatrick had left the government. She stuck to her vow to leave the United Nations at the end of Mr. Reagan's first term and resigned in April 1985. She was succeeded by Vernon A. Walters, a former deputy director of central intelligence. The next year, as the Iran-contra story began unfolding, Mr. Casey urged the president to make her secretary of state, but Mr. Reagan rejected the idea.

Her diplomacy made her a national political figure. She was a star performer at the 1984 Republican national convention, deriding Democrats as the "blame America first" party.

After leaving the Reagan administration in 1985, she changed political affiliation and seriously considered seeking the Republican nomination for president. But fearing she would split the conservative vote, putting moderate George H. W. Bush into office, she decided against running.

In March 2003, his son, President George W. Bush, recalled Ambassador Kirkpatrick to duty and sent her on a secret mission to Geneva. Her purpose was to head off a diplomatic uprising against the imminent war against Iraq. Arab ministers planned to condemn it as an act of aggression. Alan Gerson, who had served as her general counsel at the United Nations, explained, "The marching orders we received were to argue that pre-emptive war is legitimate."

Kirkpatrick's answer was: "No one will buy it. If that's the position, count me out." Instead, her position was that the attack was justified by Saddam Hussein's violations of UN resolutions dating from 1991. Her arguments convinced the ministers not to protest the invasion of Iraq.

Kirkpatrick spent the rest of her career commenting on policy instead of making it. She remained among the most highly regarded members of the Republican establishment, and her voice remained one of the strongest echoes of the Reagan era. Among her many honors, awards and honorary degrees, the Kirkpatrick professorship of international affairs was established in her honor at Harvard in 1999.

In a 1996 interview, she said that power is based not merely on guns or money but on the strength of personal conviction. "We were concerned about the weakening of Western will. We advocated rebuilding Western strength, and we did that with Ronald Reagan, if I may say so."

Jeane Kirkpatrick died on December 7, 2006 in her home in Bethesda, MD, leaving her other two sons and five grandchildren.

Suggested Reading:

(1) *Who's Who of American Women 2006-2007*. Marquis Who's Who, LLC, 2005., p. 1059.

(2) "Jeane Kirkpatrick, Reagan's Forceful Envoy, Dies" by Tim Weiner. *The New York Times*, December 9, 2006.

(3) "Jeane Kirkpatrick: Her Anti-Communist Views Made Her an Ideal UN Envoy for Reagan" by Harold Jackson. *The Guardian Weekly*, December 15-21, 2006.

Section L

Lucero, Beatriz Merino .

Prime Minister of Peru (June 2003-December 2003).

Beatriz Merino Lucero was born on November 15, 1947 in Peru. After receiving an undergraduate degree in Peru, she came to the United States and took a Master's degree in law from Harvard University. She returned to Peru and entered private practice. In 1990 she entered politics, running for a senate seat. She was elected and served until 1992. In 1995 she was elected to the Congress and served until 2000. In June of 2003, she became Prime Minister, the highest ranking position ever held by a woman in Peru. She had a very high approval rating (60%) until December of that same year, when she was fired by President Alejandro Toledo after rumors circulated that she was a lesbian. In that Roman Catholic country, the accusation was enough to finish her career.

Suggested Reading:

(1)   Wildman, Sarah. "Prime Minister's Peril." *Advocate* 907, 2004.
(2)   Initial Signitaries to the Global Action Plan." Win with Women Global Initiative. NDI Women's Programs. July 7, 2005

Section M

Mankiller, Wilma Pearl

Chief of Cherokee Nation (1985-1995)

She was born in 1944, the daughter of Charlie and Irene Mankiller. Her father was full-blood Cherokee; her mother was Dutch-Irish. She and ten brothers and sisters grew up in a four-room frame house with no plumbing located on the family allotment in Mankiller Flats in Adair County in eastern Oklahoma. In 1956 when she was eleven years old the family was moved to San Francisco by the Bureau of Indian Affairs as part of a government program to force the assimilation of Native Americans. The family lived in a tenement in Hunter's Point, then a high crime primarily poor black neighborhood. After high school, at age 17, she married Hector Hugo Olaya di Bardi, an Ecuadorian college student, and toured Europe with him. They had two daughters, Felicia in 1963 and Gina in 1965. She studied sociology at San Francisco State University, where she became interested in bettering the plight of Indians. The nation's attention was focused on the problems of Native Americans when a group, including some of Mankiller's relatives, occupied Alcatraz Island for 19 months (1969-1970). A number of celebrities went to Alcatraz to show their support, but Mankiller remained on the mainland working for Native American causes.

In 1971 her father died and was returned to Oklahoma to be buried. When her activist work to help the Pit River Indians recover their lands and her other civil rights struggles led to her divorce three years later, she felt compelled to return to her roots. She returned with her daughters to Oklahoma and completed her degree in 1975 at Flaming Rainbow University. It was not until that year that the U.S. government granted the Cherokees self-determination. In 1977 she began working for the then 65,000 known members of the Cherokee tribe as an economic coordinator and commuted to the University of Arkansas to work toward a master's degree in community planning. An auto accident enroute to classes in 1979 resulted in 17 surgeries in one year. The following year she contracted myasthenia gravis and had surgery on her thymus gland. Despite her difficulties, in 1983 she was elected Deputy Chief of the Cherokee nation, which had grown to 108,000 registered members. In 1985 she moved from the second spot to become the first female Chief when Chief Ross Swimmer became head of the Bureau of Indian Affairs. Many U.S. tribes trace their ancestry matrilineally, and Chief Mankiller looked upon her ascension as a return to the historical role women held in tribal affairs. Historically, a woman selected the chief; the head of the women's council had a great deal of power, Mankiller has explained. In 1987 she ran for a full four-year term and was elected on her own merits. In 1991, despite a recent kidney transplant—donated by her brother Donald Mankiller, she ran again and was re-elected by a majority of 82 per cent. She was the tribe's first Principal Chief in recorded history. She lives with her second husband, Charlie Soap, a full-blood Cherokee, and his son Winterhawk in Tahlequah, Oklahoma, capital of the Cherokee nation, located 80 miles east of Tulsa. Of her duties, she said, "It is sort of like running a small country and sort of like running a middle-sized corporation." Mankiller has attributed her resilience to her Cherokee blood. She noted that most Cherokees were marched from their southeastern U.S. homeland by soldiers in the 1838 Trail of Tears. Although 4000 died along the way, those who survived quickly established themselves as a literate nation. They opened the first school west of the Mississippi and established several Cherokee language newspapers. Mankiller said in an interview, "We are fighters and survivors. We were not shy about war, but we also fought a lot of battles in court. We were devastated, uprooted and driven like cattle to this land, but we made the best of it."

Mankiller worked throughout her time in office overseeing tremendous growth in tribal membership and encouraging new business ventures for the Cherokee nation. She was inducted into the National Women's Hall of Fame and received the Humanitarian Award from the Ford Foundation. Following her decision not to run for another term, she was honored by President Clinton for her many years of public service in a special ceremony at the White House.

Suggested Reading:

(1) Flood, Mary. "First Female Cherokee Chief Ready for Job." *The Houston Post.* 7 April 1984: A 1, A 26.
(2) Whittemore, Hank. "She Leads a Nation." *Parade Magazine.* 18 August 1991: 4-5.

(3) Mankiller, Wilma with Michael Wallis. *Mankiller*. New York:, 1994.

(4) Zakin, Susan. "Woman Chief Blazing An Indian Trail." *Mother Jones.* September 1986: 8, 10.

(5) "Who's News." *USA Weekend.* 2-4 March 1990: 2.

(6) Sowers, Leslie. "Wilma Mankiller: The First Woman Chief of the Cherokee Nation Is as Comfortable in the White House as She Is at a Stomp Dance." *Texas.* 20 January 1991: 10-11.

Mary Bosomworth

"Princess", ruler of Ossabaw, Sapelo, and St. Catherines Islands (1747-?)

A Creek Indian, she was the daughter of "an Indian woman of no note," according to one Georgia account. She served General James Oglethorpe, the founder of Georgia, as an interpreter to the Creek Indians. As her third husband she took the Reverend Thomas Bosomworth, Oglethorpe's chaplain. Together they persuaded the Creeks that Mary was their princess in the maternal line. The Creeks accepted her and honored her request to give her three islands to command off the Georgia coast: Ossabaw, Sapelo, and St. Catherines. The British attempted to recover the islands, but Mary raised an army of Creeks and marched into Savannah, threatening a massacre. The British backed down, but eventually ransomed Ossabaw and Sapelo for large sums. Mary kept the island of St. Catherines.

Suggested Reading:

(1) Cerutis, James. "Sea Islands: The South's Surprising Coast". *National Geographic 139*. March 1971: 373-374.

Merino Lucero, Beatriz

Prime Minister of Peru (June 2003-December 2003)

Beatriz Merino Lucero was born on November 15, 1947 in Peru. She earned a law degree from the Universidad Nacional Mayor de San Marcos in 1970 and completed postgraduate studies on taxation at the London School of Economics in 1972. She received her LL.M. from Harvard University Law School in 1977. She was employed at the law firm of Estudio Merino and Reano and was a faculty member at Lima University, where she directed the

Master's program on fiscal policies and also directed the program of foreign cooperation. She entered politics in 1990 and was elected to the Senate, serving until 1992. In 1995 she was elected to the Congress, where she served until 2000. A tireless proponent of women's rights, she is director of the Women's Leadership Program (PROLEAD) sponsored by the Inter-American Development Bank which financed projects to advance women's options in Latin America. She served on the Commission of Andean Jurists, the first Peruvian woman so honored. She is a member of the board of directors for the International Women's Forum and is on the steering committee for the Business Women's Initiative against HIV/AIDS. On June 23, 2003, she became the Prime Minister of Peru, the highest ranking position ever held by a woman in Peru's history of Peru. While in office, she successfully conducted the Peruvian Tax Reform. More than 28 tax laws were enacted. In addition, she initiated and publicized the guidelines for Peruvian State Reform. Her approval rating was sixty-six percent when she traveled to the United States to further cooperation between her country and the U.S. During her absence rumors were circulated in her Roman Catholic nation that she was a lesbian. She was unmarried and had purchased a house with a female colleague. On December 12, 2003, President Alejandro Toledo removed her from office. She learned of her dismissal on her return from the trip. She held office between 23 June 2003 and 12 December 2003. Merino now serves as a senior specialist in the Public Sector at the World Bank, based in Washington, D.C. She specializes in the areas of tax administration and policy, state reform, customs, the modernization of government agencies and the strengthening of Latin American congresses. She has written two books, *Peruvian Women in the XX Century Legislation* and *Marriage and Rape: Debate of Article 178 of the Peruvian Criminal Code.*

Suggested Reading:

(1) Wildman, Sarah. "Prime Minister's Peril." Advocate 907 (2004): 15.
(2) "Initial Signataries to the Global Action Plan." Win with Women Global Initiative. NDI Women's Programs. 5 Apr. 2008.
(3) Crawford, Franklin. "Beatriz Merino, Peru's First Female Prime Minister, To Speak September 1." *Cornell News*, August 18, 2005.

Section N

Naah Ek'

Snake Lady of Palenque (520)

Palenque was located in present-day Mexico. Naah Ek' was the first Snake Lady to arrive in the kingdom. She was the wife of Tuun K'ab' Hiix, who ruled ca. 520-ca. 550. He was one of the Snake Kingdom's greatest early rulers. Her name, u nahtal ix kan ajaw, means "the first Snake Queen, and Naah Ek' means "House Star." Her position was one of great authority and political power.

Section O

O'Connor, Sandra Day

Justice of the U.S. Supreme Court (1981-2006)

She was born in El Paso, Texas on March 26, 1930, the daughter of Ada May Wilkey and Harry Alfred Day, ranchers. Although she grew up on a cattle ranch near Duncan, Arizona, she went to elementary school and Radford School for Girls in El Paso while living with her maternal grandmother. In 1950 she received a BA degree in economics from Stanford University, then earned her LLB degree from Stanford Law School, serving on the Stanford Law Review. She graduated third in a class of 102. First in the class was future Chief Justice William Rehnquist, whom she occasionally dated. In spite of her outstanding record at law school, because of her gender, no California firm would hire her, although she was offered one job as a legal secretary. She took a position as Deputy County Attorney of San Mateo County (1952-1953) and as a civilian attorney for Quartermaster market Center in Frankfurt, Germany (1954-1957). In 1952 she had married John Jay O'Connor III, and the couple had three sons. For most of two decades John O'Connor suffered from Alzheimer's and eventually had to be institutionalized. From 1958 to 1960, she practiced law in Phoenix and served as Assistant Attorney General of Arizona from 1965 to 1969. In 1969 Arizona Governor Jack Richard Williams appointed her to the Arizona State Senate, and she was then twice re-elected. In 1973 she was elected majority leader. In 1975, she was elected judge of the Maricopa County Superior Court, where she served until 1979, when Governor Bruce Babbitt appointed her to the Arizona Court of Appeals. From there, President Ronald Reagan appointed her to the U.S. Supreme Court in 1981. She was the first woman to become Justice of the Supreme Court of the United States. In the first few years, her rulings were conservative, but as time went on, she often cast the swing vote, siding with moderates on some issues, In 2001 *Ladies' Home Journal* named her the second most powerful woman in America. In 2004

Forbes listed her as the sixth most powerful woman in the world. The only American women preceding her were National Security Advisor Condoleezza Rice, Senator Hillary Clinton, and First Lady Laura Bush. In 2005 *Forbes* again listed O'Connor among the world's most powerful women, tagging her at number thirty-six. On July 1, 2005, she announced her intention to retire from the bench as soon as a successor could be confirmed. This occurred in January, 2006 when Samuel Alito took her place. O'Connor accepted a position as Chancellor of the College of William & Mary and she served on the board of trustees of the National Constitution Center in Philadelphia.

Suggested Reading:

(1) Greenburg, Jan Crawford. *Supreme Conflict: The Inside Story of the Struggle for Control of the United States Supreme Court.* New York: Penguin Books, 2007.

(2) Greenhouse, Linda. *Becoming Justice Blackmum.* New York: Times Books, 2005.

(3) Krauthammer, Charles. "Philosophy for a Judge." *The Washington Post,* July 7, 2005.

(4) "Supreme Court's first woman justice Sandra Day O'Connor announces retirement." *Court TV,* July 18, 2005.

Section P

Palin, Sarah

Governor of Alaska (2006-2009)

Sarah Louise Heath was born February 11, 1964 in Sandpoint, Idaho, the daughter of Charles R. Heath, a science teacher and track coach, and Sarah Sheeran Heath, a school secretary. She was third in a family of four children. While she was an infant, the family moved to Alaska. She graduated from Wasilla High School in 1982 and spent the first semester of her college career at Hawaii Pacific College in Honolulu. She then transferred to North Idaho Community College in Coeur d'Alene where she spent two semesters. In 1984 she entered and won the Miss Wasilla Pageant, then finished third in the Miss Alaska Pageant, winning the "Miss Congeniality Award." She transferred to the University of Idaho for two semesters then transferred to Palmer, Alaska's Matanuska-Susitna College for one semester. She returned to the University of Idaho to major in journalism, receiving her bachelor's degree in 1987 after a total of five years of college-hopping. In 1988 she married Todd Palin, a commercial fisherman and employee of British Petroleum. The couple had five children. She went to work in television as a sports reporter in Anchorage and also wrote for the *Mat-Su Valley Frontiersman*. She also helped in her husband's commercial fishing business.

In 1992 she was elected to the Wasilla city council, where she served until 1996. She ran successfully for mayor of Wasilla in 1996, serving until 2002. She ran for lieutenant governor in 2002, but was defeated. She chaired the Alaska Oil and Gas Commission from 2003 until she resigned the following year. In 2004 she was elected Governor of Alaska, the first female and youngest person ever to hold the office in that state. Prior to her election Congress had passed a $442-million earmark bill to build two bridges in Alaska. The Gravina Island Bridge received national bad press as an example of pork-barrel spending, because the island has a population of 50, although it is the site of Ketchican Airport. The bridge had become known as "the bridge to nowhere. Palin had run on a strong platform of "build the bridge" and urged speedy work on its infrastructure while there was still support in Congress. After a large public outcry, Congress eliminated the bridge earmark but gave the funds to Alaska for its general transportation fund. Following Palin's election, Alaska chose not to return the $442 million to the federal government, but Palin reversed her pre-election stance supporting the project and cancelled it in 2007.

She was tapped by Senator John McCain to be his running mate in the 2008 presidential elections, but the ticket was soundly defeated.

In July 2009 she announced her resignation as Governor of Alaska effective that month. She said she would not be a candidate for re-election in 2010. A week before she was to leave office, the Associated Press revealed that an independent investigator had found evidence that Governor Palin may have violated ethics laws by trading on her position in seeking money for legal fees. The report from the investigator for the state Personnel Board says Palin was securing unwarranted benefits and receiving improper gifts through the Alaska Fund Trust, which had been set up by supporters and that there was probable cause to believe Palin attempted to use her official position for personal gain because she authorized the creation of the trust as the "official" legal defense fund. However, since she was leaving office, it was doubtful that she would be indicted.

Suggested Reading:

(1) Will, George. "Impulse, Meet Experience." *The Washington Post.* September 9, 2002.
Nichols, Jon (August 30, 2008).
(2) "Clinton Praises Palin Pick." *The Nation,* June 21, 2009.
(3) D'Oro, Rachel, "Investigator rules against Palin in ethics probe." Associated Press, July 21, 2009.

Pascal-Trouillot, Ertha

Provisional President of Haiti (1990-1991)

Born Ertha Pascal in 1943/4, she was a member of the wealthy mulatto professional elite that dominated Haitian politics prior to the rule of Francois Duvalier. She married Ernst Trouillot, a prominent lawyer who presided over the Port-au-Prince Bar Association until his death in 1989. The couple had one daughter. She earned her own law degree in 1971 and soon gained respect as a legal scholar. She authored several books on law; the first and best known, *The Judicial Status of Haitian Women in Social Legislation*, was written only two years after her graduation. She worked to reform Haiti's outmoded laws affecting the rights of women. Although Haiti's constitutions have provided for women's suffrage since 1950, until the 1970's, women were considered "minors" and were not permitted to conduct business or have a bank account without the signature of their husbands. In 1984 Ertha Pascal-Trouillot was named Appeals Court judge, and in 1986, after the fall from power of Jean-Claude Duvalier, Minister of Justice Francois Latortue appointed her to a ten-year term as Supreme Court Justice. Although other women had served as judges in Haiti, Mrs. Pascal-Trouillot was the first woman to sit on the Supreme Court. On March 10, 1990, Haitian ruler Lt. Gen. Prosper Avril resigned during a popular uprising against his military regime, turning over power to acting army chief of staff Major Gen. Herard Abraham, who promised to transfer power to a civilian leader within 72 hours. According to the constitution, Chief Justice Gilbert Austin was next in line; however, the opposition coalition Unity Assembly rejected his claim on the grounds that he was a puppet of the military. Austin extracted a pledge from the other 11 justices not to accept the nomination over him, and three other justices refused to accept the nomination. On the evening of March 11 the nominating committee visited Mrs. Pascal-Trouillot, the court's newest justice, to offer her the nomination. After a brief consultation with her sister and brother-in-law, she decided, in the interest of unity, to forego her commitment to Justice Austin and to take a leave of absence from the bench so as to preside over the provisional government for several months to oversee, with an advisory council of 19 members, the democratic election of a Haitian president. Because roving assassination squads threatened her life, she was taken into hiding until her inauguration the following day. In her inauguration speech, delivered in both French and Creole, she said, "I have accepted this heavy task in the name of the Haitian woman, who for the first time in the history of our country, has been called upon to go beyond her traditional daily sacrifices made with courage and true patriotism . . . In the short time I have, I will work to clean the face of Haiti." In Haiti's first free election, Catholic priest Jean Bertrand Ariste was chosen to succeed her (January 1991). However, before due process could be enacted, on January 7, 1991, the capital was attacked by a military coup led by the former defense minister, Col. Christofe Dardompre, who declared himself ruler. Ertha Pascal-Trouillot announced that she was resigning immediately. She disappeared and word reached the capital that she was held hostage. The *coup* failed and Dardompre, who headed the National Palace Guard under ousted military ruler Prosper Avril, was arrested in April, 1991. Earlier that month, Pascal-Trouillot had been arrested and questioned about the January *coup*. She was actually held at gunpoint by Roger Lafontant, a former interior minister during Duvalier's dictatorship.

Suggested Reading:

(1) Norton, Michael. "Pascal-Trouillot Blazes a Trail for Women". *Houston Chronicle*. 13 march 1990: 8A.

(2) Treaster, Joseph B. "Civilian Sworn In as Haiti's President". *The New York Times*. 14 March 1990: A3.

(3) "Haiti Coup Suspect Held". *Houston Chronicle*. 21 April 1991: 23A.

(4) French, Howard W. Haiti's Class Divisions Deepen, Threatening Efforts to Return Aristide to Presidency". *The New York Times*. 3 November 1991: 9.

(5) French, Howard W. "New Leader of Haitians Offers U. S. a Wary Hand". *The New York Times*. 23 December 1990: 2.

Pelosi, Nancy

Speaker of the United States House of Representatives (2007-)

Nancy Patricia D'Alesandro was born on March 26, 1940 in Baltimore, MD. Her father, Thomas D'Alesandro, Jr., represented Baltimore for five terms in Congress, then served as Mayor of Baltimore for 12 years. Her brother, Thomas D'Alesandro III, also served as Mayor of Baltimore.

She graduated from Trinity College in Washington, D.C. in 1962 with a BA in Political Science. She married Paul Pelosi, a native of San Francisco, and the couple has five children: Nancy Corinne, Christine, Jacqueline, Paul and Alexandra, and five grandchildren.

Since 1987, Nancy Pelosi has represented California's Eighth District in the House of Representatives. The Eighth District includes most of the City of San Francisco including Golden Gate Park, Fisherman's Wharf, Chinatown, and many of the diverse neighborhoods that make San Francisco a vibrant and prosperous community. Overwhelmingly elected by her colleagues in the fall of 2002 as Democratic Leader of the House of Representatives, Nancy Pelosi is the first woman in American history to lead a major party in the U.S. Congress. Before being elected Leader, she served as House Democratic Whip for one year and was responsible for the party's legislative strategy in the House.

As a senior member of the House Appropriations Committee, Pelosi fought for America's families. She has been a leader in increasing educational opportunity, protecting workers, and promoting health care, including women's health and the creation of a nationwide health tracking network to examine the links between environmental pollutants and chronic disease. She has been a strong proponent of increased investments in health research, and has secured funding to double the budget for the National Institutes of Health. Pelosi also has successfully defeated repeated attempts to reduce funding for international family planning programs.

One of her first legislative victories was the creation of the Housing Opportunities for People with AIDS program. She has also worked to accelerate development of an HIV vaccine, expand access to Medicaid for people living with HIV, and increase funding for the Ryan White CARE Act, the Minority HIV/AIDS Initiative and other programs vital to people living with or at risk for HIV/AIDS.

Pelosi also increased access to health insurance for people with disabilities by ensuring continuation of their health care coverage. She was instrumental in passing legislation to assist nonprofit organizations in the creation of affordable housing.

As a member of the House Permanent Select Committee on Intelligence for 10 years (the longest continuous period of service in the committee's history) including two years as the Ranking Democrat, Pelosi worked to ensure that policymakers and military commanders are provided with the timely and accurate intelligence necessary to guide diplomatic initiatives, succeed in combat, and protect U.S. military forces.

In meetings around the world with U.S. and foreign intelligence leaders, Pelosi has urged greater attention to the threats to international security posed by the proliferation of technologies associated with the weapons of mass destruction and global terrorism.

In the wake of the September 11 terrorist attacks, Pelosi led congressional reviews of the U.S. intelligence and security agencies and authored legislation to create an independent national commission to assess the overall performance of the federal government before, during, and after the attacks.

Long known as an advocate for human rights around the world, she has fought to improve China's human rights record, attempting to tie trade to increased human rights standards. She has also been a leader on efforts to free the people of Tibet.

A leader on the environment at home and abroad, Pelosi secured passage of a provision in the International Development and Finance Act of 1989 which requires the World Bank and all the regional multilateral development banks to review the potential environmental impacts of development projects for which they provide funding and to make these environmental assessments publicly available. Known as the "Pelosi Amendment," it has become a significant tool for indigenous, nongovernmental organizations around the world.

Pelosi has also served on the Committee on Standards of Official Conduct (Ethics) and on the Banking and Financial Services Committee. She has chaired the Congressional Working Group on China and has served on the Executive Committee of the Democratic Study Group.

In 2006, when the Democratic Party captured a majority of the seats in the House of Representatives, Pelosi was elevated to Speaker of the House, third in line for the Presidency, the most powerful position ever held by a woman in the United States. Long a vocal critic of President George W. Bush, she vowed to bring civility back into government and to work in a bi-partisan fashion with the Bush administration. However, throughout Bush's term of office, their relationship had been marked by mutual disdain.

"He is an incompetent leader. In fact, he is not a leader," she said in a 2004 interview. "He's a person who has no judgment, no experience and no knowledge of the subjects that he has to decide on." Bush painted her as a tax-loving Democrat.

Suggested Reading:

(1) *Who's Who of American Women 2006-2007*. New Providence, RI: Marquis Who's Who/ Reed Elsevier, Inc. 2005, p. 1525.

(2) "The woman two heartbeats away from the presidency" by Dan Glaister. *The Guardian Weekly*, Nov. 17-23, 2006.

Perón, Isabel (Isabelita)

President of Argentina (1974-1976)

She was born María Estela Martínez in 1931, one of five children of a small town bank manager in northwest Argentina. The family moved to

Buenos Aires in 1933, and her father died four years later. Her mother worked to keep the family together, but María Estela quit school after the sixth grade to pursue a career in music and ballet. She studied ballet and piano and became a qualified piano teacher. When she was 20 she joined a professional ballet company, changing her name to Isabel, her saint's name. One story claims that in mid-tour of her dance company in 1956, she was stranded in Panama City and met the exiled Juan Perón, president of Argentina from 1946 to 1955. She became his personal secretary and traveling companion and settled with him in Madrid. In 1961, at the age of 30, she became the 65-year-old Perón's wife. Since she was not in exile, she was free to return to her homeland, so in 1964, she began to travel around Argentina, speaking on behalf of Peronista candidates. In 1973 Perón was recalled to Argentina and elected president, with his wife Isabel as vice president. Isabel had the handicap of following Perón's popular second wife, Eva (Evita). Later in 1973, Juan Perón, who was 78 and in poor health, fell ill, and he delegated full power to her. In 1974 he died and Isabel acceded to the presidency, becoming the first woman chief of state to serve in her own right in South America. Although the liberal unions had always been the bastions of Peronist support, the right-wing military had supported Peron as well. These two factions had warred for years. To combat the terrorism which had interrupted the government from time to time for years, Isabel suspended constitutional rights and imposed defacto martial law. Inflation was running at 200 percent per year, so she imposed austere fiscal measures which precipitated a union strike which crippled the nation. Eventually she had to give in to union demands for large wage hikes just to get the country moving again. In 1976, while she suffered a gall bladder attack, her regime was overthrown by a military junta. She went into self-exile in Spain in 1981 but returned in 1983 for the inauguration at the request of the new constitutional president, Raul Alfonsín. Then she retreated again to exile in Spain. According to a BBC report, on January 12, 2007, she was arrested, charged with being connected to Argentine death squads.

Suggested Reading:

(1) "Isabel Perón's Return Confirmed". *The Houston Post*. 27 August 1982: 3A.
(2) "Isabel Perón Pardoned". *The Houston Post*. 10 September 1983: 4A.
(3) "Intelligence Report". *Parade*. 27 February 1983: 2.

(4) Egan, Edward W. et. al., eds. *Kings, Rulers, and Statesmen*. New York: Sterling Publishing Company, 1976. p. 18.

(5) "BBC World" report by Cassie Kay. British Broadcasting Company, January 17, 2007.

Pulecio, Yolanda

Senator in Colombia (1990-1991)

Yolanda Pulecio Vélez, also known as "Mama Yolanda," was born c. 1939 in Colombia. In 1955 she was a beauty queen in the Miss Colombia contest, representing the Department of Cundinamarca. That same year she married Gabriel Betancourt, a former minister of finance and diplomat. The couple had two children: Astrid Betancourt and Íngrid Betancourt. In 1958 she founded the *Hogares Infantiles de Bogotá*, a shelter to help the street children and other poor children of Bogotá.

In 1961, Gabriel Betancourt was appointed as Adjutant Director of the UNESCO of Colombia in France, and the family moved to Neuilly-sur-Seine outside Paris for a period of five years. In 1966 President Carlos Lleras Restrepo appointed Betancourt Minister of Education and the family returned to Colombia, where the mayor of Bogotá appointed Yolanda Director of the Department of Social Welfare.

Back in Colombia, Pulecio was appointed by the Mayor of Bogotá as Director of the Social Welfare Department. She served until 1969, when Gabriel was named Ambassador of Colombia to UNESCO, and the family returned to Paris. With reluctance, Pulecio gave up her work with the foundation for Bogotá's homeless children.

However, she missed her work and eventually returned to Colombia, leaving her daughters to complete their studies at the *Institut de l'Assompition*. She developed a more active interest in politics and decided to remain in Bogotá permanently. She divorced her husband, for which the press crucified her. Her daughter Íngrid later wrote: "She separated from her husband to recover her active role in society, but she found herself judged, in defamation, criticized and condemned by the Colombian society of the time."

She ran for Congress, representing the poor southern district of Bogotá. Later her daughter Ingrid returned to Colombia and entered public service as well. When Íngrid, campaigning for President, was kidnapped by the Revolutionary Armed Forces of Colombia (FARC), Yolanda Pulencio began to devote her entire resources advocating for her daughter's release and the hundreds of others held as hostages.

Pulencio has criticized both Presidents Andres Pastrana and Alvaro Uribe for not doing enough for the release of the hostages, as well as not collaborating on achieving a possible humanitarian exchange of prisoners for hostages between the government and the FARC guerrilla. When senator of Colombia, Piedad Cordoba and Venezuelan President Hugo Chavez were named as facilitators by the Uribe government, Pulecio supported their initiatives declaring that they had achieved in a few months what had not been done in five years since the kidnapping of her daughter. Meanwhile, the deteriorating health of the hostage made her release even more critical. Claims have been made that she has Hepatitis B and is "near the end."

Suggested Reading:

(1)   Betancourt, Íngrid, *Letters to My Mother: A Message of Love, A Plea for Freedom*. Trans. Steven Kendall.

Section R

Rice, Condoleezza

U.S. Secretary of State (2005-2008)

Born in segregated Birmingham, Alabama on November 14, 1954 to John Wesley and Angelina Ray Rice, Condoleezza was encouraged by her parents to excel. She skipped two grades in school, graduating high school at age fifteen. She was an accomplished musician, and when she first entered the University of Denver, she planned on becoming a concert pianist. But a course taught by Josef Korbel, a former Czech diplomat and the father of Madeline Albright, changed her life forever. She decided to major in Political Science, earning a BA cum laude and Phi Beta Kappa in 1974 at the age of nineteen. She earned her master's from the University of Notre Dame in 1975; and her Ph.D. from the Graduate School of International Studies at the University of Denver in 1981. She is a Fellow of the American Academy of Arts and Sciences and has been awarded honorary doctorates from Morehouse College in 1991, the University of Alabama in 1994, the University of Notre Dame in 1995, the National Defense University in 2002, the Mississippi College School of Law in 2003, the University of Louisville and Michigan State University in 2004.

After receiving her PhD in 1981, Rice joined the faculty of Stanford University, where she won two of the highest teaching honors: the 1984 Walter J. Gores Award for Excellence in Teaching and the 1993 School of Humanities and Sciences Dean's Award for Distinguished Teaching. At Stanford, she was a member of the Center for International Security and Arms Control, a Senior Fellow of the Institute for International Studies, and a Fellow (by courtesy) of the Hoover Institution.

From 1989 through March 1991, the period of German reunification and the final days of the Soviet Union, she served in the Bush Administration as Director, and then Senior Director, of Soviet and East European Affairs in the National Security Council, and a Special Assistant to the President for National Security Affairs. In 1986, while an international affairs fellow of the Council on Foreign Relations, she served as Special Assistant to the Director of the Joint Chiefs of Staff. In 1997, she served on the Federal Advisory Committee on Gender Integrated Training in the Military.

In June 1999, she completed a six-year tenure as Stanford University's Provost, during which she was the institution's chief budget and academic officer. As Provost she was responsible for a $1.5 billion annual budget and the academic program involving 1,400 faculty members and 14,000 students.

She was a member of the boards of directors for the Chevron Corporation, the Charles Schwab Corporation, the William and Flora Hewlett Foundation, the University of Notre Dame, the International Advisory Council of J.P. Morgan and the San Francisco Symphony Board of Governors. While Rice concentrated on building relationships within large corporations, her cousin, Constance Lamay Rice, a Radcliffe graduate and NYU-educated lawyer, recipient of the Peace Prize, worked among the disadvantaged in Los Angeles. When asked by Bill Moyer about the differences between the cousins, Constance Rice commented that while she herself found gratification helping those less fortunate, Condoleezza preferred to make her way among the board rooms of the wealthy. Of her success, Condoleezza Rice commented: "In America, with education and hard work, it really does not matter where you come from; it matters where you are going." She was a Founding Board member of the Center for a New Generation, an educational support fund for schools in East Palo Alto and East Menlo Park, California and was Vice President of the Boys and Girls Club of the Peninsula. In addition, her past board service has included Transamerica Corporation, Hewlett Packard, the Carnegie Corporation, Carnegie Endowment for International Peace, The Rand Corporation, the National Council for Soviet and East European Studies, the Mid-Peninsula Urban Coalition and KQED, public broadcasting for San Francisco.

In January 2001 she was appointed by President George W. Bush as Assistant to the President for National Security Affairs, commonly referred to as the National Security Advisor, a post she held until January 26, 2005, when she became the Secretary of State.

Her books include *Uncertain Allegiance: The Soviet Union and the Czechoslovak Army* (1984), *The Gorbachev Era* (1986) with Alexander Dallin, and *Germany Unified and Europe Transformed* (1995) with Philip Zelikow. She also has written numerous articles on Soviet and East European foreign and defense policy, and has addressed audiences around the world in settings ranging from the U.S. Ambassador's Residence in Moscow to the Commonwealth Club to the 1992 and 2000 Republican National Conventions.

Suggested Reading:

(1) *www.whitehouse.gov/government/rice-bio.html.
(2) *Who's Who of American Women 2006-2007*. New Providence, RI: Marquis Who's Who/ Reed Elsevier, Inc. 2005. pp. T18, 1636.

Rojas, Clara

Colombian Vice Presidential candidate (2002)

Clara Rojas was born on December 20, 1964 in Bogotá, Colombia, and trained as a tax lawyer. She was working as a university lecturer in 2002 when she was tapped by her friend, former senator Íngrid Betancourt, to manage her presidential campaign. On February 23, 2002, while on a campaign junket with Betancourt near San Vicente del Caguán, she was kidnapped along with Betancourt by the FARC guerrilla group. After the kidnapping, Rojas was named as Betancourt's vice-presidential candidate.

In 2003 the FARC released a video which showed Rojas as a prisoner. No other word about her until 2006, when it was revealed that Rojas had given birth to a boy named Emmanuel while in captivity. The father was said to be a FARC guerrilla.

In December of 2007 Colombian President Álvaro Uribe announced that there was information about the child being held by the Colombian Institute for Family Welfare (ICBF). On January 2, 2008, the institution confirmed that a child, allegedly the son of Clara Rojas, was in custody of the institution. On January 3 the Colombian Government announced that the child was subjected to a mitrocondrial DNA test, which verified that he is the son of Clara Rojas. Emmanuel had become ill as a baby, and Rojas had allowed her son to be taken to a doctor for care on the condition that he would be returned to her. Instead, he was placed with a peasant who did not know to whom the child belonged. There was much criticism regarding the way in which both the Colombian government and FARC have handled the situation.

On December 27, 2007, the FARC guerrilla group was said to be planning the imminent release of Rojas and former congresswoman Consuelo

González in a one-sided prisoner release negotiated by Venezuelan president Hugo Chávez, using Venezuelan aircraft and the support of the International Red Cross.

After being temporarily suspended, the operation resumed and, on January 10, 2008, a humanitarian commission headed by the International Committee of the Red Cross flew in two Venezuelan helicopters to a location in Colombia that had been designated by FARC the previous day. Rojas and González were then released to the care of the commission. On January 13, 2008, Clara Rojas was reunited with her son, Emmanuel; the first time she had seen him for more than two years.

Suggested Reading:

(1) See Betancourt entry.

Section S

Sauvé, Jeanne Mathilde

Governor-general of Canada (1984-1990)

She was born Jeanne Mathilde Benoit in 1992 in Prud'homme, Saskatchewan. In 1925 her family moved to Ottawa, where she was educated, graduating from the University of Ottawa. In 1942 she became president of Jeunesse Étudiante Catholique in Montreal, where she remained for five years. She married Maurice Sauvé, an economist, and the couple lived in Europe for four years. On their return to Canada as union organizers, she worked as a TV commentator on CBC.

In 1972 she was elected as a Liberal to the House of Commons, and shortly afterward Prime Minister Elliott Trudeau named her successively Minister of Science and Technology, Environment, and Communications. In 1980 she became the first woman to be Speaker of the House. In 1984, she assumed the post as Canada's first woman Governor-general, replacing Edward R. Schreyer.

The Governor-general is the nominal head of the government, appointed by the reigning monarch as the representative of the British crown. Following the Prime Minister's advice, the Governor-general appoints the cabinet, which submits its decisions to the Governor-general, who in turn, in most cases, is constitutionally bound to approve them. In theory, the Governor-general is the head of the national government; the actual head is the Prime Minister, who is appointed to that post by the Governor-general on the recommendation of the House of Commons.

Ms. Sauvé retired in 1990 and died in 1993.

Suggested Reading:

(1) *Funk & Wagnalls New Encyclopedia*, Vol. 23, 1986. p. 175.
(2) Filon, John, Canadian ed. *The World Almanac and Book of Facts*. New York: Newspaper Enterprise Association, Inc., 1994.pp. 522-523.

Simpson-Miller, Portia

Prime Minister of Jamaica (2006-)

Portia Simpson-Miller, known by many as "Sista P," was born on December 12, 1945, in Wood Hall, St. Catherine, Jamaica. She received a BA Degree in Public Administration from Union Institute in Miami, Florida. While completing her degree, she also completed a diploma in Computing, Programming and Public Relations and first won a seat in parliament in 1976 at the age of 30. She became vice president of the People's National Party in 1978 and held that position for almost three decades. In a male-dominated culture, she managed to serve in several portfolios, including Minister of Labor, 1993-2000, Minister of Labor, Welfare and Sports, 1989-1993, and Minister of Tourism and Sports, 200-2002. An avid fan of both golf and boxing, she often criticized the behavior of Jamaica's sports visitors, saying their behavior clashed with the island's traditional morals.

When she launched her bid to head the People's National Party, her detractors in the media considered her an intellectual lightweight and labeled her as a "serial kisser" at rallies. But her popularity at the grassroots level and her ability to ignore her critics made a run for the prime ministry obligatory. An advocate for the poor and dispossessed and a spokesperson for women's rights, she also promised to crack down on crime, especially the drugs trade, and bring greater economic development to the country. She vowed to bring her friend, Asafa Powell, the 100m world record holder, to help put an end to drug-related killings, particularly in the slums of Kingston, the capital. She was swept into office in a landslide on February 25, 2006 and was sworn in in March, 2006 as the nation's first female leader.

She is married to Errald Miller, a former CEO of the Jamaican arm of Cable & Wireless.

Suggested Reading:

(1) "Half the World" by Diane Dixon, the *Guardian Weekly*, June 10-22, 2006.

Six Sky, Lady

See Wac-Chanil-Ahau

Snake Lady of Palenque

Lady of Palenque (677)

No name has been found for this Princess, who arrived in the Maya Kingdom of Palenque on the day of one of the greatest victories for the Kan Kingdom. This Snake Princess married the local ruler, King K'in ich Yook (ruled 667-ca. 682), who as vassal or "vajaw" in turn paid tribute to Yukno'm Ch'e'n II (636-686), the greatest king of Calakmul. On the day that Snake Lady arrived, the army of Calakmul had defeated the forces of its greatest rival, Tikal. Her appearance may have taken on great significance because of this victory.

Sotomayor, Sonia Maria

Associate Justice of the United States Supreme Court (2009-)

She was born June 25, 1954 to Puerto Rican parents in a poor neighborhood of the Bronx, New York. Her father, Juan Sotomayor, came from San Juan, had a third grade education, and did not speak English. Her mother, Celina Báez, was from the rural area of Santa Rosa, Puerto Rico. Sonia was diagnosed with diabetes when she was eight. Her father died when Sonia was only nine, and her mother Celina raised Sonia and her younger brother Juan on a nurse's salary and still managed to send her to Catholic schools. Sonia graduated in 1972 and entered Princeton where she studied history. She graduated in 1976 summa cum laude and Phi Beta Kappa. She entered Yale Law School, where she was an editor of the *Yale Law Journal*. By that time she had married her high school sweetheart, Kevin Edward Noon, but they couple divorced in 1983.

From 1979 to 1984 she was an assistant district attorney in the office of Manhattan district attorney Robert Morgenthau, and then she went into private practice with a firm specializing in business cases. She practiced law until 1992, when President George H.W. Bush nominated her as a federal judge in the Southern District of New York. She was easily confirmed, but when President Bill Clinton nominated her for the Second Circuit Court of Appeals, Republicans held off a confirmation vote for more than a year. In May of 2009, when President Barak Obama picked her for the Supreme, she was its first female Hispanic nominee. She took her place on the bench of the Supreme Court when it convened in October, 2009. No one expects her appointment to change the ideological balance of the court. Sotomayor tends to write rulings that focus on close application of the law.

She has received honorary law degrees from Lehman College (1999), Princeton (2001), Brooklyn Law School (201), Pace University School of Law (2003), Hofstra University (2006), and Northeastern University School of Law (2007).

Suggested Reading:

(1) "A Justice Like No Other," by Richard Lacayo. *Time.* June 8, 2009. pp. 24-27.
(2) "A Changing Court," by Massimo Calabresi, Jay Newton-Small, Michael Scherer, Mark Thompson and Karen Tumulty. *Time.* June 8, 2009. pp. 28-29.
(3) "The Limits of Empathy," by Christopher Caldwell. *Time.* June 8, 2009. p. 32.
(4) www.wikipedia.org.

Section T

Tejada, Lidia Gueiler

President of Bolivia (1979-1980)

During a tumultuous period in Bolivia's history, the elections of July 1979 pitted three candidates representing three equally strong factions: military, political, and union. The election produced no majority, and an interim president, Walter Guevara Arza, was chosen by the parliament to serve until elections could be held in 1980. However, he was seen as being too biased against the military, and on November 1, 1979, he was deposed by Colonel Alberto Nalusch Busch, who held power for slightly over two weeks, until November 16. During that time a non-controversial, compromise candidate, Lidia Gueiler Tejada, was chosen by leaders representing the union, political, and military interests. Tejada, born in 1926, had been active in politics and had held a number of committee positions, but she had the reputation of being open-minded. She became Bolivia's first woman president, chosen to serve a one-year term. She was ousted in a military coup in 1980 before her term expired.

Suggested Reading:

(1) *Britannica Macropaedia*, 1983. vol. 3, *Bolivia, History*. p. 13.

Tí, Lady

Snake Queen of Palenque, Mexico (721)

Lady Tí is depicted in an early Mayan tablet as a Snake Queen of Calakmul and the *vatan* (consort) of King Yuknoom Too K'awiil, last great ruler of Calakmul (r. ca. 702-ca. 731), having arrived at Sak Nikté in the Petén in

721. Her arrival suggests that the Snake Kingdom was once again asserting its influence over Tikal and the Petén.

Suggested Reading:

(1) Schele, Linda and David Freidel. *A Forest of Kings The Untold Story of the Ancient Maya*. New York: Quill/William Morrow, 1990.

Tuckabatchee, Queen of

Legendary queen of Tuckabatchee Creek (late 18th. c.)

According to Janice Woods Windle, family lore maintains that the queen of Tuckabatchee was a "full-breasted woman" whose relationship to the Woods family is legendary. She was said to have been the mother of Cherokee Hawkins Lawshe and the grandmother of Texas pioneer Georgia Lawshe Woods.

Suggested Reading:

(1) Windle, Janice Woods. *True Women*. New York: G. P. Putnam's Sons, 1993. pp. 169-170, 174-175.

Section U

Uicab, Maria

"Queen" of Tulum (1871)

Maria Uicab was a Mayan woman living on the Yucatan Peninsula who was known as the patron saint of Tulum and was given the title of queen. In 1871 the sacred Mayan ruins of the city of Tulum became an Indian shrine where a "talking cross" was set up. The city of Tulum, and especially the "talking cross" were placed in the care of Queen Maria.

Suggested Reading:

(1) *Las ruinas de Tulum*. Ciudad de Mexico: Instituto Nacional de Antropologia e Historia, 1969. p. 14.

Section W

Wac-Chanil-Ahau, Lady ("Six Celestial Lord", also Lady 6 Sky)

Maya Queen, Regent of Naranjo (682–c. 699)

She was the daughter of Flint-Sky-God K, king of the Maya of Dos Pilas (r. 645—?). Following the Caracol-Tikal-Naranjo wars in which both Naranjo and Tikal fared badly at the hands of Caracol, Flint-Sky-God K set up the new kingdom called Dos Pilas near Lake Petexbatún and the Pasión River in the southern lowlands of the Yucatán. To solidify his position, he sent women, possibly sisters or daughters, to marry rulers of El Charro and El Pato, and, in 682, he sent lady Wac-Chanil-Ahau, with an elaborate wedding caravan, to Naranjo to marry a nobleman and establish a new royal family.

On her arrival in Naranjo, she performed a three-day blood-letting sacrificial ritual (August 30-September 1, 682). She did not marry a king, and her husband was not important enough to be depicted on a stela. Their son, Smoking-Squirrel, was born on January 1, 688 and acceded to the throne at the age of five. Only twenty days after his accession, Naranjo warriors attacked the neighboring kingdom of Ucanal, taking prisoner one important lord named Kinichil-Cab. A stela depicting this capture shows Lady Wac-Chanil-Ahau standing on the captive's body (June 20, 693). Although Kinichil-Cab survived, in April 19, 699, Lady Wac-Chanil-Ahau conducted a public ritual in which she is again depicted standing on his body. This is the last date of which there is any record of her activities.

She lived many years into his reign, and every time Smoking-Squirrel erected a monument commemorating his accession, he erected another dedicated to his mother. These monuments depict her engaging in the same rituals of state as her son. She was never given the designation "king" but appears to have ruled, first as viceroy or regent for her father from 682 to 693, and then as regent for her son for a number of years. She not only waged war in her son's name, but also had herself portrayed on monuments and military records, and she led various yearly rituals. She died at the age of 77 in 741.

Suggested Reading:

(1) Schele, Linda and David Freidel. *A Forest of Kings The Untold Story of the Ancient Maya*. New York: Quill/William Morrow, 1990, pp. 168, 183-186, 221, 459, 460, 461, 478.

Waka Queen

Queen Regnant of Waka (ca. 650/750)

Waka was a Maya kingdom in present-day Guatemala. In 2004 researchers uncovered her grave that contains the trappings of a royal personage, but they have not found her name. Relics in the tomb are dated between 650 and 750.

Werleigh, Claudette

Prime minister of Haiti (1994-1995)

In 1991 Haitian President Jean-Bertrand Aristide was arrested in a military coup and expelled from the country. Over the next two years thousands of Haitian refugees attempted to enter the United States to escape the military dictatorship. In 1993 the United Nations imposed a worldwide embargo of arms, oil, and financial aid upon Haiti. In 1994 the United Nations Security Council authorized an invasion of Haiti to unseat the usurpers, but at the last minute the military agreed to step down and allow the duly elected president to return. After thousands of U.S. troops arrived to assure his safety, Aristide returned to resume his office October 15, 1994. Claudette Werleigh, a member of a distinguished family to jurists in Port au Prince, and a minister of the Ministry of Foreign Affairs, was chosen to serve as prime minister. A U.N. peacekeeping force took over responsibility of Haiti on March 31, 1995. In the elections held at the close of the year, René Préval was voted Aristide's successor, and Rosny Smarth was chosen as the new prime minister. Préval took office on February 7, 1996.

Suggested Reading:

(1) *Who's Who in the World 1996.* New Providence, NJ: Marquis Who's Who/Reed Reference Publishing Company, 1995. p. 1432.
(2) Famighetti, Robert, ed. dir. *The World Almanac 1998.* Mahwah, NJ: KIII Reference Corporation, 1997. p. 772.

Section Y

Yohl Ik'nal, Lady

See Kanal Ikal, Lady

Palenque was a Mayan kingdom located in the present-day Yucatan area of Mexico. Yohl Ik'nal ascended to the throne following the death of Kan B'alam I, who was probably her father. She was also called Lady Kanal Ikal, Ix Yohi Ik'nal, Lady Olnal, Kan-Ik, Lady Ik, or K'anal-Ik'al. She was one of a very few Mayan women to bear full royal titles and to rule in her own right for an extended period—in her case, more than two decades. She had at least one son, Ai Ne' ohl, who succeeded her.

Ywahoo, Dhyani

Cherokee Nation clan chief (fl. 1969-1998)

She is the chief of the Green Mountain (Vermont) Ani Yunwiwa, laying claim as holder of the Ywahoo lineage, said to be 2,860 years old. Her teachings were passed to her by her grandfather, Eonah Fisher (Bear Fishing), who received them from his father-in-law, Eli Ywahoo; and from her grandmother, Nellie Ywahoo. In 1969 the elders of the Etowah Band and the Ywahoo bloodline conferred and concluded that their teachings should be shared with the world. Venerable Dhyani Ywahoo founded and directs the Sunray Meditation Society, near Bristol, Vermont.

In addition to leading her clan of the Cherokees, Dhyani Ywahoo is a champion of Native American cultures and the author of *Voices of Our Ancestors*. She has taken as part of her mission educating the world about the gifts to humanity from Native Americans. She informed a reporter that there are 128 foods now consumed worldwide that were cultivated by Native Americans for thousands of years. In addition, much of Western pharmacopoeia can be traced to Native American herbal knowledge. The

Native Americans have led the world in their concern for living in harmony with nature and with protecting their environment.

As the countries of the Western Hemisphere celebrated the 500th anniversary of the arrival of Christopher Columbus in the New World, Dhyani Ywahoo traveled to Spain, where she met with Queen Sofia and others. She was invited to participate in the opening of Madrid's Casa de Americas, Europe's only institute devoted to Native American Studies.

Suggested Reading:

(1) "Thanksgiving 1991: Food for Thought". *Parade*. 24 November 1991: 11
(2) www.sunray.org.

Section Z

Zac-Kuk of B'aakal, Lady

"King" of the Mayas of Palenque (October 22, 612-A.D.-615 A.D.), co-ruler (615 A.D.-640 A.D.)

Palenque was a Mayan city-state in present-day Mexico. Lady Zac-Kuk the daughter of Pacal I (d. March 9, 612 A.D.), the younger brother of a king: Ac-Kan (d. August 11, 612 A.D.) She was the granddaughter of woman ruler, Lady Kanal-Ikal (r. 583-604). Zak means "white" and Kuk means "quetzal." She was married to Kan-Bahlum-Mo', but she did not come to the throne as a consort, for her husband was never king. Nor was she regent for a king. She inherited the throne, presumably as her uncle's next-of-kin. She is depicted in Mayan art as having crossed eyes and tattoos over her whole body. She took the throne in 612 A.D. and ruled through "three pregnancies" until her son Hanab Pacal (b. 603 A.D.) reached the age to twelve. At that time she handed her royal headdress over to him, as depicted in an ancient tablet carving in the Oval Palace. Even then Zac-Kuk continued as co-ruler, not just until Pacal became a man, but for many years beyond that time.

In the Temple of Inscriptions are two great vaulted chambers containing three panels carved with glyphs recounting the history of Pacal's ancestors. He started the pyramid and after his death in 683, his son Chan-Bahlum (crowned January 10, 690 A.D.) finished it. On these panels, Zac-Kuk is designated as being analogous to the mother of the gods, thus inferring Pacal's own god-like status. In his case, the mother was the parent critical to his claim to the throne.

Apparently, Zac-Kuk kept a tight hold on power until she died (640 A.D.), because no major works were commissioned by her son Pacal until after that time. In 647, at the age of forty-three, he dedicated the first of his construction projects, Temple Olvidado. It had been seven years since her death, and four years since his father's death.

Suggested Reading:

(1) Schele, Linda and David Freidel, *A Forest of Kings. The Untold Story of the Ancient Maya*. New York: Quill, William Morrow, 1990, pp. 221-225, 227-228, 266, 467, 468, 478.

About the Author

Guida Jackson has worked as a newspaper editor, magazine editor, book editor, English teacher (University of Houston), and Creative Writing teacher (Montgomery College). She has a BA in Journalism, MA in the Humanities specializing in Latin American Literature, and PhD in Comparative Literature specializing in Third World Literature, particularly West African. She is founder of *Touchstone Literary Journal* (1976) and Panther Creek Press (1999), and author of 18 fiction and non-fiction books, published by Simon & Schuster, Oxford University Press, Barnes & Noble Books, and others. She has written two other books about women rulers and two other books about women writers. Both *Women Who Ruled* and *Women Rulers Throughout the Ages* were named to the Best References List of the *Library Journal*. She lives with Jack, Hunter, and Lili Hume in Houston, Texas.